# RENWICK'S GUIDES

# SELF BUILD CAMPERVAN CONVERSIONS

A guide to converting everyday vehicles into campervans & motorhomes.

BY KENNY BIGGIN

**© Kenny Biggin 2017**
All rights reserved. No part of this book may be reproduced or transmitted in any form by any means without the prior written permission of the publisher.

Photos & Diagrams by Kenny Biggin except where otherwise stated.

**ISBN 978-0-9926065-3-4**
A catalogue record of this book is available from the British Library.
1st Edition by Kenny Biggin 2017. 3rd Impression.
Published by Renwick's Guides.
www.renwicksguides.co.uk

Renwick's Guides is a trading name of SkiMountain Ltd.

**Advertising**
If you would like to hear about advertising opportunities in future editions of this book or others in the series, please contact us at publish@renwicksguides.co.uk.

**Feedback**
We have put a lot of effort into producing this book, and we hope that it is a high quality and (most importantly) useful addition to your book shelf. If you find any corrections, have some feedback for us, or want to share your project with us, please email us at publish@renwicksguides.co.uk.

MIX
Paper from
responsible sources
FSC® C023105

"I am only around five miles from home, and yet as I drive northwards in my newly converted van, with the sun shining through the window, I recognise a familiar sensation beginning to wash over me ... freedom!"

# PREFACE

My interest in converting campervans and motorhomes began a couple of years before I could drive, when I was around 15. I was into windsurfing and remember reading an article in 'Boards' magazine about converting vans for the sport. I must have spent many dull classes in school fantasising about getting the biggest van I could, loading it up with toys, and going on tour. For a long time I wanted to drive all the way to America from the UK, right across Europe, Russia and Siberia, and across the ice into Alaska.

Fast forward a few more years to 1997 and I ended up on a white-water kayaking trip in British Columbia, Canada. That was when I had my first real campervan experience, except it was actually a car – a 1974 Buick Station Wagon to be exact. It was a great vehicle – it had an 8-track stereo, cruise control, seats for eleven people including a three seat bench in the front, and a seven and a half litre engine. It needed that big engine because it weighed almost two and half tons – more than my current panel van.

Although this wasn't a proper campervan we certainly treated it as such – we had a big foam mattress in the back, cooked on an MSR Whisperlite camping stove, and ate outside on deckchairs. Whatever its shortcomings as a campervan, that station wagon provided the backbone for a three month adventure that set a high bar for future trips to live up to.

Ten years on from the BC Buick, I had been through numerous vehicles from a string of clapped out cars, to a Mazda Bongo and a Mitsubishi 300 in New Zealand, to Ford Transit conversions. But in 2007 I finally had enough cash, know-how, and time to convert my first 'good' campervan. It was a Volkswagen T5 that had a pretty high mileage and was utterly filthy having been used to transport live crickets from Greece to the UK to feed snakes in a zoo. It took the whole first day just to clean all the cricket shit out of it, and another three months before the conversion was complete. Then we went away in it for three months, following the white-water around the Alps, down to the Pyrenees, and up through Germany and Denmark to Norway.

That first T5 was when I finally felt like I had made a conversion breakthrough – it had a comfy rock-n-roll sliding bed, good storage space, windows in the sides, running water, a sink / stove combo, a proper 12V electrical setup, and a heater.  Living in it was relatively comfortable, especially when it wasn't raining too hard.  I went on to have numerous trips in that van, and the lessons I learnt with it have informed all projects since.  I also started writing about campervan conversions after coming back from that trip in the summer of 2007, as well as opening a small shop selling conversion parts, and this book can trace its roots back to then – ten years in the making.

Since that first T5, I have been through a number of vehicles, most of which have been bigger conversions – some fairly basic, some all singing all dancing with bathrooms, hot water showers, fancy joinery… the works.

It was almost twenty five years ago when I first imagined my perfect campervan conversion, and along the way I have explored many enjoyable diversions, not least of which has been the process of converting vehicles.  The act of taking an everyday vehicle and converting it into a campervan, the epitome of freedom, will always hold a certain draw for me.  And although I still haven't made that trip across the Siberian tundra, I've yet to make a plan for next summer…

I've tried to share much of my knowledge of campervan conversions in these pages and, as the old cliché goes: "this is the book I wish I'd had when I started".  Whatever your conversion plans, be they big or small, bold, complex, or basic, I hope this book helps you along the way.  Most important of all is to remember why you're doing it – don't spend forever on the conversion: throw a mattress in the back, drive somewhere new, and enjoy the adventure!

Kenny Biggin
Scottish Highlands, October 2017

# CONTENTS

# INTRODUCTION

So much of owning a campervan or motorhome is about freedom – freedom to go where you want, when you want, and to take whatever and whoever with you. You don't need to pay for expensive hotels and you don't even need to decide where you want to go, or for how long. You can adopt a degree of flexibility that few other ways of travelling offer – wait and see what the weather does, follow the surf, see where the road leads. If you find yourself somewhere with a great view, you can spend the night there and watch the sunrise in the morning. Travelling with such freedom can even invite serendipity into your life – meet new people, explore new places, have new adventures… with your own campervan at your disposal, who knows where you might end up!

Unfortunately for most of us, a professionally built campervan or motorhome can be prohibitively expensive – in some cases they can attract price tags not dissimilar to a small house. Fortunately for the less well heeled amongst us, there is an alternative: build your own! Armed with a small selection of DIY skills along with a bit of enthusiasm, and this book of course, it is possible to go out and buy yourself a nice base vehicle for whatever price you can afford and convert it into your ideal home on wheels.

Not only does the 'self build' approach save a lot of hard earned cash, but it is also hugely rewarding and ensures that you end up with a vehicle designed specifically around your own needs. If you want a big garage space for your bikes or boards, or a fancy stove to cook up luxury meals by the beach, or a couple of cages for your dogs, a store for your work tools, or a hanging space for wetsuits… no problem – it's your van, build it your way!

This book's fundamental goal is to provide you with the information and know-how you need to convert a wide variety of everyday vehicles into campervans or motorhomes designed around your needs. The book tries to cover everything from buying a good base vehicle, to insulating and lining it, to installing heaters and windows, dealing with water and gas, installing electrics, and many other subjects. To add a little inspiration the book is littered with colour photos of other self built conversions alongside the vital info. You need to have a crack at it yourself.

# Task Breakdowns and Step-by-steps

Certain sections of the book are presented as specific tasks, often with step-by-step instructions. At the start of each of these sections there is a graphic panel designed to help you get a sense of what is involved. This is purely designed as a visual guide and shouldn't be taken too literally.

| | PREREQUISITES | Windows, Flooring |
| --- | --- | --- |
| | DO BEFORE | Wiring, insulation |
| | COMBINE WITH | Constructing Furniture |

# Difficulty Rating

At the left of the visual task panel there is a "Speedo" difficulty rating graphic which is intended to provide an at-a-glance hint as to how easy, tricky or involved the task being described is. Of course this rating will be a huge generalisation but it should help provide a little guidance. If the rating for a task seems beyond your current skill and confidence level it may be a task worth seeking some professional or more experienced help with. That said, hopefully the information within this book will help encourage you to step out of your comfort zone a little and tackle conversion jobs that would previously have seemed like mystic dark arts to you.

| Task Rating | Guidance |
| --- | --- |
| EASY 1/5 | These are the simplest and most basic of conversion tasks that require very little if any skill or knowledge. Anyone reading the book, including complete novice self-builders, should feel happy to take these tasks on. |
| EASY / MODERATE 2/5 | These tasks are still very accessible to the majority of readers. They may require slightly more care and attention to detail or neatness than 'Easy' tasks. |
| MODERATE 3/5 | Tasks that are challenging but perfectly achievable for the majority of DIY'ers. Having a bit of experience behind you will be a big help with these tasks, but everyone learns by doing so don't be too put off. |
| ADVANCED 4/5 | The tasks marked as Advanced will require some skilled work and you should probably only take these on if you have done similar (if not identical) bits of work before, or if you have someone else with more experience helping you out. |
| DIFFICULT 5/5 | There are very few tasks described here under the Difficult rating as the majority of such tasks are firmly in the realm of the professionals. If you are a very experienced self builder or DIY enthusiast you may decide to take these on, but probably only when the task in question aligns with your existing skill-set. Some of these tasks will have consequences if you don't get them right and, as with all tasks, safety should be of paramount importance when considering taking them on. |

# Skills and Tools Icons

| PREREQUISITES | Windows, Flooring |
| DO BEFORE | Wiring, insulation |
| COMBINE WITH | Constructing Furniture |

The skills and tools icons are intended to give an at-a-glance indication of the type of skills and tools that might be required to take on the task being described. Many tasks will have a number of the icons highlighted, indicating that carrying out the task will require a number of differing skills and tools to complete it. There is a chapter discussing the common tools required towards the back of the book.

**Joinery / Woodwork** – The handsaw icon will often be on as working with timber is common when converting vehicles. Some basic woodworking skills and tools will be a great help for these tasks although a huge amount can be achieved using a handsaw, a tape measure, a cordless drill / driver, a jigsaw, and the odd bit of sandpaper.

**Metalwork / Structural** – The drill icon will often be highlighted when structural changes to the vehicle are taking place, such as fitting windows. The drill is just one of the tools that may be required – for example jigsaws, angle grinders, and files.

**Water & Plumbing** – The water droplet icon is displayed wherever the water system is involved. Since most campervan plumbing is either flexible hose or push-fit, the tools and skills required aren't too onerous.

**Gas** – The flame icon indicates tasks requiring interaction with gas. Since gas is a regulated trade you are likely to need to enlist a gas engineer to finalise your installation, though much groundwork can be carried out yourself.

**Mechanical** – The spanner icon shows some basic mechanical skills and tools are required, though this frequently only involves using a socket set or adjustable wrench to do up bolts etc.

**Soft furnishings** – When the scissors icon is highlighted it indicates the task involves 'soft' skills such as trimming carpet, spray gluing fabric, making curtains, upholstery, etc. Time to get your sewing machines out chaps!

**Electrics** – The lightning bolt or spark is used for tasks involving the electrical system. This could be either 12V or mains and of course there are safety issues with both to consider (especially with mains power).

**Tea Break** – This universal tea / coffee break icon will be lit up in all tasks and aims to remind you to enjoy the conversion process. Stop frequently to think, plan, design, and discuss… and whenever you hit a hurdle, it's probably time to stick the kettle on and have another brew!

# Task Ordering

| | |
|---|---|
| PREREQUISITES | Windows, Flooring |
| DO BEFORE | Wiring, insulation |
| COMBINE WITH | Constructing Furniture |

EASY
1/5

At the right hand side of the visual task panel there are three categories aimed at providing some guidance related to the order you carry out your conversion. The "Prerequisites", "Do Before", and "Combine With" headings are purely intended to provide some general hints and shouldn't be taken too strictly as the whole conversion process is frequently very fluid.

| Task Ordering | Explanation |
|---|---|
| **Prerequisites** | Items listed here should be done before the task being described. For example you should insulate the van before putting the panels on. |
| **Do Before** | In most conversions it makes sense to do the task described before those listed here. For example you should install windows before insulating. |
| **Combine With** | It will often make sense to combine this task with those listed. For example it makes sense to combine your kitchen unit design with the rear seat and bed construction. |

# How to Use This Book

The information in this book covers a diverse collection of topics. Although it should be possible to read the book cover-to-cover, it is more likely that you will want to browse through and pick and choose those chapters that are of most interest at any particular time. Since there is no definitive order to completing a conversion project, the chapters are not presented sequentially – that said, the initial chapters including Choosing & Buying a Vehicle and Planning & Preparation cover some of the crucial information to consider from the outset of a project, especially if you are new to the conversion game.

It is well worth taking a good look through the rest of the book before deciding on the type of conversion project you plan to take on – with luck you will find some inspiration and good ideas. Some tasks you thought straightforward might turn out to be more involved, but likewise others that you previously wouldn't have dreamed of taking on will hopefully become achievable.

In general, chapters start off with a short overview of the topic, followed by a more in-depth discussion broken down into subsections with photos and step-by-step task descriptions on the subsequent pages. This book aims to provide a good starting point for your conversion project with enough detail to see you through key tasks. There are many different ways of converting vehicles and lots of different techniques, so it is almost impossible to provide a definitive tutorial. This book concentrates on providing you with some of the simpler and more common ways of skinning the conversion cat - happy converting!

---

"With luck you will find some inspiration and discover new ways to skin the conversion cat."

---

# Exceptions

The book doesn't attempt to provide information aimed at professional converters, although many professionals start out as self-builders, and many of the techniques described here will be similar to (or basic versions of) those used by conversion companies. In a professional setting there is frequently access to a greater selection of tools, a better indoor workspace, a variety of skilled workers, economies of scale for parts, and of course there is a customer who is paying a price for the work being done. Where possible the techniques described within are chosen because they are reasonably accessible (in terms of both skills and tools) to many DIY converters. If you start outgrowing the methods covered in this book – for instance by creating luxurious curved kitchen units, extendable bathrooms with tambour doors, or by making dramatic alterations to the structure of the vehicle – then you are probably entering the realm of producing professional quality conversions yourself, and your services may well start to be in demand. The book also doesn't cover "coach building" or coach-built motorhomes where a custom shell is built onto a chassis – this requires specialist techniques that are well beyond the scope of this book.

# Terminology

Since this book is more about relaying the conversion skills rather than prescribing the precise end product, there are any number of different vehicles that you could apply this to, including buses and lorries, Land Rovers and other 4WD's, sports utility vehicles, ice cream vans, panel vans, horse boxes, even boats, sheds, and no doubt countless other variations. However, for ease of reading the two terms generally used to describe the vehicle being converted are either 'campervan' or 'van'. Often the term 'motorhome' will also be used, but the line between a campervan and a motorhome is hazy to the point of being impossible to define. Other terms such as motor caravan, leisure vehicle, overlanders, etc. have also, for the purposes of readability, all been pulled back under the general umbrella terms of 'vans' and 'campervans'. In essence, please read the book with whatever your chosen vehicle is in mind, and know that the information within these pages can be readily applied to pretty much anything with wheels.

# Quick Tour of a Conversion

There are around twenty detailed chapters within this book, each dealing with the various conversion related subjects in more depth. Before delving into the detail of it all, it's worth having a quick tour of a conversion project. A simple conversion might just involve doing a little insulating, tidying up some panels, perhaps installing a seat swivel or two, and doing a little woodwork to create a bed platform and perhaps a small kitchen unit for a sink and stove in the back. More complex conversions projects can get fiendishly complicated, but most will still follow a similar pattern. If you're new to converting you may well want to start with a reasonably simple project, and then get more ambitious as you gain experience and work out what does and doesn't work for you.

The first stage in any project is usually to choose, find, and buy a base vehicle. Related to buying your vehicle is planning your conversion and the combination of these two first steps is likely to have a dramatic effect on the eventual outcome of the project. It is worth spending time and effort up front to make sure you have worked out the sort of conversion that will suit your needs, and then patiently seek out the right vehicle to pour your conversion skills and effort into. Once you have bought the base vehicle it is usually a case of stripping everything out to give yourself a clean sheet to work from. Starting off by removing all panels, flooring, any existing rear seats, shelves, ambulance sirens, etc. gives you a much clearer view of the space you're working with.

If there are any structural changes to be made to the vehicle, such as installation of windows, pop-tops, rooflights, etc., these are best carried out at the start. If you have a clear idea of where items that require cutting holes in the van are going – such as heaters, water heaters, cassette loos, mains hookup sockets, etc. – then installing these near the start as well can make a lot of sense, and likewise for under-floor water and LPG tanks which usually require bolts going through the floor.

Inevitably you won't know where everything is going at first, which isn't too much of a problem – it just means you may later have to remove panels etc. in order to retrofit the item. The next big items on the list are usually insulation and 'first fix' wiring (i.e. running cables); wiring and insulation can be done in either order really but both will usually be done before the panels are put back on. Once the vehicle is nicely insulated and you have cables running roughly where you think you need them, the next step is making, covering, and fitting panels onto walls and ceiling, as well as fixing new flooring in place. It is common to make and loosely fit panels before taking them off while struts and bare metal such as wheel arches are lined.

Adding in your chosen rear seat and bed solution is usually next on the list, often done in conjunction with a reasonably lengthy stage including designing, building, and installing a kitchen unit and whatever other storage units you are building. If you are building a bathroom cubicle then this will be built now as well.

Once panels are on and most furniture is built and in place, a 'second fix' electrics stage is required, when battery charging, lights, switches, sockets, and appliances all get installed and wired up using the wires that were laid during the first fix stage. Water and gas plumbing will need to be done at various points through the project, and can also be split roughly into first and second fix stages – with pipes being run out of sight near the start of the project, while appliances are plumbed in once units are built etc. You may need to enlist some professional help, for instance from a registered gas engineer or an electrician, to finalise the project and ensure it is safe for habitation.

The final step in most conversion projects, is to take it away on that all-important first night away. All being well, you will be able to park up, flick the lights on, crack open a beer or a bottle of wine, and toast your ingenuity and your new creation while soaking up your new found freedom of life on the road.

# CHOOSING & BUYING A BASE VEHICLE

Arguably the most important part of any conversion project comes right at the start – if you manage to choose and buy the right base vehicle you are on to a winner from the off. Conversely, if you make a bad choice of vehicle at the start you may end up fighting against an inevitable series of problems throughout the project. This section should help you to home in on a suitable vehicle for your needs, and provide a little advice on how to source it without blowing your budget.

When it comes to base vehicles there are a myriad of options to choose from and, as with the rest of your project, this is a very personal choice and really anything goes. Base vehicle options range from a panel van, to a minibus, or perhaps something more exotic like a horsebox, an ice cream van, a four wheel drive, a school-bus, or even an ex-military truck. By far the most common type of vehicle to convert is the standard panel van, so this book focuses heavily on these while providing plenty of good information for the conversion of all other vehicles.

Campervan paradise – vans of all shapes, sizes, and ages parked up next to the beach in Tarifa, Spain.

## How Big?

Of all the questions to ask when choosing a vehicle to convert, 'how big?' is probably the most defining. Do you want a nice small van, nimble for tight parking spaces and zipping around tight country roads, where the main criterion is to be as car-like as possible while having space for some sort of bed in the back? Or do you have a wish-list of features including such items as standing room, a bathroom, kitchen and dining area, lots of storage space, and a full size fixed bed? Are you willing to sacrifice a little on drivability in order to have a more luxurious home from home?

The blue van is small... the white vans are far away. Right to left: A Vauxhall Combo, VW T5, Renault Trafic, Iveco Daily.

The question of how big you want your campervan to be is a very personal preference that involves making a series of choices and inevitably compromises will also need to be made. Try to home in on which items on your wish-list are high priority, work out how much space you need to accommodate them, and let that steer you towards the right size of vehicle. Be careful not to get carried away and end up with an enormous vehicle that you won't want to drive around – the challenge is to fit everything you need into the smallest possible vehicle, without unduly sacrificing the level of comfort that you will be happy with.

Other things to think about when trying to decide which van to go for are things like the engine size. Bigger and more powerful engines tend to cost more, but if you are likely to be driving long distances and you don't want to be sat behind the wheel forever then it is probably worth investing in a higher spec. engine.

## How New?

Alongside the question of what size of vehicle you get, another critical question tends to be the rough age, mileage, and condition of the vehicle. Of course this is almost always constrained by your budget, however it is important to try to hit a sweet-spot. Your aim should be to get something that you can afford that will also provide a good base vehicle to make the effort (and cost) of the conversion worthwhile.

A Citroen C35, still going strong!

A classic VW campervan.

A sad tale to tell is that of the converter who purchased a supposed 'bargain vehicle', poured their heart and sole into the conversion, only to find their vehicle was already nearing the end of its life. It is true that a well looked after vehicle can be made to last a long time, but this requires a fair amount of nurturing and TLC that, if lacking in the earlier years, can be hard to come back from once a critical amount of rust and mechanical decay sets in.

----------

"…get the newest and lowest mileage vehicle you can afford,
and adjust the level, cost, and effort of your conversion to
match the condition of the vehicle"

----------

A major benefit of converting your own vehicle is that you should be able to afford a newer base vehicle than if you were buying a pre-converted campervan. Old professionally converted campervans and motorhomes can fetch eye wateringly high price tags despite their age (especially if they retain a low mileage). One of the strongest recommendations this author can give you is to get the newest and lowest mileage vehicle you can afford, and adjust the level, cost, and effort of your conversion to match the condition of the vehicle.

In other words, if you are buying a fairly new, low mileage vehicle, then spending good money and effort carrying out an all singing / all dancing conversion may well be worthwhile; however, carrying out the same standard of conversion on a much older, high mileage, heavily rusted vehicle is a blighted enterprise from the outset.

Many people fall into the trap of mismatching the standard of their conversion to the standard of their vehicle. By all means, stick to a low budget and pick up a characterful old vehicle nearing the end of its days… but limit yourself to spending a proportionately low amount on the conversion, bearing in mind that you may well need to upgrade the vehicle in a few years time. By the same token, if you decide to invest in a new or nearly new vehicle then investing in a high standard, relatively expensive conversion will make more sense… assuming your pockets are deep enough.

# How Many Passengers?

Before even starting to look at vehicles you need to have decided roughly what you want to use your van for and especially how many people are likely to be using it. If you are confident that it will only ever be you and maybe one other person, then finding a van with two (or three) good travelling seats in the front should be straightforward. However, if you are a family with several kids, all requiring both good seats with seat belts, and beds, and space for everyone's stuff, then the options may start to look more limited.

# The Ideal Van

In order to home in on the sort of vehicle you'd like to end up with, try jotting down some criteria to help focus the mind. By picking out a list of things you'd like to have in the van, and by defining what you'd like to use the campervan for, you are more likely to be able to see the wood for the trees.

## What will you want to put in the van?

| Useful Items…? |
| --- |
| Cooker / stove and gas |
| Fridge |
| Sink and/or water tank |
| Heater |
| Second battery |
| Bed / seating (how many people?) |
| Swivel seats |
| Table |
| Storage units |
| Toilet / shower |
| Pets? |
| Kit / toys (bikes, boats, skis, surfboards etc...) |

## What will you use the van for?

| Trip Types |
| --- |
| Long trips |
| Short trips |
| Dual Use (e.g. work and holidays) |
| Daily driving |
| Good / bad roads / 4WD needed? |
| At home / Abroad / Overland |
| Just you or 2, 3, 4 people etc... |

"…the challenge is to fit everything you need into the smallest possible vehicle, without unduly sacrificing the level of comfort…"

# Panel Vans

At first glance, there is a bewildering array of different vans out there… and to be honest the full range of options stays fairly mysterious even to those immersed in the industry. However, without going into all the intricacies, a run through of the main panel van options and how they compare to each other should help the uninitiated start to make inroads into deciding which van would be about right for their needs. Van models can be roughly broken down into different size categories, although there is of course a fair degree of overlap. Even when the information here was compiled it was never comprehensive, and since vehicle models are constantly evolving this should only be used as a starter for ten in your search for your ideal vehicle. The make and model names are those currently used in the UK, but note that sometimes the names and availability differs slightly overseas.

A VW Caddy next to a long wheel base, high roof Fiat Ducato.

# Car Derived Vans and Microvans

For those of you looking for the smallest of vehicles, some of these models may suit your needs. They are too small to do much more than sleep for the odd night in, but to paraphrase an old saying "one man's mini is another man's palace". The car derived van models are self explanatory in that they are basically the same shape as the car with the same name, but usually without seats or windows in the back. Models such as the Ford Fiesta, Vauxhall Astra and Corsa, and even the classic Mini Van are examples of this category.

The microvan category, including models such as the DFSK Loadhopper, is also included here but in many ways it is difficult to place it – these vans are decreasingly common in the UK, but are still popular in some countries and, although currently few are sold new here, they can still be found on the second hand market.

# Small Vans

The vans in this category are still a little too small to be considered conventional campervans, but in many ways they are great vehicles to switch to from a car.

Some of the smallest vans are, in reality, no bigger than a car which makes them very good as general run-around vehicles, but quite small if you want to do any more than just sleep in them. Most converters will stop short of using the smallest car-derived vans like Vauxhall Astra or Ford Fiesta vans; but many people will find the next size up quite appealing – vans such as the VW Caddy, Ford Transit Connect, and others can provide a great compromise between an estate car and a bigger panel van, and there are some ingenious solutions to small campervan layouts which can make these diminutive vehicles work very well.

A long wheel base Transit Connect conversion.

Other vans that fit somewhere into this size category are the Citroen Dispatch, Fiat Fiorino and Doblo Cargo, Fiat Scudo, Nissan NV200, Peugeot Bipper, Peugeot Expert, Peugeot Partner, Vauxhall Combo, Renault Kangoo, and Mercedes Citan. In other words, plenty to choose from! Take some time researching sizes of current models and alternatives on the web – Wikipedia usually contains good breakdowns of models including their sizes, engines, and histories.

## Mid-size Vans

Next up in size are vans like the VW Transporter, Ford Transit Custom, Mercedes Vito, and Renault Trafic / Vauxhall Vivaro. Note that the Trafic and Vivaro are a joint project and therefore essentially the same vehicle. Similar in size but slightly different in style are vans such as the Mazda Bongo, Mitsubishi L300, and Toyota HiAce. The ubiquitous VW Transporter vans, now in their sixth generation (the T6), are in this size category, and for a lot of people this is what they will think of when they hear the word 'campervan'. These vans are a great size for a campervan because they are big enough to fit a good living area into (bed, kitchen facilities, seating) without being overly cumbersome to drive and park. You still have to be fairly space conscious at this size, and cunning solutions like seat swivels, rock and roll beds, and pop-top roofs help make the most of the relatively limited space.

Different generations of VW Transporters, all with pop-tops fitted.

Most of the models here come in a short and long wheelbase, and there are often high top versions as well. Long wheel base (LWB) vans give you that bit more space - for example a LWB VW T5 has an extra 30cm in between the front and rear wheels; 30cm may not sound like a lot but the extra length can actually make quite a difference. The downside of long wheel bases is they are a little harder to manoeuvre, although this is mainly psychological and you quickly get used to the small difference.

A number of the models in this category have pop-top roofs available for them, and rock n roll style beds are aimed squarely at these vehicles. Although there are exceptions, these vans are too small to fit a bathroom in, but as many people have shown over the years, it is perfectly possible to live and travel in this size of van for months on end.

A basic Mitsubishi L300 conversion.

A VW T4 conversion.

Most mid-size vans have a choice of rear doors – either a single tailgate door which raises up and can be good for sheltering under, or two barn doors which tend to be better suited for bike racks. Swivel seats are available for most of these vans with the frequent exception of the HiAce, L300, and Bongo in which some models have the engine under the front seats making swivelling seats tricky to achieve.

# Big Vans

Taking a jump up in size there are the Renault Master / Vauxhall Movano, Fiat Ducato / Citroen Relay / Peugeot Boxer, and the Ford Transit - these all come in a variety of wheelbase lengths and roof heights. They all make good base vehicles for conversions that become more like motorhomes than campervans. For those who want to be able to comfortably stand inside and particularly for those who list a bathroom as an essential requirement, these are probably the size of van for you. In their long wheel base / high roof sizes these vans are big enough to fit a decent living area, a bathroom, and a fixed full-size bed without being so big as to become a pain to drive around. The vans in this category are frequently used by professional converters to make motorhomes (rather than campervans).

A long wheel base, high roof Fiat Ducato.

A medium wheel base, high roof Vauxhall Movano.

The really big vans are the Mercedes Sprinter / VW Crafter, and the Iveco Daily, as well as the extra long wheel base (also known and 'jumbo' and 'maxi') versions of the vans mentioned previously. These vans are suitable for larger motorhome style conversions and you can fit loads into them, but they do feel really quite big to drive. It's worth noting that even the biggest panel vans are still narrower than most coach-built motorhomes which can be a major advantage, especially on narrow roads.

A prominent feature of this category are the three joint manufacturing projects:

- the VW Crafter and Mercedes Sprinter are essentially the same vehicle with different badges on them.

An Iveco Daily conversion – one of the bigger panel van options.

- the same applies to the Ducato / Boxer / Relay trio which are rebadged models of the same vehicle.

- the Renault Master / Vauxhall Movano / Nissan NV400 triplet are also the same underlying vehicle.

Various details between the joint project models will usually be different – for instance the interior trim, optional extras, and engine specs., but in essence these sets of vans are fundamentally the same.

# Other Vehicle Options

One of the great things about converting your own vehicle is that you can choose whatever vehicle takes your fancy. Your imagination and enthusiasm are the only real limitations here, so don't feel constrained to follow the norm – pick something that inspires you and go forth. Be aware that some of these vehicles (particularly the bigger commercial ones) may need special licences to drive, and the servicing and MOT requirements may differ and need specialist garages.

Not just a potential home, but a potential business

- **Minibuses** – These are frequently just window versions of popular panel vans and they are commonly available on the second hand market.  One of the big attractions of using a minibus is that you won't need to add windows – in fact, you may end up with the opposite problem and want to block some of them off.  The passenger seats can easily be unbolted and removed and at a push you may be able to re-use or even sell some of them.

- **Ambulances** – Essentially panel vans with a load of medical kit in the back, ambulances can be great options for a campervan conversion.  They have often been driven a lot, but are usually well serviced.  They will sometimes have provision for a leisure battery and electrics which may be re-usable.  Think carefully about whether the doors and any wheelchair ramps etc. are going to be compatible with your plans.  If you manage to find one with the flashing lights and siren still working, try not to get caught using them!

- **Buses** – If you are looking for a bigger vehicle then a bus or coach is one option.  Often school buses and smaller community buses can make good conversions, but you could also get a full size coach and convert it into a large motorhome or band tour bus.  As with minibuses, the windows and seats can be both helpful and a hindrance, depending on your plans.

- **Lutons, lorries, & trucks** – There are all sorts of different shapes and sizes of lorries and trucks, from old fire wagons to the biggest artics., but one of the most common type to be converted into a campervan is the Luton style.  Unless you plan on building a whole shell you will want one with solid walls.  There is potential for a really large conversion with this type of vehicle, although parking-up options become a little more limited.

A truck conversion prepared for expedition use.

An inspirational expedition truck from www.pan-trucks.at

- **Unimogs** – These are really just another type of truck (and there are other makes) but they are worthy of their own mention as they are often used as base vehicles to create real expedition campervans.  There's a good reason that these vehicles have been used so widely by the military around the world.  There are numerous different models but they all have 'all wheel drive' (either four or six wheel drive) and are designed to thrive in terrain and environments where few other vehicles would dare to tread.

Overland vehicles in the South of Spain, bound for Africa...

- **Pickups and Utes** – Vehicles such as the Ford Ranger, VW Amorak, Mitsubishi L200, Nissan Navara, and Toyota HiLux can also be adapted in various ways to serve as campervans. These are great off-road vehicles and are designed to be workhorses – if you want to tow heavy loads this may be what you need. Models with fully enclosed load-areas can be adapted to include your living accommodation. You can even either construct a permanent camper structure on the back of the pickup, or adopt the 'slide on camper' approach which allows the pickup to be used without the camper pod when required.

- **Four Wheel Drives** – All sorts of 4WD vehicles can make great camper conversions. In fact there is a thriving scene of people converting and using Land Rovers, Jeeps, and other 4WDs. These are obvious vehicles to consider if off-road travel is your aim, and for overland expedition use they may well be the base vehicle of choice. They are sometimes fitted with pop-tops or even highly modified with the addition of custom built bodies.

- **Horseboxes** – These vehicles offer great conversion potential and can be either be converted in their entirety into campervans or their horse-carrying capacity can be retained with a small portion split off to form accommodation when away at events and on the road.

A large horse box conversion.

- **Ice Cream Vans and Other Vehicles** – There are few vehicles that can't be converted into a campervan of some sort, given the right vision from the owner. You don't need to feel constrained by what other people think is a good idea – if you have the inspiration and the skills to make a campervan out of an old plane, or a giant fibreglass coke bottle, go for it… and send us a picture for the next edition!

Anything goes!

# 01 Buying Your Vehicle

| | |
|---|---|
| **PREREQUISITES** | Earn some cash. Think, discuss, & search! |
| **DO BEFORE** | Everything else |
| **COMBINE WITH** | Planning your conversion |

EASY / MODERATE
2/5

Once you have homed in on the sort of vehicle you want, the next challenge is to actually find one to buy.

There is almost certainly the perfect vehicle for you out there somewhere… but finding it can be a tricky business. Your search these days is likely to start online and looking at Autotrader, Gumtree, Ebay, Facebook, and no doubt many other sites will often prove fruitful. Many people have also successfully let the vehicle come to them by posting 'wanted' ads in various places. Whether you find them online or in the papers, the three main ways to buy a vehicle are:

- **Dealers** – buying a vehicle from a dealer is likely to be the option offering most ease and more peace of mind, but also the more costly route. If the dealer is offering a warranty on the vehicle, this can be worth a lot as you then know you have some recourse if things go wrong. Make sure the warranty covers a reasonable period and will cover things you are worried about – e.g. the engine and mechanical failure. It is reasonable to expect a dealer to put the vehicle through an MOT before you buy it and this is another good selling point. If you have something to part-exchange this may help sweeten the deal but be aware that dealers will always try to 'buy low, sell high'. They will often put high prices on things to start with, so that they can offer big discounts or offer you what seems like a good trade-in price.

- **Private** – buying a vehicle privately can be a way to get a good deal (often for both parties). However, there is none of the security of buying from a dealer, so you need to be happy taking the plunge before handing the money over.

- **Auction** – buying a vehicle at auction is not for the faint hearted and is only a good option for those who both know what they are looking at and are willing to take a certain amount of risk. That said, there are some good deals to be had if you keep looking. You should plan on attending more than one auction before buying as it takes quite a bit of getting used to. Remember that auction fees and usually VAT will be added onto the hammer price. You will need to pay a deposit straight away so make sure you have the means to do so before bidding.

A commercial vehicle auction - more vans than you can shake a stick at.

# What to Look For

If you don't know what you are looking for then it's best to get some help. Take along a friend who knows about vehicles and engines or invest in an AA check. Here's a quick list of some key things you should look at:

- **Age** - this is probably the single biggest factor that will affect the price - the price drops dramatically with each year, and for good reason. Get the newest vehicle you can afford, with the lowest miles.

- **Mileage** - the importance of this does vary with van makes and models. High mileage but newer vehicles will generally last longer than older low mileage vans. An old campervan, driven only on the odd weekend in the summer and stored over winter will have a very low mileage, while an ex-delivery van, even only 2 or 3 years old may already have 100,000+ miles on the clock. Mileage isn't everything - bear it in mind, find out what is average for the make and age, but put that in the context of how other aspects of the van fit what you want.

One tip to help you home in on how much life a van might have left in it is to look through all the vans of that make that are for sale as 'non-runners' and see what the average mileage is. For some vehicles it is common to see 'non-runners' with under 100k miles logged, while some vans are rarely seen as 'non-runners' until their engines have several hundred thousand miles on the clock. Some manufacturers will also list the vehicle's designed for serviceable life – after which some vehicles may well soldier on for a long time, but all bets are off.

- **MOT** - getting a vehicle with as close to a year long MOT as possible is a good start. Be suspicious if the MOT is almost up - work will almost certainly be required, which may be fine so long as you budget for it and so long as you haven't missed something major.

- **Leaks** - check door and window seals and look for wear or evidence of water (e.g. staining). For existing conversions / campervans, check where anything has been added which breaks the integrity of the van e.g. vents, windows, rooflights, or a pop-top roof.

- **Rust** - check the vehicle all over for rust. Look underneath, wheel arches, door sills, exhaust pipe, etc. If the vehicle is quite old some rust is probably inevitable – this is ok if repairs have been done well or you feel you have identified all the problem areas and are confident you can fix them.

- **Service History** - a full service history (FSH) is a must for a relatively new van but is much more unlikely to find with older vehicles. An incomplete but current record of repairs and services is better than nothing and can help you to plan when major components should need replacing.

Finally, take the vehicle on a test drive (make sure you are insured first, minimum 3rd party) and try out all the features; this includes appliances if you are buying an existing campervan. Be highly suspicious of any vehicle you are not able to see or allowed to test drive. Beyond the basic mechanics and engine power you want to think about comfort for sitting (drive position, head height, passenger comfort etc.) as well as the manoeuvrability, especially how easy it is to park.

Once you've made your wish list, searched long and hard for the perfect vehicle, as well as having thoroughly checked it over and driven it… your next step is to pluck up the courage to buy it and start converting… Good luck!

_____

"Pluck up the courage to buy, and start converting!"

_____

# PLANNING & PREPARATION

In many ways, the planning stage for your project should come before you go out and buy the vehicle. The better honed your vision of the end-product, the more likely it is that you will end up with a vehicle that suits your needs. Your planning should start by answering some broad-brush questions such as:

- Number of passengers requiring seats with seatbelts?
- Frequent wild / offgrid parking up or often campsite based?
- Number and type of berths (beds) required?
- Winter use?
- Sporting equipment to be carried (inside or outside the van)?
- How important is it to be able to stand up?
- Any pets?
- How important are kitchen facilities?
- Do you plan to stay in the van for extended periods or just for the odd night?
- Do you have specific requirements such as a fixed bed, a good dining area, a bathroom?
- Mainly day-van use?

Answering some of these questions will drive your choice of vehicle, and you may well need to go back and forward over your requirements before you come up with a set that works for you. All choices when planning a conversion have implications – for space needed, for cost, for amount of work required – and therefore coming up with a final plan for your project will almost always require a series of compromises to be made. For instance you can't have a stand-up bathroom in a low roof van, and you can't have a luxury conversion including all mod-cons for a really tight budget.

A conversion being designed around bikes fitting under the bed in the back.

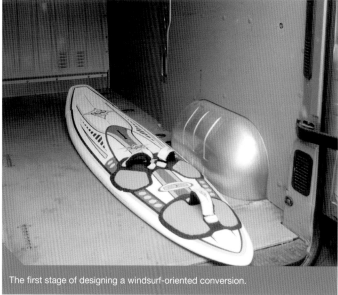
The first stage of designing a windsurf-oriented conversion.

You need to come up with a wish-list of features and then weigh them up against each other, considering the implications of each decision, until you come up with a basic plan that will work for you. To complicate matters further, this process is frequently a team effort requiring careful consideration of the priorities of each of the eventual users of the vehicle.

Many experienced converters will tell you that they went through numerous differing vehicles and layouts before finding out what really worked for them. Even just after completing a new conversion, many converters will already be thinking "next time I'll do X, Y, and Z differently". It is well worth re-iterating that compromise is a necessary evil – a major attraction of converting a van yourself is designing it to your own requirements, but be under no illusion that you will be able to satisfy every single item on your ultimate wish-list… the best you can aim for is to come up with a well balanced set of compromises.

# Planning Choices

When planning a conversion project it is useful to go through various lists of choices to help you come up with a shortlist of requirements.  Try going through the following lists and see what you end up – you might be surprised at the outcome.

"All great conversions utilise every last bit of available space,
and every item has its own little cubby-hole"

## Storage

Come up with a comprehensive list of all the items you will have with you on your travels.  Your aim should be to find a space in the vehicle for everything.  All great conversions have one thing in common – they tend to utilise every last ounce of available space, and every item of kit, clothing, food, and all the other accoutrements of travel have their very own little cubby-holes to be tucked away in.  The following is just a small list of suggested items to get you started.

- Food
- Pans, plates, cutlery, utensils
- Clothes
- Shoes
- Sports equipment
- Sports accessories (e.g. wetsuits, bike spares, etc.)

- Tools including vehicle jack / spare wheel
- 1st Aid and fire extinguisher
- Cleaning products, loo roll, etc.
- Washing line, deckchairs, picnic table
- Books, maps, magazines, etc.
- Wine and beer

Everyday items need to be easy to get at whilst less frequently used things can be tucked away.  Remember you will want things to be secure and not rattling about when you drive.

## Appliances

What appliances will your campervan have?  How basic or luxurious do you want your campervan experience to be?  This list will have a major effect on your budget, so think carefully about what you really need!

- Fridge / Electrics
- Stove (number of rings / oven / grill)
- Sink / running water
- Hot water / Heating
- Bathroom – shower, toilet, sink

In addition to answering yes or no to these items, also consider what size they should be and where they will be located?  Do they need to be near something else?  Most of the items above are considered further in their own chapters later in the book.

It makes the conversion process easier if you can gather most of the items to be installed near the start – time for a shopping trip!

# Layouts

Once you've worked out what you want in your van, you need to work out how to fit it all in... squeezing beds, seats, kitchen, bathroom, sports equipment, and storage inside a cramped van can often seem unlikely at first glance. A quick sketch might help you see how (or if) everything will fit. Use the dimensions for your chosen vehicle and draw out the floor plan or even a number of 3D internal views of your van. It can be handy here to rope in a friend who is skilled with a pencil and paper (or a CAD package) if you're less than artistic. You can also flip this around and draw your ideal van layout and then find a vehicle with dimensions to suit.

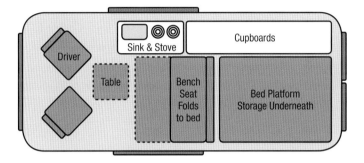

**Classic Camper with 'Rock-n-roll' Bed**

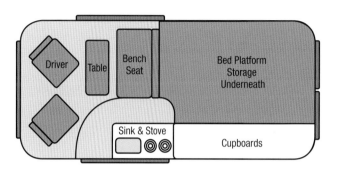

**Fixed Full Length Bed Platform with Dinette**

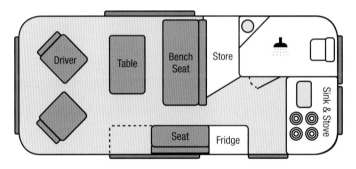

**Rear Kitchen with Bed in High-roof**

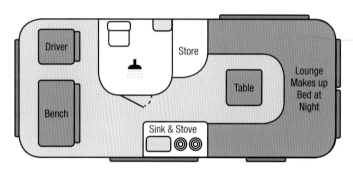

**Rear Lounge with 3 Cab Seats**

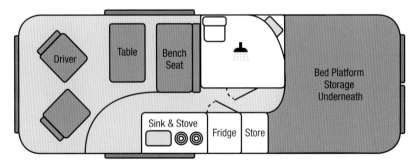

**Transverse Bed Platform with Dinette**

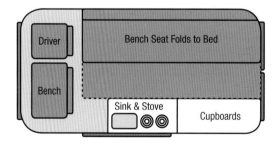

**Compact Camper with Side-on Bench/Bed**

A small selection of the endless different ways to layout a campervan. Seek out common tried-and-tested layouts online as these are well worth using as a starting point.

For the less able sketchers amongst us one of the best ways of getting a better handle on the layout is to physically mock it up. This can be as simple as moving various objects – seats, surf boards, bits of wood – around in your living room. It can also be useful to chalk out floor layouts (either in the van if you have it already, or in a garage or outside if not) or create rough cardboard cut outs of furniture so you can get an impression of how things will look, and more importantly, fit.

If you are starting completely from scratch, it can be really hard to know where to begin. Deciding on a couple of big-ticket essential items which you can't cope without is the best way to start – after factoring the dimensions of these high priority items into your plan, you will start to see your design emerge and get a better feel for what other items you will be able to fit in.

Another top-tip is to look extensively at layouts produced by others – both those of your friends, but also have a look at layouts used by professional converters (they often have images on their websites of the various models they produce). One good way to see lots of different layouts in one place is to go along to one of the campervan and motorhome shows of which there are a number at various big exhibition centres each year.

# Preparation

By now you've done your research, decided what your ideal campervan will look like, searched high and low, and eventually found yourself the perfect vehicle. Your shiny new (well, new to you at any rate) base vehicle is sitting in the driveway waiting for you to start… what now?

> "…the best thing you can do to get your project off to a good start is give yourself a nice clean sheet to start from…"

No matter what sort of vehicle you are converting, the best thing you can do to get your project off to a good start is give yourself a nice clean sheet to start from, and make sure you have at least a reasonable proportion of the various tools and materials you are going to need. It can be hugely counterproductive and usually a false economy to try to retain or work-around existing features – those that are inexperienced will often bend over backwards to retain an existing panel, or some rotten flooring, or a rather shoddy set of existing shelves, thinking that they are saving some effort or cash, but in fact working around these will almost always prove more effort in the long run. On the first day you get the vehicle, the best thing you can do is strip it out, right back to bare metal.

Old floor boards should be removed but they are useful as templates.

Sometimes the first task is to give the floor a good clean!

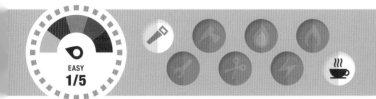

| PREREQUISITES | Buy your base vehicle |
| --- | --- |
| DO BEFORE | Starting your conversion |
| COMBINE WITH | Planning, Removing Bulkhead |

EASY
1/5

Start by stripping out all and any panels, writing numbers on the backs and keeping a note of where things went if you think you might forget. If there are panels and flooring in place it can be tempting to leave them in situ, however unless they are in good condition and you don't need to get under or behind them for any reason this is often a mistake. If there are existing floor boards and panels that are rotten or otherwise in a poor state, keep hold of the old boards as you can often use them as templates to create replacements.

Flooring will often be screwed down to the metal floor so carefully find all the screws and try to get them out – this can be tricky if the screw heads have long since been hidden by grime or become unusable. If required you can either drill the screws out or lever the boards up over the screw heads and then you will be able to extract them by gripping them with a pair of pliers or mole grips.

A good van to start converting – the panels, and bulkhead all came straight out to allow insulating, but in this case the floor was good enough to leave in place.

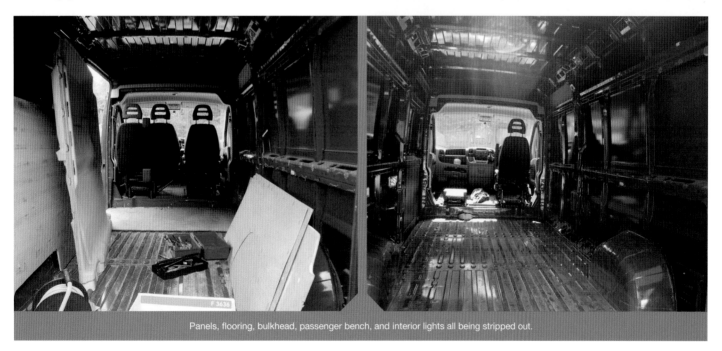

Panels, flooring, bulkhead, passenger bench, and interior lights all being stripped out.

Panels are usually either screwed or riveted in place, or attached using a variety of plastic fixings. Obviously screws can be unscrewed as normal. Any metal rivets will need to be drilled out using a metal drill-bit. Plastic fixings can usually be levered out with a large flathead screwdriver (or a plastic pry-bar or similar is better if you have one) – you may be tempted to reuse the fixings but if you are planning to carpet line the panels it is more likely that you will be using new fixings (probably screws) so don't worry too much about getting them out intact.

# 03  Removing the Bulkhead

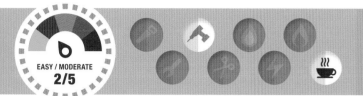

EASY / MODERATE
2/5

| PREREQUISITES | Buy your base vehicle |
|---|---|
| DO BEFORE | Starting your conversion |
| COMBINE WITH | Planning, Removing Panels |

If the van has a bulkhead behind the cab seats, this will usually need to be taken out – this may just be a case of undoing the bolts and man-handling the large sheet of metal out.  Frequently however, bulkheads are fitted with some 'security bolts' that are designed to make it difficult for an intruder to access the cab from the cargo area and vice versa.  These bolts are usually impossible to remove without damaging them in some way – for this, an angle grinder is your friend!  Often you can grind a slot in the head of the security bolts and then unscrew them with a flat head screwdriver… or grind the head off completely and then once the bulkhead is out you can use some mole grips to grab the remaining bolt shaft and unscrew it.  There is a slim chance you may be able to sell the bulkhead, but it is more likely that it will clutter up your garage for the next twenty years… so you may want to put thoughts that "it might come in useful for something" to one side, cut your losses, and take it straight to your local scrap and recycling yard.

A good first step is often to remove the bulkhead.

Most bulkhead bolts can be undone with a socket set.

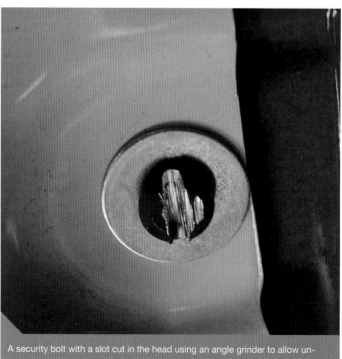

A security bolt with a slot cut in the head using an angle grinder to allow unscrewing using a flathead screwdriver.

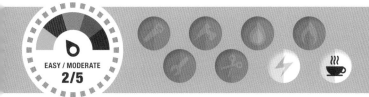

**EASY / MODERATE 2/5**

| PREREQUISITES | Buy your base vehicle |
|---|---|
| DO BEFORE | Starting your conversion |
| COMBINE WITH | Removing Panels |

Your base vehicle will probably have some existing wiring – for example some lights in the cargo area that come on when the doors are open. The temptation here again is to try to reuse these existing electrics but tread carefully – internal lights in the backs of vans (especially older models) are frequently inefficient and they will be wired into the vehicle starter battery. These are almost always best removed and replaced with efficient LED lights wired off a new leisure battery. The best plan is to unscrew or lever the existing lights out of their positions, unplug the wires from the back, tape the wires up and push them back into the strut. Ideally you should also disconnect the wires at the fuse end (or simply remove the fuse) but this may be tricky to do without affecting internal cab lights.

Remove original lights and replace with efficient LEDs.

"There is a slim chance you may be able to sell the bulkhead, but it is more likely that it will clutter up your garage for the next twenty years…"

# INSULATION

In recent years there has been an explosion of detailed information about pretty much everything on the internet, and no subject exemplifies this trend more than how to insulate a campervan conversion. Despite this flood of information, there remains huge doubt amongst the converting public about how best to insulate their vehicles. Debate rages online about materials, strategies, whether to leave air gaps and all sorts of other details which only serve to confuse and debilitate the would be converter. In fact, insulating a campervan should be remarkably straightforward – and the simpler you keep it, the quicker your conversion will be completed and the sooner you'll be on the road exploring your new found freedom.

You insulate your vehicle primarily to keep it warm. If you use your vehicle in warmer climes, the insulation will also help to keep it cool or at least stabilise dramatic swings in temperature. At the same time as keeping your van warm, the insulation will also help combat two other big problems associated with van-dwelling – condensation and sound-proofing (more on those soon).

# 05  Install Insulation – Keep it Simple

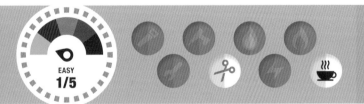

| | | |
|---|---|---|
| EASY 1/5 | PREREQUISITES | Remove original panels, Fit windows / other structural work |
| | DO BEFORE | Replacing panels |
| | COMBINE WITH | Running cables |

You don't need to agonise over the details of insulating your vehicle – keep it simple:

1. Remove the panels.

2. Fill all voids with your chosen insulation (quilt / wool, solid, or closed cell foam for example – more info. below).

3. Cover everything with a sheet of polythene (or other vapour barrier).

4. Put the panels back on.

That's it – it should take you a day or so, then you can move on to more interesting aspects of the project.

# Insulation Materials

Having said you should keep it simple, for those of you who want more information a quick look through the various insulation types may be useful. They all have pros and cons – from being most efficient, to being cheap, thin, environmentally friendly, easy to use, and no doubt any number of other attributes used by marketing gurus to extol the virtues of their particular insulation product. In reality, you are insulating a pretty small space so try not to get bogged down in this choice – pick one, buy it, use it, move on!

Foil insulation covering rock-wool in the cavities, with wiring and panels over the top.

Different insulation types – closed cell foam sandwiched in foil / rockwool / PIR solid insulation boards.

# Insulation Wool

This type of insulation is great for its versatility and availability (but see the Saggy Soggy Wool Warning below). Despite being referred to as 'wool', it is usually not wool from animals, though the manufactured products are modelled on nature. It works by trapping small pockets of air which creates an effective brake on heat passing through it. The domestic housing market uses insulation wool rolls in abundance so all local building merchants will always stock it in one form or another. There are many differing forms of insulation wool, all of which come in rolls of various thicknesses (usually 25mm, 50mm, 100mm, and 150mm). Two rolls of the same thickness can have different insulating values and the better ones will have correspondingly higher price tags.

Empty cavities waiting to be filled with insulation.

# Wool Types

- **Glass and Mineral Wool** – glass wool is made from recycled glass and sand melted at high temperatures and spun into fibres. Similarly, mineral wool is made from molten rock fibres (hence one brand is called Rockwool). They share similar properties – both good insulators, both commonly used forms of insulation; both often irritating to skin and eyes, especially while being installed (wear gloves, dust-mask and goggles). For many this stuff will be the cheap, easy, and effective option to go for when using wool to insulate a vehicle.

- **Natural Wool** – from an environmental and user-friendly point of view, it is hard to beat the use of natural materials. Evolution has spent millennia tweaking and perfecting the stuff that keeps sheep and other animals warm, so there's no reason why it shouldn't keep us warm as well. You can either source wool directly from a farmer, or there are a few companies who clean and refine the raw wool into a more formal insulation product. Either way, pay attention to the section on vapour barriers as damp natural wool not only won't perform very well but will also quickly degrade and smell. If considering natural wool you may also want to consider hemp which is a fast-growing crop.

- **Polyester** – polyester fibre insulation quilt is usually lightweight and thin. It's very user friendly since there aren't any nasty glass fibres or similar in it, so is especially suitable in places where it may not get sealed from the living space. It is also used for wadding in clothing where Thinsulate is one brand example.

# Wool Installation

No matter which type of insulation wool you use, it can be cut with a sharp long bladed knife using a number of passes (ideally cutting onto a concrete floor or plywood offcut rather than your living room carpet). Garden hedge shears can also be used to cut thick quilt. Once cut to size, the wool can either be tucked into the void or if required it can be glued roughly in place using spray adhesive. You don't need to worry too much about this as once the panels go back on they will hold it in place to a reasonable degree. Bits of wool can be stuffed diligently anywhere there are holes in the struts or other small nooks and crannies.

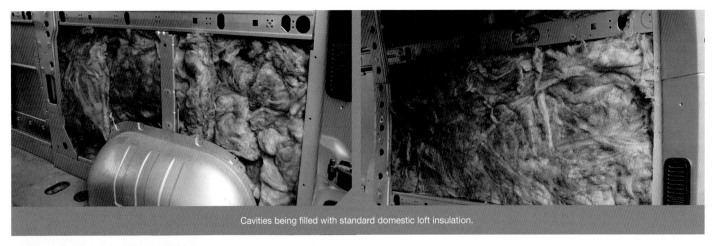

Cavities being filled with standard domestic loft insulation.

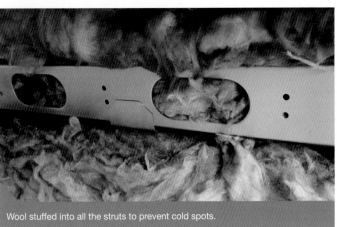

Wool stuffed into all the struts to prevent cold spots.

## Saggy Soggy Wool Warning

Insulation wool is great for its ease and cost, however many professional converters will tell you they have lost count of the times they've pulled sagging, soggy, and rotting wool out from behind panels when renovating vehicles. Wool can still be a good material to use but to avoid these pitfalls it must be paired with an effective and well sealed vapour barrier that prevents moisture getting at the insulation, and the wool batts should be thick enough that it will stay in place behind the panels rather than compressing and sagging over time.

# Solid Insulation (PIR)

Solid insulation panels are often viewed as a top-end insulation product and the price tags often match that. Although frequently referred to by the brand name 'Kingspan', there are numerous other brands making similar products (e.g. Celotex, Quinn-therm, Recticel, EcoTherm, and others). Solid insulation boards are usually made of PIR (Polyisocyanurate) which for the chemists amongst you is a thermoset plastic. The boards are often faced on both sides with foil. Although great from an insulation point of view, the solid boards tend to be fairly pricey. The other big problem with PIR insulation in vehicles is that (especially in the thicker sizes) the boards are fairly rigid so don't easily follow curved panels in the way that more flexible options do.

## PIR Installation

Just as with glass and mineral wool, solid insulation boards tend to irritate skin, lungs and eyes so cover up accordingly. The thinner boards can be cut using a knife, while thicker boards are best cut using a hand saw. You can either hold a batten against the board to guide the saw or follow one of the lines marked on the foil. Thinner boards (e.g. 25mm) can usually be pushed up and fixed onto curved ceilings using spray glue. You may want to supplement rigid insulation with some wool stuffed into gaps to avoid any unwanted cold spots.

# Foam

There are so many differing types of foam available that you could probably write a whole book on the subject (and no doubt people already have). Suffice to say, that there are numerous foam products out there that are great for use as campervan insulation. The stuff that's probably most useful in this context is 'closed cell rubber foam' (which is similar to the stuff that swimming floats are made out of) and it comes in rolls or slabs of varying thicknesses. It sometimes comes with an adhesive backing (though you could easily spray glue it). It is well suited to conversions because it's highly flexible, reasonably thin, and very user friendly. Varieties with foil backing etc. are also available.

You should try to use the thickest insulation that will fit in each void – in other words at the base of the walls the insulation will be pretty thick, but then thinner on the upper walls and ceilings.

## Foam Installation

Foam can simply be stuck to the metal of the vehicle using high temperature spray glue.

Closed cell foam with foil on one side and adhesive on the other makes for easy installation.

"…you are insulating a pretty small space so try not to get bogged down in this choice – pick one, buy it, use it, move on!"

# Condensation, Ventilation, & Vapour Barriers

Condensation forms when warm air laden with water vapour comes into contact with a cold surface. Inside a vehicle warm moist air is produced in abundance – primarily from cooking and from people breathing, but also from wet clothes, showers, outdoor kit drying out, wet dogs, etc. Your objective is to prevent the warm moist air inside the van from touching any cold surfaces, and provide ventilation so that the moisture can escape outside before it gets a chance to condense and cause problems.

> "…prevent warm moist air from touching any cold surfaces, and provide ventilation so the moisture can escape…"

The insulation you install will help keep the moist air inside the van warm. The concept of a vapour barrier is to create a sealed living space, inside the insulation envelope, where the warm moist air is prevented from touching any cold surfaces. The vapour barrier also stops moist air from soaking into your insulation (especially important in the case of wool type insulation).

Polythene over the entire panel to form a vapour barrier.

Thin layers of mineral wool being used on the ceiling before being covered by the vapour barrier.

The simplest material to use for your vapour barrier is polythene but you can also use a layer of thin aluminium foil (often combined with layers of bubbles or closed cell foam) which can double as a radiant barrier as discussed below.

Ventilation must go hand in hand with this system in order to allow the moisture to escape outside in a timely fashion. The ventilation could be as simple as opening a window or two, although there is substantial merit in having ceiling vents or rooflights that you can open. Installing ventilation in places closest to moisture creation is a good idea – for instance a vent above the stove or at least an open-able window; likewise a vent, window, or rooflight in a bathroom (especially with a shower) is essential.

Ventilation is also essential when sleeping in a vehicle, particularly with multiple people – you only need to think of horror stories of smuggled people suffocating in shipping containers to realise that letting some fresh air in at night is a good idea.

# Insulation Physics

Heat moves in mysterious ways… or to put it more precisely, heat energy can travel via conduction, convection, and by radiation. By understanding these basic concepts, you will be better armed to retain as much warmth as possible in your nice snug campervan.

- **Conduction** is the transfer of energy from one particle to another within a solid, liquid, or gas. Metal is a very good heat conductor while air is a poor conductor.

- **Convection** is the transfer of energy with the physical travel of particles from one place to another in a gas or liquid.

- **Radiation** is the transfer of energy via electromagnetic waves.

Each of these types of heat energy transfer need to be considered for effective temperature control. Heat is lost through the van walls, ceiling, and floor primarily by conduction. Insulation slows down conduction, and therefore the thicker the better. If insulation gets wet from condensation (or from leaking windows or rooflights) it loses its effect – hence a vapour barrier is important. Places in the van where metal is exposed or insulation is thin can form 'cold bridges' and these need to be minimised.

After conduction, the main loss of heat is via convection through ventilation or draughts… however, there has to be a compromise: there must be sufficient ventilation to get rid of the moisture from cooking and breathing but not so much that all your precious heat goes out of the window. Ventilation is extremely important if you are cooking or heating with an open flame device - there are sad cases of deaths caused by the build up of carbon monoxide; this risk can be made worse in cold conditions by the potential for ventilation to be blocked by frozen condensation.

Heat loss by radiation can be at least partially addressed by reflecting the electromagnetic waves back into the vehicle – and that's where foil comes in.

———

"…people suffocate in shipping containers so letting
some fresh air in at night is a good idea"

———

# Radiant Barriers & Foil

There are numerous products on the market which are sold on their merits of reflecting heat radiation, and the idea of preventing heat loss by reflecting the heat energy back into the vehicle with one or more thin layers of foil is an attractive one... however the installation details are important otherwise it won't work. A radiant barrier (i.e. a layer of aluminium foil) needs to face an air-gap in order to reflect radiation. If a layer of foil is sandwiched in-between two solid layers, it will just work as a good conductor since it's made of metal.

> "Use a large dollop of pragmatism: aim for a good ratio of effectiveness to effort"

Polyester fibre insulation is nice and thin for ceiling cavities – covered here by foil + closed cell foam to act as both radiant heat and vapour barrier.

There is varying advice about how big an air-gap is needed for the foil to be effective, with some saying a relatively small gap is sufficient (partly due to the short wavelength of infrared radiation) while elsewhere figures of at least half an inch are quoted, with the effectiveness of the foil decreasing as the size of the air-gap gets smaller, though good data on this is hard to come by. How you achieve an air-gap when the foil is sandwiched in your walls is a tricky issue – in a domestic house the barrier is usually draped between rafters in attics or in walls the foil can be separated from contacting other surfaces with one or two inch battens. In vehicles there is much more limited space, so achieving this air-gap is far harder.

A large dollop of pragmatism is required when considering this issue – aim for a good insulation solution that doesn't compromise your budget, or the rest of your project, and more importantly find a solution that provides a good ratio of effectiveness to effort. You could start constructing fancy walls containing battens and air-gaps, but in reality it just isn't worth sacrificing the limited space, adding the extra weight, or the additional effort. That's not to say adding in a layer of foil or one of the many foil / bubble or foil / foam products isn't worth doing – if nothing else they do a good job as vapour barriers, add a certain amount of sound deadening, and certainly provide a tidy finished appearance to the insulated van.

The place where radiant barriers definitely do come into their own is on the windows, because here retaining an air-gap on the inside of the vehicle is easy. More on window insulation a little later.

# Soundproofing

After you have bought your vehicle, taken out the bulkhead, and stripped it back to the bare bones, if you take it for a drive the amount of noise can be quite daunting. Especially with bigger panel vans there is a loud cacophony of noise created by the combination of road noise, panels banging and wobbling, and wind whistling past. Don't be too worried at this stage, as every layer of material that gets added back into the empty shell helps to further reduce the noise levels. If you do a good job of insulating the van for warmth, and then add a nice carpet (or similar) lining on-top of all the panels, you will also gain the side-effect of a reasonable level of sound reduction.

If you want to pay additional attention to sound deadening, there are a number of good areas to focus on:

- The floor and wheel-arches – much of the road noise comes up through the floor and especially through the wheel-arches, so even simple measure such as adding an extra layer of thin foam or other insulation to these areas will pay big dividends. Adding a layer of thin closed cell foam insulation underneath plywood flooring helps a great deal.

- Large panels – most panel vans already have sound-deadening struts and/or pads on the panels, but there is nothing to stop you adding some more to further improve things.

- Holes – seal up any holes, especially in the floor, that aren't required for ventilation purposes.

- The engine – particularly in older vehicles and at higher speeds, the engine noise can be quite off-putting. Engine soundproofing blankets are available that can be a big help with this, although most modern vehicles have already paid significant attention to this.

Going the extra mile and adding a layer of insulation over the wheel-arches before carpeting helps reduce road noise.

Unfortunately there is a paradox at play when it comes to soundproofing: the best sound deadening materials are also dense and heavy, and you don't want to add too much additional weight to your vehicle. The reality is that, as already stated, if you do a reasonable job of insulating the van for warmth and make it comfortable you will probably also be relatively happy with the soundproofing.

# Window Insulation

After going to the time and effort of insulating the walls and ceiling of your van, why throw away valuable heat by letting it all escape overnight through the windows?  The simplest solution to window coverings is curtains, but these do little to stop heat escaping.  It is also possible to fit blinds (such as those made by Remis) and these are often seen installed on professional motorhomes.  If you have chosen to fit framed windows these often have the advantage of being double glazed with integrated fly screens and blinds – good reasons to opt for these windows instead of single glazed bonded windows.

Cab window insulation mats in a Fiat Ducato – foil facing out in this case to reflect the sun and keep the van cool.

For DIY converters, material window insulation mats which attach to the window either directly via suckers or using press-studs around the perimeter are one of the simplest and best solutions to window insulation.  Window mats, much like the rest of your insulation, can regulate in two directions – not only do they trap heat inside the van for warmth, they can also reflect sunlight stopping the air inside your van from heating up excessively and thereby keeping the vehicle pleasantly cool in summer.

The benefits of covering the windows when not driving aren't purely about temperature – the mats do a brilliant job of making your van interior private and dark at night.  They also make an impressive difference to the amount of condensation you get on your windows over night, though eliminating it completely on single glazed windows is tricky.

Most window insulation mats are reversible with a foil aluminium coating on one side and a plain (usually grey) material on the other.  The different finishes are there for a reason - the foil acts as a radiant barrier and reflects heat whilst the plain material absorbs it.  If you want to keep the inside of the van warm you put the mats up foil side in, and vice versa if you want to keep the inside of the van cool (in hot weather) face the shiny side outwards.

Window insulation mats with foil facing in to reflect the heat back into the vehicle.  Mats do a much better job than curtains at retaining heat and blocking out light.

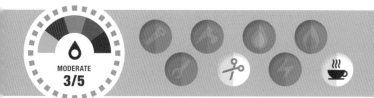

# 06 Making Window Insulation Mats

| | |
|---|---|
| **PREREQUISITES** | - - |
| **DO BEFORE** | - - |
| **COMBINE WITH** | **Do in parallel with rest of conversion** |

MODERATE 3/5

Like many stages in converting a van there are choices: either you can buy the mats ready made or you can have a go at making them yourself. Often a combination of the two is a good approach: the cab windows are awkward and hard to make yourself, so buying a set of pre-made mats for these windows makes sense; side and back door windows are relatively straight forward to make yourself.

## Materials needed:

- Insulation mat material
- Eyelets
- Suction cups
- Edging Trim

## Making the mats:

1. Calculate the lengths and amount of everything required based on the windows to be covered. Always include a reasonable contingency in this calculation as it's far better to have a little too much than too little.

2. Trim the insulation material to size for your window and round the corners, this makes sewing on the hem much simpler as well as helping them to fit more snugly against the van windows.

3. Pin and sew the hemming material, ensuring that it folds around the edge of the insulation material and is sewn on both sides.

4. Finally measure the mat back up against the window and mark where the suction pads should go. Remember that the suckers need to be in full contact with the glass to work so don't put them too close to the edge of the mats.

5. Using the eyelets as a guide, carefully cut out the eyelet holes and clip in the eyelets. Fit in the suction pads and stick them to the windows

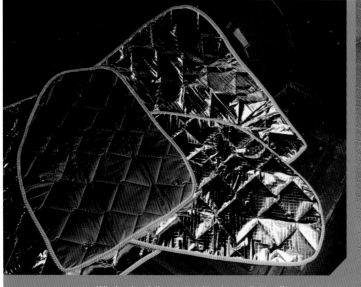
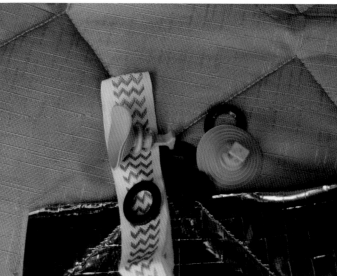

Window insulation material is also available off the roll to make your own mats along with hemming tape, suckers, and eyelets.

# The Extra Mile – False Floors and Framing

For some, a well insulated vehicle becomes close to an obsession and for those of you that fit into this bracket only the best will do. Of course if you are carrying out a full-on conversion project intended to be of high-end quality and for use in colder climes, perhaps even in winter, then there can be plenty of justification for doing this stage of your project well. There is still much debate about what 'the best' actually is, but if you are still reading then the following may provide some useful points to consider.

## Framing

If you don't feel you can get enough insulation to suit your needs into the cavities behind the panels, you may decide to build an internal frame inside the vehicle. You can build an internal frame for the walls, the ceiling, or both. One advantage of this approach is that you end up with vertical walls and a horizontal ceiling, with easy fixing points wherever you need them, all of which does make panelling, cubicle making, and furniture construction easier. If you are building an internal frame you can make it as deep as you need to accommodate your chosen insulation. Bear in mind though that building an internal frame will add effort and significant weight to your project, not to mention taking up valuable space. The approach will be overkill for most (though not all) panel van converters but can certainly be put to good use in big vehicles such as Luton trucks.

The frame construction can be adjusted to suit the situation, but using 2 x 2" softwood is probably about right (certainly any thicker is unnecessarily bulky). Studs should be placed at 400 or 600mm centres which will suit both insulation and plywood panel sizing. Ensure the frame is securely fixed to the vehicle struts and remember to plan for windows, rooflights, etc. before you start. Every time you add another bit of timber, imagine it shaving more miles off your maximum speed and using up slightly more fuel.

## False Floor

If you have anything other than the highest of vehicles, you probably want to retain as much head room as possible. In most vehicles adding a thin layer (e.g. 5mm) of closed cell foam or similar material laid directly on top of the metal floor, underneath plywood floor boards, will do a perfectly acceptable job of both insulating and sound deadening. This also adds a bit of 'give' to the flooring which provides a comfortable feel.

Adding a thin layer of foil backed foam directly to the floor with plywood on top is simple and effective.

If you are converting one of the higher vehicles – for example a Sprinter / Crafter or maybe a horse box or Luton truck – you have more head height to play with and you might want to consider building a false floor. The floor can be constructed by laying a grid of battens at spacing of 400 or 600mm. 2 x 1" or 2 x 2" softwood timber should be plenty for the battens and these can either be stuck or screwed to the floor of the vehicle. You can then fill the voids in between the battens with insulation as you see fit, and then place plywood floor boards across the top of the battens. If required you can make the false floor much deeper in places to accommodate water tanks or additional storage etc. Note that if there are wide spans between battens you will need to use thicker plywood (e.g. 18mm) for the floor boards, whereas if the boards are lying directly on the vehicle floor 12mm ply will be fine.

Softwood batten framing can be added if you want to add extra insulation or raise the floor level up – in this case to match the seat rails in a VW T5.

"Imagine every extra bit of timber slowing you down and using up fuel."

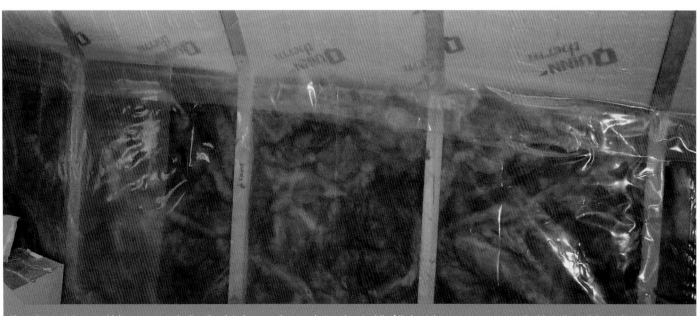

If you frame out your vehicle, you can make it as insulated as your house – but each extra bit of timber takes up more space and adds to the weight you're carrying.

# PANELLING, CARPET LINING, & TRIMMING

Once your vehicle is nicely insulated, and once you have finished cutting any holes and running whatever wiring is required, it is time to make the space a little more comfortable. In a simple conversion, all you might want to do is stick some insulation in, panel and line the space, and throw a mattress in the back – and many a comfy night have been spent in such vehicles.

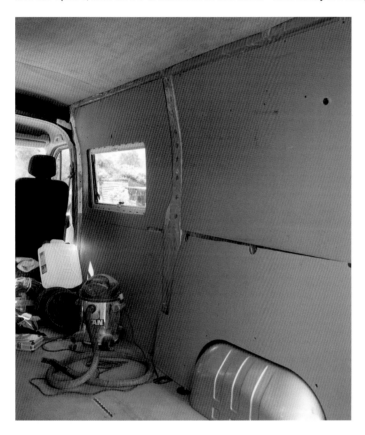 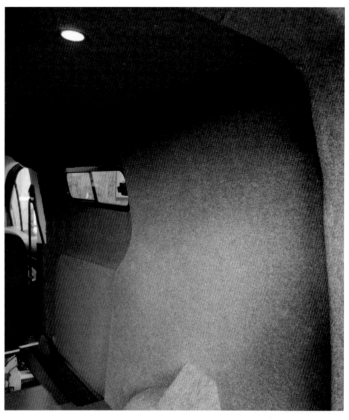

By far the most common way to get a good finish on a home conversion project is to use a combination of nice looking wood, coupled with some form of lining material. The same approach is taken in most cars, with the bulk of a car's structure nicely hidden using fabric covered panels. Professional converters sometimes get moulded fibreglass or plastic panels made, which can look great, but this is rarely an option for the home converter.

# 07 Making Panels

EASY / MODERATE
2/5

| PREREQUISITES | Windows & structural changes, insulation, run cables |
|---|---|
| DO BEFORE | Furniture construction, seats & beds |
| COMBINE WITH | Making floor boards |

Many base vehicles purchased for conversion already have panels on the walls and ceilings, but some won't have any. If you can re-use any panels that are there, it will save you both time and money. If panels are present but damaged, you will probably still be able to make use of them as templates to make a replacement so don't be too hasty in throwing them out. Sometimes original panels made by the vehicle manufacturer are present – these are usually some form of plastic and you should be able to reuse these, perhaps with a little trimming here and there to fit around windows, bed boards, etc.

The panels are fixed on the inside of the vehicle's struts – with the bonus side-effect of creating a natural void to be filled with insulation.

Original panels can often be re-used. Remove them by levering out the plastic rivets which can be replaced with self-tapping screws.

If you have to make new panels from scratch, this is best done using thin 3mm plywood (normally actually 3.6mm) or if on a budget 3mm hardboard can also be used. If you are planning to leave the wood on show instead of covering it then you can pick some nice hardwood plywood or thin 'wallboard' is also available (which is usually paper or vinyl covered plywood that can be picked to match your 15mm furniture ply).

It is helpful to pencil mark an ID onto each panel – e.g. 'left lower back panel' – as they can quickly start to look the same once removed, especially ceiling panels that were cut several weeks or months before. Also mark on a direction arrow and mark which is the front (i.e. internal) side as this is important when you come to lining the panel with material. If you plan on leaving your plywood panels bare, make sure you mark them with pencil and rub out the marks before varnishing.

Original damaged panels should be removed but retained for use as templates to cut new plywood panels.

Start by measuring the maximum height and width of the space your panel is for and cut out a rectangle to match. Then you need to shape it to get a good fit. Long straight cuts are best made using a circular saw, but smaller cuts and curved cuts should be made using a jigsaw. If there is an intricate curve to be cut use fine toothed narrow jigsaw blades.

Thin plywood panels in a Fiat Ducato.

## Scribing a Panel to Fit

One way to get a panel to fit is to take a guess at the right shape, make a cut, hold it up, refine it, hold it up again, refine it some more, etc. You can also try creasing a paper or card template to get the shape. However there is a better, more technical way of getting the right shape and that is to 'scribe' the panel. Scribing is described in more detail in the 'Joinery Skills' chapter elsewhere in the book.

Hold or temporarily fix the panel in place above the wheel-arch and scribe it to get the cut-out shape right (see Joinery Skills chapter).

Panels are scribed to fit around curves and awkward shapes.

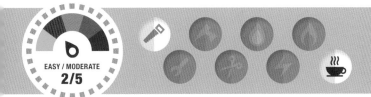

EASY / MODERATE
2/5

| PREREQUISITES | Insulation & first fix wiring |
|---|---|
| DO BEFORE | Furniture construction, seats & beds |
| COMBINE WITH | - - |

If the vehicle you are converting has internal ribs or struts, the chances are you will be able to screw your panels onto these. Almost all panel vans are constructed with numerous hollow metal struts dividing up the sections of the vehicle. You need to be careful not to accidentally drill or screw through the external metal skin of the vehicle, but usually the struts are at least an inch deep (often substantially more) so there should be plenty of room. Start by holding the panel in place and drilling a pilot hole through the panel and on through to the strut being fixed to. The job gets easier once you get the first couple of screws in to hold the panel in place.

Fix panels with self-tapping screws. You will need to drill a pilot hole into the metal strut, ensuring that neither the drill bit or the screw will hit the van's exterior.

The best screws to use are 'self-tappers' which means they create their own threads. The screws should be long enough to go through your panel (with lining material on it), and into the strut, but then stop well before hitting the external skin of the vehicle.

You will need to drill a pilot hole for the screws and this should be done with a drill bit with a smaller diameter than the screw thread. Just how much smaller the drill bit should be depends on the material the screw is going into – if it's into a thin and soft bit of metal, make the drill bit the same size as the shaft of the screw; if it's going into a thicker piece of metal the pilot hole will need to be only just under the diameter of the screw's thread. Trial and error is your friend here – if it's too hard to drive the screw in then take it out and drill a slightly wider hole (otherwise the screw-head may well snap). Note that the hole drilled through the panel itself can be a slightly bigger diameter than the screw.

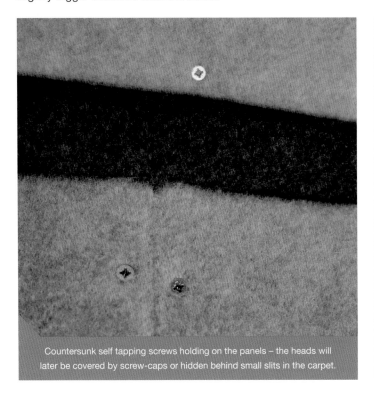

Countersunk self tapping screws holding on the panels – the heads will later be covered by screw-caps or hidden behind small slits in the carpet.

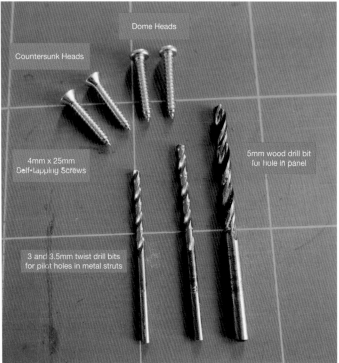

Dome Heads

Countersunk Heads

4mm x 25mm Self-tapping Screws

5mm wood drill bit for hole in panel

3 and 3.5mm twist drill bits for pilot holes in metal struts

Screw heads can be covered neatly with small screw caps at the end of the project. Another approach to getting a neat finish with no screws showing is to cut a small slice through the carpet lining with a sharp blade, put the screw through, then glue the carpet back over the top – done well, this can create an almost seamless finish. The only drawback to the latter approach is if you need to take the panel off it makes it trickier to re-find the screws.

There are other approaches to fixing things to the wall of the vehicle:

● Gluing (or screwing) on battens that things can then be screwed onto.

● Rivet nuts (also known as blind fastenings, rivnuts, nutserts, plus-nuts and other variations) – these are great for giving you some more solid anchor points for heavier items and are particular useful when you want to be able to take things in and out on a regular basis – for instance if you plan to have a removable unit to make the vehicle multi-use.

● Also potentially of interest for those looking for a particular fixing solution are clip nuts, cage nuts, lug nuts, and other variations.

Spending time making, fixing, and lining the panels is well worth the effort to give the conversion a homely and comfortable finish.

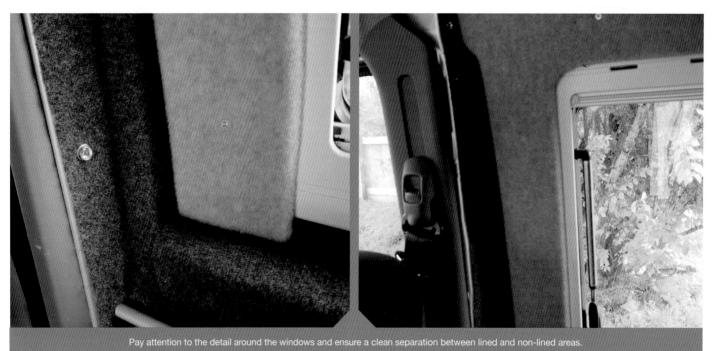

Pay attention to the detail around the windows and ensure a clean separation between lined and non-lined areas.

# Ceiling Panels

Ceiling panels can be curved to follow the contoured ribs of the vehicle. You may well need to add some extra wooden ribs in places to provide fixing points for the panels, especially at the rear end of the ceiling. The wooden ribs can simply be glued on to the metal with high-temperature spray adhesive.

Use spare bits of timber to prop. panels up until you get the first couple of screws in.

3.6mm ply ceiling panels fitted loosely in place – they will be removed and carpet lined before being fixed permanently. It is useful to take a photo at this stage so that you know which struts etc. will need to be lined (the sections where green plastic is showing here).

The rear ceiling panel may need some extra timber ribs added as attachment points.

Cut holes as required for spot lights, rooflights, windows, etc.

# Lining Materials

The choice of which lining material you use is one of the best opportunities to stamp a mark of uniqueness to your conversion. The standard material to use is a thin lining carpet which often has a degree of stretch to it – this comes in numerous colours and there are several similar products on the market ('Easyliner' is one such brand). The thinner lining carpets are great to work with as you can stretch them to fit round most curves, however if you want something a bit harder wearing slightly thicker versions are available which, although less easy to work with, also tend to have better fire-resistance ratings.

Choose a colour and material to make your conversion individual and stand-out. Automotive lining carpet is a popular choice as it has enough stretch to make lining awkward shapes relatively easy.

You can also opt for something other than carpet – there are no hard and fast rules and really any fabric could be used. You could consider using fabrics such as velour or vinyl (perhaps matching seating fabric), or get imaginative and find something to really give your conversion the edge such as corduroy, velvet, or even denim, suede, or leather. Whatever material you go for, care and attention are required to get a neat finish, particularly if the fabric is thick and / or non-stretchy.

# 09  Lining Wheel-arches

| | | |
|---|---|---|
| **PREREQUISITES** | Insulation | |
| **DO BEFORE** | Flooring & fixing panels in place | |
| **COMBINE WITH** | - - | |

MODERATE 3/5

Not only do well trimmed wheel-arches provide a satisfying finish to your conversion, they also play a big part in cutting down on road noise while driving. A substantial proportion of road noise heard in campervans comes through the wheel-arches, so a bit of effort here is time well spent. An alternative approach is to box the wheel-arches in and this has the added side-effect of providing a flat surface e.g. for bed boards to sit on, as well as creating some useful cubbyholes for items such as wheel jacks, roofrack straps, etc.

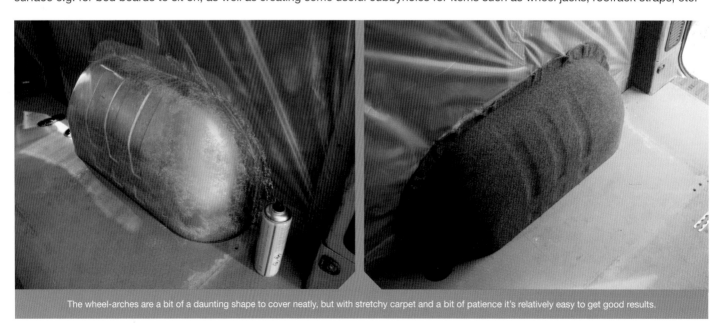

The wheel-arches are a bit of a daunting shape to cover neatly, but with stretchy carpet and a bit of patience it's relatively easy to get good results.

# Lining Wheel-arches, Step-by-step

At first glance the shape of a wheel-arch can be quite a daunting object to cover neatly. This is where a nice stretchy material such as thin lining carpet comes into its own.

1. Cut a large rectangle of your lining carpet with plenty of spare material to easily cover the whole arch, bearing in mind it needs to be big enough to bend over the top and ideally you want a couple of inches spare all the way round.

2. Cover both the wheel-arch and the material with high temperature spray glue and give it a minute to dry.

Use high temperature spray adhesive to coat both surfaces. For extra soundproofing and insulation, a layer of thin closed cell foam (foil backed in this case) can be added under the carpet lining. Give the glue a minute to dry and then make a start.

3. Take your time, get comfy, and start in the middle. Work the material out in one direction and pull it, push it, and stretch it into the right shape. If you're not happy with a bit don't be afraid to peel it back and have another shot – you can be reasonably rough with it, peeling it back and re-applying numerous times.

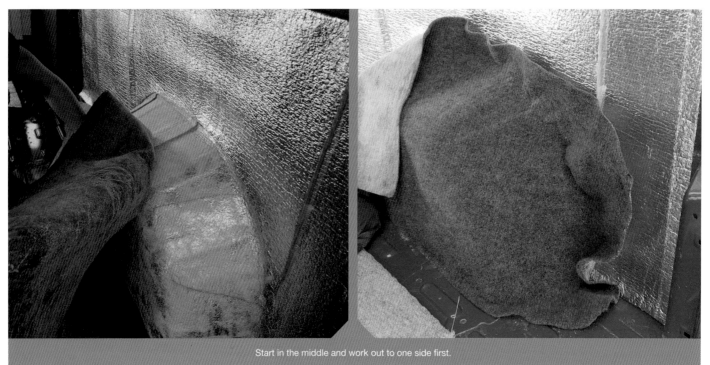

Start in the middle and work out to one side first.

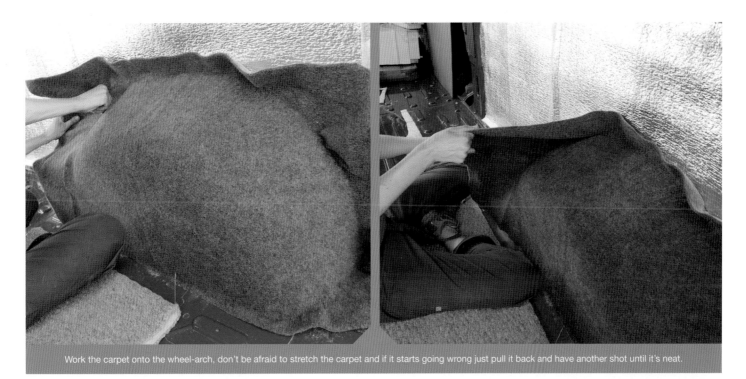

Work the carpet onto the wheel-arch, don't be afraid to stretch the carpet and if it starts going wrong just pull it back and have another shot until it's neat.

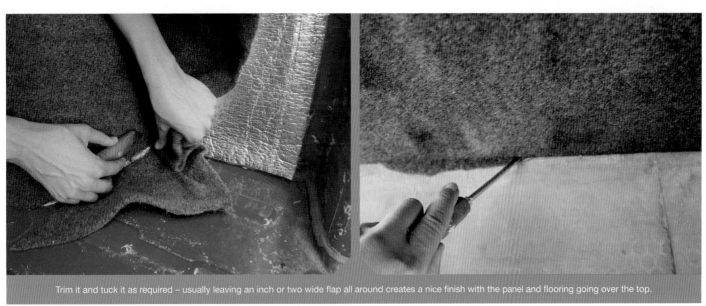

Trim it and tuck it as required – usually leaving an inch or two wide flap all around creates a nice finish with the panel and flooring going over the top.

A finished wheel-arch and panel, though struts behind still need to be done.

4. Once you get to the end you can either trim off the excess or often you can just leave the flaps of material which will be hidden under flooring or panels.

An additional touch is to add a layer of thin insulation (e.g. 5mm closed cell foam) underneath the carpet to really help deaden the road noise.

## High Temperature Spray Adhesive

Always use 'High Temperature' spray adhesive which is designed to remain stuck even when the temperature in the van soars on a sunny day – if you use conventional glue you risk coming back to your vehicle to find the carpet lining hanging off after the glue has melted.

# 10  Lining Struts

PREREQUISITES | Insulation & first fix wiring
DO BEFORE | Fixing panels
COMBINE WITH | - -

MODERATE 3/5

Anywhere that won't be covered by panels, furniture, seats or other structures, will probably need to be lined or trimmed in some way to give it a professional looking finish.  This stage can be quite fiddly but a bit of care and patience is usually rewarded with impressive looking results.  If you are rubbish at wrapping Christmas presents then you may want to rope in someone with a bit of finesse to help you out.  It is useful to see the vehicle with all the panels loosely in place before tackling this so that you can see which bits of metal will need to be covered.  You may want to take a photo or two and then take the panels out again before beginning so you have something to refer back to.

As with trimming the wheel-arches, start by cutting a long rectangular strip of material with plenty of spare.  Use spray glue and take your time stretching and moulding the material to the curved shapes in order to get a good finish.  Use a pair of sharp nail scissors when required to cut out little slices and triangles (darts) to keep things neat in alcoves, corners, etc.  You want there to be an overlap between the panels and the lined struts in order to create a continuous wall of comfort.

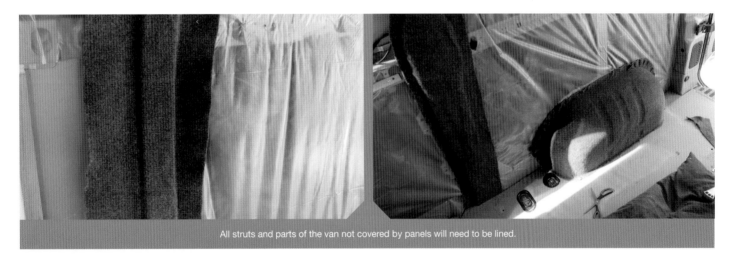

All struts and parts of the van not covered by panels will need to be lined.

Pay attention to getting a neat finish around windows and other awkward features – time spent getting this stage right will result in a far more professional finish.

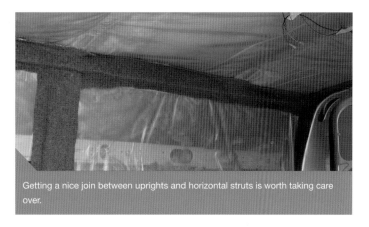

Getting a nice join between uprights and horizontal struts is worth taking care over.

With panels in place you can get a nice seamless effect between strut and panels, or (as here) use two tone colours to make a feature out of the panels.

# 11 Carpeting Panels

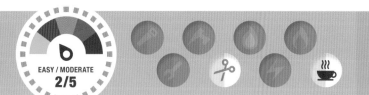

**EASY / MODERATE**
**2/5**

| PREREQUISITES | Cut panels and ensure good fit |
|---|---|
| DO BEFORE | Fixing panels in place |
| COMBINE WITH | Can be done in parallel with wiring, windows, etc. |

When you come to covering the panels, find yourself a good clean area with plenty of space to work in.

1. Cut a large rectangle of material with at least an inch or two of overlap all the way round the panel. Laying your panel on the material will give you an easy guide to cut round.

2. Spray glue over the front of the panel and the back of the material (if you get all the way through the project without getting something the wrong way round at least once you're doing well). Note that lining carpet often does have a front and back so take the time to establish which is which. Leave the glue to set for a minute or so.

3. Carefully lay the carpet onto the board, starting at one end and trying to smooth out any wrinkles as you go. If it starts to go wrong, don't panic, just peel the carpet back and reapply as required until you have a smooth finish.

4. Turn the panel over and start gluing down the overlap. At the corners cut little darts with sharp scissors to achieve a neat finish. If there are any large cut-outs in the panel – for instance to accommodate windows or rooflights – use a knife or sharp scissors to cut out the hole, leaving a good overlap to fold and glue to the back of the board.

5. Where there are holes for spotlights, use sharp scissors to cut a series of darts or triangles and fold these back for a neat finish.

Two-tone carpet lined panels starting to take shape… the screws are still visible but can either be covered with screw-caps or hidden by making small slits in the carpet and then re-sticking it over the top of the screw-heads.

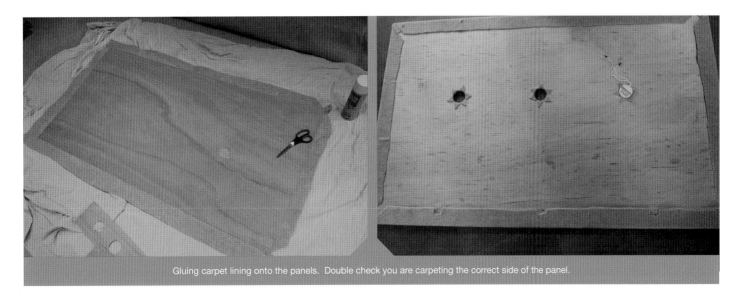

Gluing carpet lining onto the panels. Double check you are carpeting the correct side of the panel.

One way to get a neat finish at the corners and at spotlight recesses.

A finished panel nearly ready to be installed, with one spot light in place.

A van starting to look much more like a campervan. Note screws have been hidden using the carpet slit technique.

# Finishing Touches

It can be the little things that elevate a bog-standard conversion into a showstopper. You might want to add a bit of padding to a doorway to stop people banging their heads and cover it with a nice bit of material. Or perhaps make some cushions out of material to match the lining. Or maybe add some beading or piping to sub-divide spaces. Whatever it is, make the project your own and deploy as much creativity as you want to.

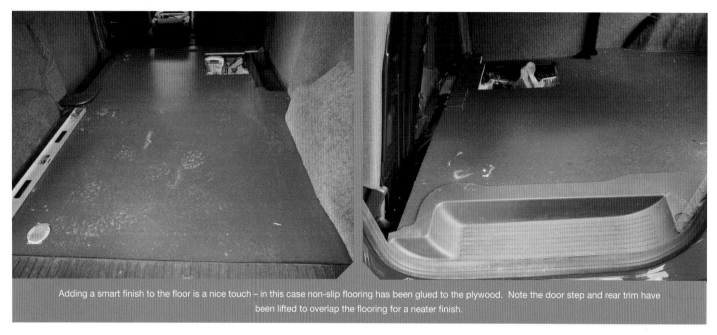

Adding a smart finish to the floor is a nice touch – in this case non-slip flooring has been glued to the plywood. Note the door step and rear trim have been lifted to overlap the flooring for a neater finish.

Here a simple domestic lino has been used to cover the flooring ply, and a length of metal profile is glued in to make a neat edge at the doorway.

# SEATS AND BEDS

In many ways, the seating and bedding in a campervan are the central feature of the whole project. The decisions you make about seats and beds will define the direction and layout of your project, so it's a topic worthy of in-depth consideration. Another way to look at it is that your seating and bed priorities should actually dictate the type of vehicle you go for, so there are few more important aspects of a conversion.

## Swivel Seats

With space at a premium in any size of campervan, being able to swivel the front cab seats round so that they face the living space makes a big difference. It gives you way more living space and makes spending time in the vehicle substantially more sociable and comfortable. Vans seldom come with pre-fitted swivels, so this is likely to be one of the top items on the agenda for a would-be converter.

Seat swivels are not available for all vehicles – there are several good manufacturers producing swivels for the majority of panel vans used for conversions, but you are unlikely to find a good swivel solution in the following cases unless you apply a good degree of ingenuity:

- Small vans (e.g. a VW Caddy, Ford Connect, etc.)

- Vans with the engine under the cab seats (e.g. Mazda Bongo, Toyota HiAce, etc.)

- Passenger bench seats (with a couple of exceptions – more on this below).

It's a fairly straight-forward job to fit a seat swivel; they consist of two plates of metal on-top of each other separated by a pivot. The bottom plate stays fixed to the seat base (the seat base is the metal box mounted to the floor of the van), while the top plate is fixed to the bottom of the actual seat (or more accurately to the sliding runners on the bottom of the seat). You pull a handle to unlock the two plates and the top one swivels around – simple really.

Swivel seats in a VW T5. This relatively small change to a vehicle makes a dramatic difference to the living space

# 12 Fitting Seat Swivels

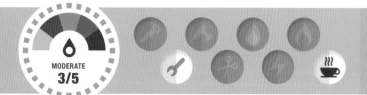

| PREREQUISITES | Relatively independent of other tasks |
| --- | --- |
| DO BEFORE | - |
| COMBINE WITH | Fitting under-seat batteries / wiring |

MODERATE
3/5

Assuming you have a straightforward seat arrangement (i.e. two single seats) the process of fitting seat swivels is easy. Usually all you need to do is unbolt the seat from the base, bolt the swivel plate onto the base, then bolt the seat and runners back onto the swivel plate. The steps in more detail are as follows:

1. If your vehicle has airbags fitted, disconnect the battery (if you don't, there is a danger the airbag will go off while dismantling the seat). After disconnecting the battery, disconnect any wiring underneath the seat.

2. Remove any plastic trim and coverings preventing you from getting at bolts. If the seatbelt is bolted at one end to the seat, undo it using a socket set.

3. Use a socket set to undo the bolts attaching the seat runners to the seat base. This should allow you to remove the seat (with runners attached to it) and leave you with the seat box bolted to the floor.

4. Bolt the bottom plate of the seat swivel onto the seat box, passing electric cables up through the central hole as required. You usually need to put the swivel plate in a 'half-swivelled' position in order to get at the bolt holes.

5. Place the seat on the seat swivel and bolt its runners to the top plate of the seat swivel. Double check that the seat swivels freely – you may need to cut bolts down to size (using a hacksaw with the bolts held in a vice) or even source new bolts to prevent snagging. Only high tensile (HT) bolts with the same rating as the originals should be used.

6. Reattach the seat belt and any bits of trim etc. as required.

7. Reconnect the wiring and then reconnect the battery.

Seat boxes (or seat bases) in a Ducato or Movano prior to the swivel plate being added.

The swivel plates are bolted on top of the seat box. Wires are passed through the central hole.

The seat is bolted on top of the swivel plate through the seat runners. Slide the seat forwards and back as required to access the bolt holes.

A good quality swivel plate which is sandwiched between the seat and the seat base.

A Fiat Ducato seat mounted on a swivel plate. The swivel seat will be several centimetres higher but significantly improves the living space. Lowered seat boxes are available if (in rare cases) the extra height is a problem for very tall drivers.

# Bolt Hole Corrections

Sometimes, even when you have carefully checked that you are buying the correct swivel for your van, the hole centres don't quite line up. This can be for a number of reasons, usually manufacturing discrepancies, a subtle change between models or versions of the van, or because a previous owner has changed something about a seat. Alternatively, your ideal seat swivel may not be available and you need to modify a close match. Don't worry if this is the case, just drill new holes in the swivel to line up with the hole centres on the seat box. Ensure any new holes aren't too close to the edges or compromising the plate's integrity – seek advice from a local engineering / welding firm if in doubt.

# Handbrakes and Seat Swivels

The main complication you may come across with fitting seat swivels is that the handbrake can get in the way on the driver's side. For example, when fitting a seat swivel to a Volkswagen Transporter T5, you have to mount the handbrake lower down using a bracket that should come with the swivel. A similar bracket is available for the Sprinter / Crafter. Once the handbrake is mounted lower down it means you have to reach down slightly when putting the handbrake on, but that isn't a big issue.

The main difficulty with lowering the handbrake is that you then need to tighten up the slack created in the handbrake cable – fairly easy to do lying on your back under the van, but get a garage to do it if you're unsure. Make sure the vehicle is on a flat surface, is firmly in gear, and put chocks under the wheels before going underneath. An awkward scenario is where you find there isn't enough adjustment available in the handbrake cable – a problem that can require some inventiveness to solve, although if it comes to it there are companies that specialise in adjusting handbrake cable lengths. Once you've moved the handbrake you may also find you need to modify some of the plastic seat trim – just take your time, use a sharp knife (or a saw if you can take the trim off), and try to make a neat job of it!

The handbrake in a Vauxhall Movano / Renault Master is particularly awkward and in the author's case an engineering company was enlisted to physically modify the handbrake in order to lower it enough for the seat to swivel freely over it. You may come across other examples of awkward handbrakes – there is usually a solution given the right degree of persistence and ingenuity, but you may also need to recognise when it doesn't warrant the effort required. Remember that the handbrake is a safety-critical part of the vehicle so whatever your approach it must be robust… apart from anything else the handbrake will always be tested in your MOT so botched solutions are not acceptable.

A problematic handbrake preventing the seat swivelling in a Vauxhall Movano / Renault Master.

A custom modified handbrake solution – but remember that safety should always be the primary consideration.

New 'captain seats' can replace the existing seats to add a touch of class to your conversion, though these days original seats are already very comfortable and keeping them can have advantages.

# Airbag Warning Lights

This is another little nugget of frustration for converters to deal with. The problem comes when you swap a cab passenger bench for a single seat – modern vehicles then complain (usually via a warning light on the dash that won't go off) that there is a problem with the wiring for the middle air bag. Ideally, you would be able to tell the vehicle's computer that there is no longer a middle seat, and therefore no longer a need for it to complain about this. However, manufacturers seem to have made this tricky to do, even for dealers who can hook the vehicle up to their computer. If you can't find a dealer who can turn off this annoyance for you, you may have to resort to one of the following options, all of which come with a major health – **Do not mess with the airbag system unless you know what you are doing.** That said, options to consider include:

1. Get a van with an original single passenger seat – the least problematic option, but usually a rare find in the second hand van market.

2. Enlist professionals or dealers to change the seats using official brand parts – likely to be an expensive option.

3. Leave the warning light on and ignore it – a cheap but frustrating 'solution' (and you may not pass your MOT). Again there are safety implications as you need to be confident that the remaining airbags will still work, despite the warning remaining active.

4. Remove the air bag sensor from the bench seat that has been removed (the sensor is often attached to or integrated with the seat belt mechanism). Tuck this mechanism under the new single seat and plug the cable into it, hopefully tricking the vehicle into thinking there is still a middle seat with all being well in the world. You should decide for yourself whether you're happy with the safety implications of this approach as it certainly wouldn't be recommended by the manufacturer, nor is it a recommendation of this book.

5. If you are electronically savvy, you may be able to find another way around this, but ensure whatever you do won't affect the operation of the other airbags which are of course still required and a crucial safety feature of the vehicle.

Remember to disconnect the battery if you are dealing with airbag electrics.

# Passenger Benches

Most panel vans come with a double passenger seat bench as standard, and at the time of purchase you may have bought the vehicle without realising how hard getting the bench to swivel was going to be.  You might decide that having three seats in the front trumps any other requirements, if not read on.

"… bench swivels can be awkward to operate and the seat can end up at a funny angle when facing the other way."

It is quite hard to find passenger bench seat swivels.  Often, there just isn't enough room to spin a bench around, and demand is such that only the more popular vans (e.g. VW T5 / Renault Trafic) have begun to have this problem resolved.  Even if you can find a bench swivel solution, they can be quite awkward to operate and because the back of the bench isn't adjustable it can end up at quite a funny angle when facing the other way.  For the adventurous out there it may be possible to use a swivel mechanism from somewhere else (or manufacture something), but the bottom line is there may not be sufficient space in the front to allow the bench seat to swivel.

The majority of panel vans have three seats in the front as standard – this may be perfect for you but a common approach is to replace the passenger bench for a single seat and make the two single seats swivel.

Double bench seat swivel plates are available for a few van models but can have drawbacks worth considering.

It has become fairly common practice to replace the passenger bench seat with a single passenger seat – unfortunately you will probably struggle to sell your bench for very much while you may have to pay through the nose for a single seat… such is life. This is a good reason to buy a van with a single passenger seat instead of a double bench, though often that's easier said than done. Once you get hold of a single passenger seat it is a pretty easy task to remove the bench and install the single in its place – assuming it's a seat for your particular vehicle the bolt patterns will match up, so it's just a case of doing the bolts up with a socket set.

The bench seat can be unbolted relatively easily with a socket set.

Before unbolting the seat, disconnect the battery and then unplug any wires attached to the seat. Failure to do this may result in an accidental airbag deployment which is to be avoided!

Beware of trying to use a driver's side seat (which are cheaper and easier to source) as a passenger side seat – they are usually subtly but frustratingly different in terms of seat belt anchors, arm rest position, and adjustment mechanisms. In theory you should be able to use a driver's seat from a left hand drive vehicle (or vice versa) but again these tend to be tricky to come by without going on a hunt around Europe.

One attractive option is to re-use your passenger bench as a back seat, and many home converters have successfully pulled this off. This is a good way to cut costs on the project, while gaining a good quality rear seat, often with seat belts at least partially built in. Another advantage of doing this is it's an easy way to get all of your seats matching each other. See further advice below with regards to securely fixing a rear seat to the chassis.

After removing the bench, try placing it in the back to see if it will fit your plans.

Depending on your design, the bench seat may be put to good use as a fixed rear seat with the advantage that the fabrics will match the front seats.

# Seating Regulations

The precise seating regulations applicable to vehicle conversions can get quite complex, however the simple message is that all seats intended to carry passengers while travelling should have robust 3-point seatbelts (and they should be worn). All seats in the vehicle cab should either be original seats or their tested equivalents. All seats designated as travelling seats will have their seat belt fittings assessed as part of the vehicle's MOT.

Ideally, any new seats added to the rear of the vehicle should be 'tested' models, but this is frequently too restrictive a requirement for many DIY conversions and the law does not (yet) insist on this for non-commercial conversion projects. One exception is if the seat is being fitted to a brand new, unregistered vehicle, then the seat must be tested. Testing a seat is a formal and expensive process whereby the seat manufacturer submits their seat for rigorous testing before it can be certified. Tested seats are only as good as their fixing to the vehicle chassis, and for this reason some (not all) seat manufacturers are reticent about DIY installation.

If you have seats in the back of the vehicle that are genuinely not intended to carry passengers while driving (for instance a side facing bench), then do not install seat belts on these seats, and rigidly stick to the rule of not allowing people to travel on them. If your rear seat is intended to carry passengers but isn't a tested model you should satisfy yourself that it is above and beyond a reasonable safety level – i.e. a robust metal frame, fixed solidly to the chassis, with adequate headrests, seatbelts, strong hinges, etc. Seatbelts should always be attached to or integrated with the metal frame of the seat, or attached to designated points on the vehicle's sub-frame – avoid unsafe Heath Robinson follies such as seat belts attached to timber panels or plywood flooring. In essence, if you wouldn't like you or your loved ones to be sitting in it when involved in a crash, then you probably need to rethink your seating plan.

# Testing Jargon

When people talk about tested seats, they are referring to a certification process that manufacturers can put their seats through (at a hefty cost). The testing is also referred to as the M1 Test, a 'pull-test', or a crash test.

- M1 – This refers to a European standard for seats in vehicles with up to 8 seats.

- Pull-Test – A static test designed to see if the seat meets the M1 standard. The seat is secured to a fixed platform and then a variety of chains are attached to the seat, and to metal 'dummies' strapped into the seat belts. The test harness chains are then pulled – hard – at a force of 7 tonnes for a few seconds to simulate a crash.

- Crash Test – A more rigorous test that involves physically crashing the seat, either on a sledge, or actually in a vehicle. An in-vehicle crash test or an in-vehicle pull-test is the only way to formally test the connection of the seat to the chassis, but this is only performed on production-line vehicles rather than on after-market seats.

Part of the testing process (known as the H-point test) ensures that the belt anchorages are in the correct place, and things like the backrest height and seat depth are also checked to ensure they fall within the requirements. Note that some (but not all) seats that haven't been tested may be capable of passing the pull-test, but the manufacturer hasn't yet invested in the certification process.

# Seats and MOTs

An MOT does not currently check to see if seats have been pull or crash tested, and nor does the MOT check the robustness of the seat. If a seat is labelled as "MOT compliant" rather than "M1 / pull-tested", it just means that in general they pass the MOT with no problems. Saying a seat is MOT compliant isn't a guarantee that the frame is safe, as the MOT only requires the seatbelts to be in good working order with no rips or damage.

# Folding Rear Seats and Beds

The concept of a dual-purpose folding rear seat / bed is almost as old as the concept of the campervan itself. Particularly in mid-size vehicles such as VW Transporters, Mercedes Vitos, Renault Trafics, etc., this is one of the best ways to maximise the utility of the available living space. The great advantage of a folding rear seat is that during the day you can have a comfortable living space, a rear travelling seat that can carry kids or passengers, and you can sit a number of people around a table to cook, eat, and socialise; then when night comes the rear seat miraculously folds and transforms the vehicle into a comfy bedroom.

A professional VW T4 conversion with a sliding rear seat that folds back to join up with a rear platform and cushion to form the bed.

Folding rear seats are not for everyone – some people find that constantly having to change the van over from night-time to day-time mode is a hassle. Having to get up in the morning and wait until your partner is up before you can have breakfast isn't an insurmountable problem, but these little niggles have undoubtedly led some people to prefer the comfort of a bigger vehicle with a fixed rear bed. For many people though, the folding seat / bed offers the best of both worlds – allowing them to retain a reasonably small vehicle while still providing good accommodation. Including swivelling front seats in a conversion certainly helps make the most of the folding rear seat solution, so these two campervan features often go hand in hand.

The basic folding rear seat is where the back of the seat simply folds back to form a bed. Often there will be additional fixed bed boards behind the seat for the bench to link up with when in bed mode. There are numerous variations on this theme, from 'rock n roll' seats, to seats that concertina out in a number of parts, to seats that not only fold but also slide the full length of the living space on rails, to seats with both simple and complex hinge mechanisms. A rear seat that folds flat forwards can also be press-ganged into service to allow the space to double as a sleeping area.

Sometimes keeping your campervan as more of a day van makes sense – strap the kids in, put the bike in the back, and go!

# Choosing a Rear Seat

There are a number of high quality folding rear seat designs on the market, all offering various different mechanisms and advantages, and at a range of price-points from reasonable to major investment. There are also some cheaper options on the market that require a cautious approach to ensure they are both safe and robust solutions. When choosing a rear seat to buy, you should carefully consider some of the following:

- Is the seat tested or not? It doesn't have to be but if it is it's a sure sign of quality (but the reassurance usually comes at a price).

- Does the seat have integrated three-point seatbelts? Make sure the seat belts are actually attached robustly to the metal frame – anything attached to timber panels etc. should ring alarm bells. Some seats can be used in conjunction with seat belts mounted on the stanchions within the vehicle (e.g. just behind the sliding door) in which case you will need to ensure the belts are correctly installed (which may well require some welding).

- How wide is the seat and how many passengers will it carry? Check that the width fits your plans – particularly with regards to the size of bed you want, as well as with the width of kitchen unit and storage that you need. Common options are full-width or ¾ width seats and this is a key measurement that you should work out early in your conversion-planning process. Custom sizes are also available from some manufacturers, but remember there may be a lengthy waiting time while the seat is built for you.

- Is there a choice of upholstery options and will you be happy not only with the finished appearance, but also with the comfort of the foam both when sitting and sleeping? Think about things such as fabric choice – for example, leather and vinyl finishes can look good but may prove too hot and sticky during hot summer trips. Will the fabric be easy to clean? Make sure you get fabric samples or visit the manufacturer in person as online colours are never the same.

- How user-friendly is the folding mechanism? The easier it is to go from seat to bed format, the more you will enjoy using the van.

- Related to the folding mechanism is the type of hinges used – some of the less reputable and cheaper offerings on the market have been known to use basic door hinges which are not suitable for the job and certainly wouldn't pass a pull-test.

- Is the seat available for DIY installation or only supplied for professional fitting by authorised dealers?

- Some seats can be mounted on sliding rails – the classic system allows the seat to be positioned forwards while driving – great for letting passengers and drivers interact; then the seat can be pushed all the way back to create a large living area while parked up and moved again at night to form the bed. There are some real benefits to the sliding rail system but it comes at a cost and further complicates installation.

- Is the seat design compatible with your plans for the vehicle – for instance does it have enough storage space, will it let you slide your surf boards underneath?

All of these options tend to affect the price. You can spend a lot of money on a good rear seat, and for some conversions this may well be worth it as a centrally important part of your project. Current legislation does not force you to install a pull-tested seat, but if the seat manufacturer has been through this process with at least one of their products it does offer a level of reassurance that they have the know-how to create a truly robust and safe offering. Beware of cheap 'bargain' seat frames which may look OK to the inexperienced eye but might be well-disguised safety hazards. If you aren't sure what you are looking at you may be well advised to opt for a tested seat that there are no question marks over. It is worth spending time looking into the options and deciding what the right solution for your project is. Which route you choose will depend on your precise requirements, and on your budget and DIY skills.

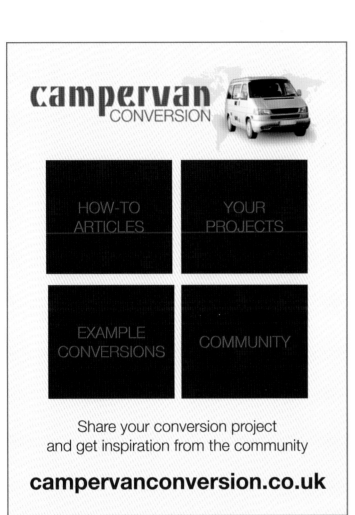

## campervan CONVERSION

HOW-TO ARTICLES

YOUR PROJECTS

EXAMPLE CONVERSIONS

COMMUNITY

Share your conversion project
and get inspiration from the community

**campervanconversion.co.uk**

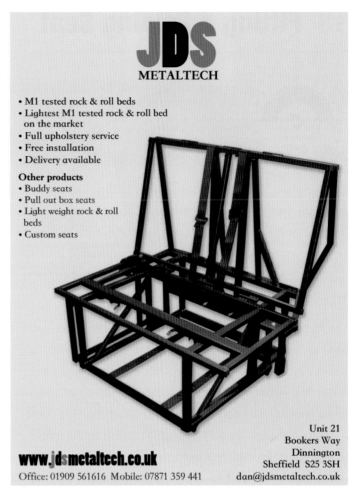
# Captain Seats & Bench Seats

# 13 Fitting a Folding Seat

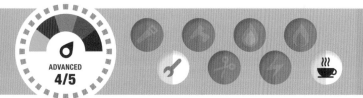

| PREREQUISITES | Insulation, panelling |
|---|---|
| DO BEFORE | - - |
| COMBINE WITH | Furniture construction, Flooring |

ADVANCED 4/5

Once you have chosen and sourced your folding seat, you need to install it into the vehicle. You should consult with the seat supplier about any specific procedures relevant to the seat in question, but the basic process is to bolt it through the floor of the vehicle. You need to remember that even though a seat may have been pull-tested, that is only any good if it is robustly fitted to the vehicle – bear in mind that the fixings should be capable of matching the 7-tonne force simulated during a pull-test. Normally seats have bolt holes at each corner of the frame, and often more intermediate bolts. There may also be adjustable bolt hole positions to allow you some flexibility when positioning the seat.

The first thing to assess is what you are bolting into – you will need to get underneath the vehicle and get a good look at where the bolts will be positioned. You will need to avoid any under-floor clutter such as brake cables, exhaust pipes, and fuel tanks – none of which are fond of being drilled into. The floors of most panel vans are either a single or double skin of metal, usually ribbed for additional stiffness. The floor is constructed over a number of structural chassis cross members. If all you did was stick a bolt through the floor and fasten it using a standard washer and bolt, the chances are that in a crash it could just pull straight up through the metal. Instead, a belt and braces approach should be taken to this task.

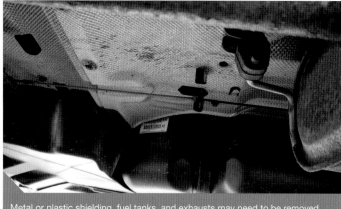

Metal or plastic shielding, fuel tanks, and exhausts may need to be removed or lowered to allow access when fitting seats – doing this job on a ramp is significantly easier.

You should only use high tensile nuts and bolts for this job – minimum 10mm diameter. High tensile bolts will have '8.8' or 'S' stamped on the head of the bolt. Even stronger are nuts and bolts with '12.9' stamped on them, while '4.6' is a weaker grade of bolt that isn't up to this job. Note that stainless steel bolts are not as strong and should not be used in this setting.

The chassis struts crossing underneath the floor are where the real structural strength comes from, so the ideal is to position the seat such that it will become attached to these. The bolts must be fastened from below using chassis brackets and / or spreader plates which will spread the load and prevent the bolt pulling through in a crash. If they are not supplied with the seat, it is relatively easy to get some good quality brackets or spreader plates made up to suit your situation – the gold standard are brackets made out of 3-5mm steel that fit around chassis members with bolts on either side.

The bare chassis of a Fiat Ducato – ideally your seats should be bolted to the structural cross-members, otherwise additional strengthening or spreader plates will be required to stop bolts from pulling through the floor in the event of a crash.

If your fixings are a distance away from chassis members, use spreader plates that link two or more of your bolts together; even better is to get some plates made up with a bracket shape half way along them so that they 'capture' a chassis member in-between bolts. In some situations (e.g. when bolts will be obscured by fuel tanks) you will need to get plates made up with 'captive nuts' so that the bolts can be installed and removed without access to the nut beneath (these plates will need to be either bolted or welded permanently in place). Give all new brackets, spreader plates, and bolts a good coating of anti-rust paint or primer before installation.

You can either site the seat directly on the metal floor, or on top of the plywood flooring – the latter approach is perhaps less hassle, but note that the plywood then becomes part of the structure and although it will help spread the load further, you must make sure the plywood is completely sound. If the seat is bolted directly to the metal floor, the plywood flooring will then need to be fitted around the seat frame, with the advantage that it can be removed separately if needed. You may find that some steel wedges or shims are required to achieve a flat surface for the seat frame to sit on a ribbed metal floor. If the frame needs to be raised higher for whatever reason, you should be able to get a local engineering or welding company to provide some steel spacers or a channel with holes drilled as required.

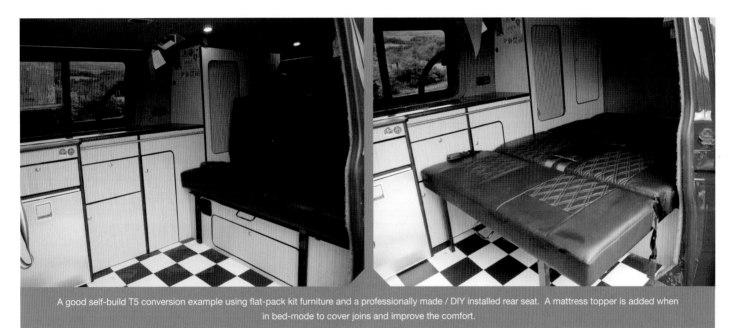

A good self-build T5 conversion example using flat-pack kit furniture and a professionally made / DIY installed rear seat. A mattress topper is added when in bed-mode to cover joins and improve the comfort.

Ensure all metal filings created when drilling through the floor are obsessively cleaned up as they will rust quickly. Ideally freshly drilled holes should also be primed to prevent rusting.

These mounting brackets are bolted around chassis members to ensure bomb-proof rear seat installations.

# 14 Constructing a Folding Seat

**PREREQUISITES** - -
**DO BEFORE** - -
**COMBINE WITH** Planning & Design

For some, constructing your own seats will be the purest form of completing a conversion project, and there is little question that there is money to be saved on this item. However, a very cautious approach is required, particularly if the seats are intended to carry passengers while travelling. You may be able to start with an existing seat frame and make modifications as required – for example a front passenger bench, or a seat out of a minibus or coach.

If attempting to construct something from scratch the base should consist of a robust metal frame. This needs to be engineered (or preferably over-engineered) to be capable of withstanding a pull-test, even though it won't be subjected to one. If you have high quality skills in this area – i.e. both the engineering and manufacturing / welding side – you may be able to construct the frame yourself. More likely is you will need to enlist an engineering / welding company (at which point it probably makes more sense to use the money to buy a commercially available seat). Some of the companies who make rear seats will also take on custom projects and it is well worth discussing your plans with these guys as they have the know-how to provide you with a robust and safe solution.

On top of the base frame, one option is to construct the seat platform and the seat back using thick plywood, perhaps connected together using rock and roll hinges (available commercially online). Then on-top of the plywood you can attach foam cushions and either upholster the cushions separately or even get the plywood and cushions upholstered together for a more professional finish.

A home-made version of a folding (and sliding) rear seat.

An old bus seat with the backrest chopped off was used as the base, with new plates welded to each side to allow rock-n-roll hinges to be bolted on.

In this case the seat was retrofitted onto a sliding rail system, but could easily be bolted directly to the floor in a fixed position.

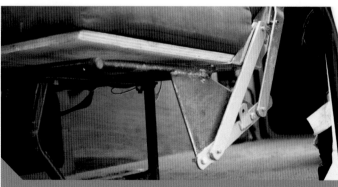

Two pieces of 18mm plywood make up the base and back boards – these are attached to the hinges using bolts and t-nuts. For a more professional finish the plywood could be upholstered along with the cushions.

# Dinette Seats

In larger vehicles, a common layout is to have a fixed bed in the back of the vehicle, with a rear seat facing the front swivel seats. This arrangement is known as a dinette seat. Many professional converters of the larger size panel vans use the dinette seat as their standard arrangement, and with good reason. The layout is tried and tested and, similarly to folding rear seats in mid-size vans, there are many advantages to this approach.

A FASP folding dinette seat (available from Leisure Vehicle Services) in a Fiat Ducato – a great solution if you need an extra couple of berths, e.g. for kids.

There are a few different options to pick from for your dinette:

- Use the front passenger bench (or a bench sourced from elsewhere).

- Buy a purpose made dinette seat.

- Construct your own (probably only a good option if not to be used for carrying passengers).

The dinette seat paired with swivel front seats and a good table provides both a great living space in addition to two additional safe seats while driving.

Here the front passenger bench has been put to good use as a (non-folding) dinette rear seat – a cost effective solution to getting four matching seats, all with good safety credentials.

# 15 Constructing a Seating Platform

MODERATE
3/5

PREREQUISITES    Insulation, panelling, flooring

DO BEFORE    Furniture construction, seats & beds

COMBINE WITH    Seat swivels. Heater installation & other under-platform work

In large panel vans such as the Fiat Ducato, Renault Master, and others, there is a step down from the front cab seats into the load area that only becomes obvious when you remove the bulkhead. The step down is great in that it gives you more head room when standing in the living space, but creates a problem from the seating point of view as when you swivel the front seats round your legs dangle off the step. If you are installing a rear seat in one of these bigger vehicles then it usually makes sense to raise it up to the same level as the front seats, creating a seating area platform.

The exact design and size of the seating platform is a perfect opportunity to add some personal uniqueness to your conversion. Often a corridor of standing height will be left leading from the sliding door towards the rear of the vehicle, with some form of curve or diagonal forming the seating platform. Whatever design you choose, the basic construction of the platform will often be similar.

1. Install some form of metal sub-frame attached solidly to the vehicle floor. In reality this sub-frame becomes part of the structure of the seat, so it should be of robust construction capable of underpinning the pull-test designed integrity of the seat attached to it. The connection of seat to sub-frame and sub-frame to chassis should be capable of withstanding crash forces (see more on this earlier in the chapter).

2. Install any sub floor elements such as heaters, batteries, etc. The space under the seating platform can also make a good storage space, provided you design in access to it somehow.

3. Build additional framing out of timber as required in order to support the platform (but do not use timber to build the sub-frame under the seat).

4. Cut and fit the platform, usually made out of thick (min 18mm) plywood.

5. Install the dinette seat on-top of the plywood, attaching robustly to the metal sub-frame that lies underneath.

6. Add a platform 'apron' to finish off the edge of the seating area.

7. Finish with flooring and trim as required.

The sub-frame for a raised platform needs to be at least as robust as the frame of the seat. Here some steel 'girders' are bolted to the floor with spreader plates beneath and the raised platform will be built on top. The seat frame can then be securely bolted through the platform and the girders.

18 or 22mm plywood is used to construct a seating platform at the same height as the cab seats.

The shape of the platform is an opportunity to get creative and choose a curve you like.

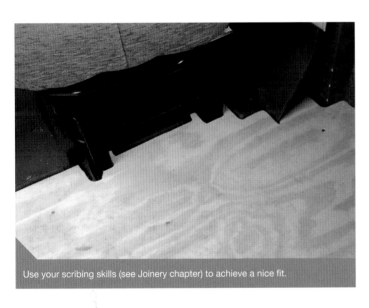
Use your scribing skills (see Joinery chapter) to achieve a nice fit.

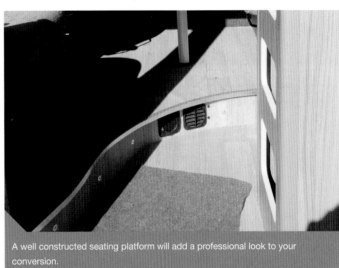
A well constructed seating platform will add a professional look to your conversion.

Use little touches such as bits of metal trim, patterned flooring, and step lights to add a touch of class.

The void under the seating platform is a great place to install a heater with the vent and air intake positioned as seen here.

# Dinette Bed-seats

If you need to create a vehicle with more than two sleeping berths, you may wish to create an extra bed area using the dinette seat. If you plan this carefully it is possible to have the dinette fold out into a bed that links up with the swivelling driver's seat. The length you need this bed to be will then dictate how far back the dinette is positioned, and as a result it will also dictate the space available in the back of the vehicle for a main bed and perhaps a bathroom.

The base cushion of the dinette flips over and lands on a lowered table.

The seat also slides out sideways to create a bigger bed possible. The backrest flips down and the headrests and top backrest cushion are slotted into the base cushion to provide the length.

The folding dinette joins with the swivelled driver's seat to create a useful extra sleeping space. Non-folding dinette seats are also available for when the extra bed isn't needed, or the front passenger bench may be put to good use.

# Side-on Seating

These days side-on seating isn't considered appropriate for carrying passengers while driving. However, if the seating is purely for use while parked up, constructing a simple side-on seating bench can be a good solution. One common design is to construct two side-on benches facing each other with a corridor and table in between – at night the table can then drop down to fill the gap and form a full width bed. Since these benches won't be used to carry passengers, they can be constructed out of timber using straight forward techniques. You can either construct the bench boxes out of softwood timber (for example planed 2x2" softwood) or construct the whole thing out of 15-18mm plywood or lightweight furniture board.

Holes can be cut in the front panels to create low-level cubby holes, or the seating platform can be made to hinge to give access to storage within. Another variation of the side-on seat is to construct an interlocked slatted seating platform that can be slid apart at night to create a comfy bed.

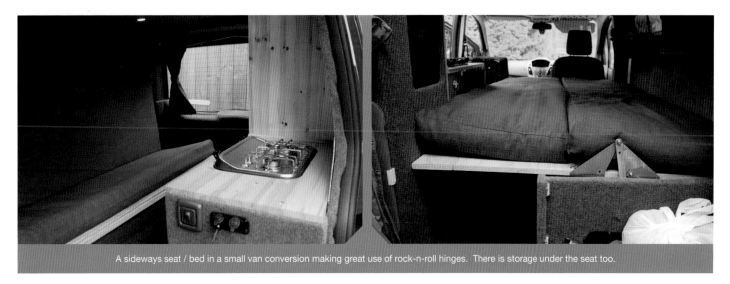

A sideways seat / bed in a small van conversion making great use of rock-n-roll hinges. There is storage under the seat too.

# Fixed Bed Platforms

One of the great benefits of larger vehicles is that they can be big enough to accommodate a fixed bed platform that doesn't need to be folded and tidied away in the morning. In the widest vehicles it is possible to design a 'transverse' bed which allows you to lie across the vehicle. The width of the vehicle (and the height of the occupants) is paramount to the transverse bed design. For example a Fiat Ducato measures approximately 1.8m across whereas a Renault Master is approx. 1.7m – only a ten centimetre difference but enough to make a transverse bed comfortable in one but less so in the other. The other downside of transverse beds is that whoever is lying at the back will always need to clamber over the other occupant to get in and out of bed.

Fixed beds facing forwards take up a lot of space, so the vehicle needs to be reasonably long to accommodate this design. Hand in hand with the lengthways bed comes a large garage space underneath that can be perfect for sports equipment. One approach to the fixed bed is to construct a timber frame underneath, with a couple of intermediate supporting walls. However, if you are keen to retain the full width of the garage space, you can install metal bars or pipes across between the vehicle wall struts.

One further bed variation is to rig up a system whereby the bed platform is attached to a rope and pulleys in such a way that during the day the bed can be folded away either against the side of the vehicle or even held up onto the ceiling. The bed can then be lowered down at night.

——

"… you can end up with a bed in your van just as comfy as in your own home."

——

The start of a lengthways fixed bed platform using steel bars sitting on the strong horizontal side ribs of the van.

18 or 22mm plywood is used to create the platform – a third middle bar was later added to provide additional support.

A well sized bed platform taking shape. Varnished 18mm marine ply is used here for extra resilience to damp from wet kit below.

You can cut a foam mattress to fit your platform for the ultimate in van comfort.

No need to be uncomfortable when you have this in the back of the van.

Strong support struts for a transverse bed platform. The platform could also be built on top of a sub-divided timber box, but with space penalties.

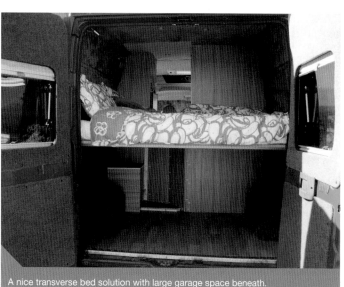

A nice transverse bed solution with large garage space beneath.

# Cushions and Mattresses

Whichever approach to beds and seats you take, you can achieve a great finish by paying attention to your cushions and mattress. The mattress can be dealt with easily by buying a foam mattress and cutting it to fit the exact shape required (a bread knife or plasterboard saw will do the trick). The beauty of this is you can end up with a bed in your van just as comfy as in your own home. Cushions for seats can also be home-made, although there are numerous upholstery companies who will do a great job of taking your exact specifications and turning them into a professional looking solution.

# Tables

Having a dining table is frequently listed as a requirement by the DVLA and insurance companies for a vehicle to be designated as a campervan or motorhome. In reality, the table could be as simple as a bit of plywood sitting on top of a couple of posts, but applying a little finesse certainly helps create a higher standard of conversion. There are a number of campervan table systems available, often involving a fixed rail mounted on the side of the kitchen unit. The table board then has a couple of clips attached to it so that the table can be clipped onto the rail and slid back and forth as required. The table leg could be as simple as a bit of timber or metal pole, but legs that can fold in the middle or be removed can also be very useful tweaks to your design. A folding table leg can be put to excellent use if the table will also double as part of the bed at night.

The table can be made out of the same material as your kitchen unit worktop for a matching finish, or in many cases just a bit of varnished plywood will suffice. Adding a nice curve or profile to the table top helps add a certain 'je ne sais quoi' to your dining experience.

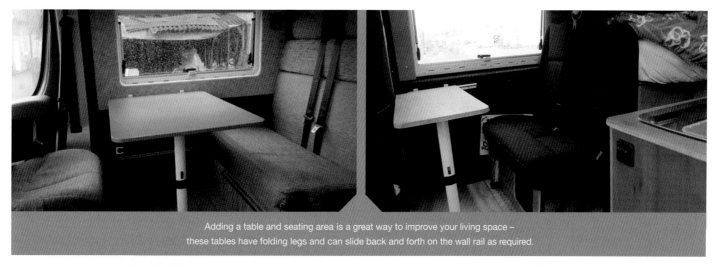

Adding a table and seating area is a great way to improve your living space – these tables have folding legs and can slide back and forth on the wall rail as required.

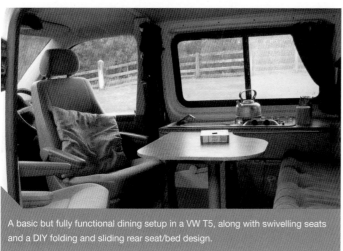

A basic but fully functional dining setup in a VW T5, along with swivelling seats and a DIY folding and sliding rear seat/bed design.

The underside of a table with clips that hook onto an aluminium rail attached to the vehicle.

# JOINERY SKILLS

The main material used in your conversion is likely to be timber – for the floor, the wall and ceiling panels, for seating and bed platforms, and for cupboards and units. Therefore, the cornerstone skill needed for the majority of campervan conversions is a bit of joinery. The good news is that it doesn't have to be complicated and if you've yet to gain any experience, the small collection of key techniques described here should stand you in good stead.

## Timber

Of all the materials that go into making a conversion, timber is probably the most important. In fact you could do an entire conversion project using nothing other than timber, and the simplest campervans are purely a timber bed board in the back of the van. At all times remember that timber is heavy and the more you use, the slower your vehicle will go!

## Softwood

Softwood is the generic term used for most framing timber stock used – it is usually pine or redwood and is called softwood to distinguish it from hardwood (e.g. oak, beech, mahogany, etc.) which is far more expensive. Softwood comes in all manner of sizes bought in lengths, usually between 1.8 and 4.8 metres long, from timber merchants and builders yards. Take a tape measure and handsaw with you when you go to buy it so that if required you can saw lengths in half to put in the car (or van).

You can buy softwood treated, rough sawn, graded for construction use, and many other varieties, but for our purposes you are mainly interested in buying PAR softwood (PAR - Planed All Round, sometimes called DAR – Dressed All Round) for interior use. The sizes of most use in a conversion are 2 x 1 inch and 2 x 2 inch – the metric equivalents being 50 x 25mm and 50 x 50mm. You shouldn't need anything bigger than that in a conversion. In fact the sizing of the timber once it's been planed in the factory is smaller than the 'nominal' sizes given and you end up with timber that is between 5 and 8mm less – so 50 x 50mm nominal is often actually 43 x 43mm or similar when you measure it. Sometimes you can also get hold of 1 x 1 inch or its metric equivalent which can be useful for lightweight framing purposes.

Softwood timber – planed all round (PAR or DAR) in useful sizes. Sizes will vary, metric examples: 18 x 18, 20 x 44, 44 x 44mm.

Assorted lengths and thicknesses of softwood.

# Plywood and Other Sheet Materials

Plywood comes in many forms, but the first thing to look at is the sizes. Plywood is usually bought in 8 x 4 foot sheets (roughly 2.4 x 1.2 metres) or similar. It varies in thickness from the thinnest at 3-4mm thick, then 5-6mm, then 9mm, 12mm, 15mm, 18mm, and 22mm. Thicker sheets are also available, but it starts to get very heavy so use them sparingly. Even a sheet of standard 18mm ply weighs around 35kg and a conversion could easily use six sheets adding over 200 kilos to the vehicle's base load. When choosing what thickness to use you should try to go for the thinnest (and therefore lightest) you can get away with while achieving the structural rigidity required for the particular task. Decide for yourself, but a suggested guide is to use:

- 3.6mm ply for wall and ceiling panels

- 12mm for flooring

- 15mm for furniture construction (or 3-5mm if using framed construction)

- 18mm for seat platforms and bed boards (going up to 22 or even 25mm for bed boards with long spans or heavy occupants).

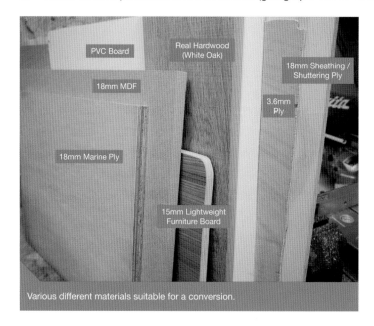

Various different materials suitable for a conversion.

You'll soon build up a collection of bits – try to resist the temptation to hoard them all otherwise your off-cuts will take over your house!

Plywood comes in a variety of forms which range from fairly cheap to pretty expensive.

- Sheathing or Shuttering Ply is the cheapest and can be used where the wood won't be seen – for instance flooring or a seating platform. Various different grades and classes are used to further categorise the ply which affects the price accordingly.

- Hardwood Ply is a much nicer plywood, and more expensive as a result. It can be used to make furniture units etc. and any situation where the wood will be on show. This makes a cheaper alternative to furniture ply and can still make a great looking conversion. A distinction is made between 'hardwood faced' and 'hardwood throughout' plywood which are fairly self-explanatory terms. Different varnishes and stains can be used to improve the finish further.

- Lightweight Furniture Ply is the stuff used in most professional conversions. It is 15mm thick and many hinges, handles, catches etc. are designed with this as the target material. Although it's called 'lightweight', that is a relative term and a sheet of this is still pretty heavy. It looks great and comes in a wide variety of colours and patterns. However, it can be expensive so is not a budget option. Thinner (e.g. 3mm) 'wall-boards' are also available in designs to match.

- Marine Ply is also fairly pricey (more than standard hardwood ply but less than furniture board) but is designed for use in places where the wood will get wet or frequently damp. With a nice varnish marine ply can also look quite attractive.

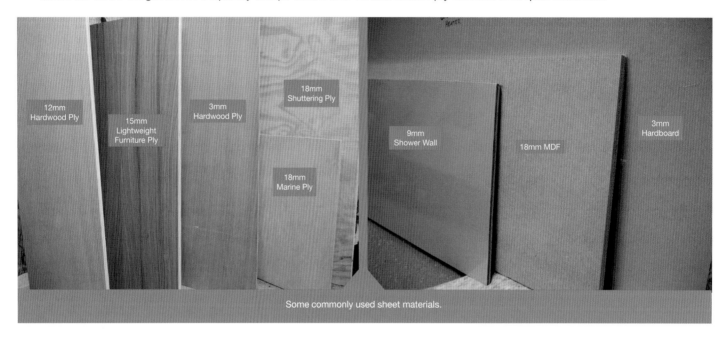
Some commonly used sheet materials.

There are also a number of other sheet materials that are worth considering:

- Hardboard is a cheaper alternative to using thin plywood to make wall and ceiling panels. Hardboard is fibrous on one side and smooth on the other. You probably won't want it on show but if covering with carpet lining it's an acceptable, if slightly inferior choice.

- MDF – Medium Density Fibreboard is widely used in domestic settings for building shelves, window cills, etc. It is cheaper but heavier than hardwood plywood of the same thickness. It doesn't hold screws as well as plywood and amongst other reasons this means it is less good for structural use. In general plywood is preferable in a conversion, but MDF can be a good option in some situations. Veneered MDF (and MFC - Melamine Faced Chipboard) is also available and this can look great if used well. MDF contains some nasty chemicals so a dust mask should be worn when cutting it and it should always be sealed or painted once installed.

# Cutting Sheet Materials

You buy plywood in 8 x 4 foot sheets (2400 x 1200mm) – sometimes they are a little bigger depending on the manufacturer, but whatever size they come as you will need to cut them up.

Some basic advice:

- Measure twice, cut once (the oldest advice in the book, but a goody).

- Use an original factory edge (not a home-cut edge) of plywood as a straight edge.  Clearly mark the edge that is perfectly straight and keep this to one side as a tool to be used throughout the project.

- Support the piece of wood as close as possible to the cut.

- You shouldn't need to force the saw – let the saw do the work and adjust your setup if it isn't working smoothly (e.g. improve the support to stop the board from bending).

- Time spent setting up will make the actual job much easier and produce better results.

- Keep your work area tidy and keep a first aid kit handy.

Take time to prepare a good platform to cut timber boards on – some old milk or beer crates are perfect.

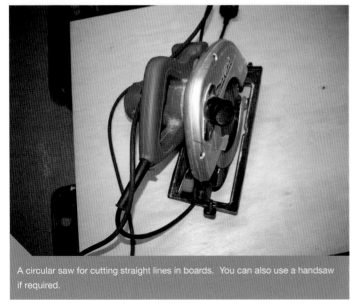

A circular saw for cutting straight lines in boards.  You can also use a handsaw if required.

"Measure twice, cut once
(the oldest advice in the book,
but a goody)."

# 16 Cutting a Sheet of Plywood

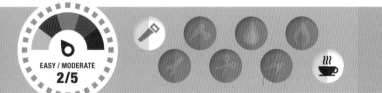

**EASY / MODERATE**
**2/5**

| PREREQUISITES | - - |
|---|---|
| DO BEFORE | - - |
| COMBINE WITH | Making furniture, panels, etc. |

The following steps show how to consistently make good clean straight cuts using a circular saw. A mains powered saw with an extension cable is fine, just don't cut through the cable. A finer toothed blade in the saw will normally make a cleaner cut, as will a newer blade. You can also cut up sheets of plywood using a standard hand saw, it's just harder work and not as quick, but a handy skill to have none-the-less. If you're finding cutting with a hand saw hard work, get a new one – yours is probably dead.

Measure the distance between the edge of the saw plate and the far edge of the blade.

The most obvious way to cut a board is to measure the board, draw a line, and cut along it. However, there is a more refined way to use a circular saw that will produce better results. Start by carefully measuring the distance from the right hand edge of the saw blade to the left hand edge of the saw's base plate – probably around 11cm but it will depend on the model of saw. Make a note of this as your 'fence offset'.

1. Lay the plywood out on milk crates, trestles, chocks of wood, or other objects that you can use to create a flat cutting platform with. The sheet must be well supported and the cut should be made close to the support. If you're right handed lay things out so that the waste side of the timber will be on your right when cutting. Lay a couple of long bits of framing timber (e.g. 3 x 2" softwood or similar) under the board if additional support is needed, for example when cutting thinner boards. The blade will stick and jam if there is any bend in the board. Often you will need support in three or four lines rather than just two as the board needs to be properly supported on both sides of the cut line (unless it's only a thin sliver being cut off).

2. Place the plywood face down (face up if using a hand saw).

3. Measure and make a couple of marks at either end where you want to cut. Now use your fence offset number to make another two marks to the left of your cut line.

4. Using a straight edge or a wide strip of 12-15mm ply with a factory cut edge, line the straight edge up between the two offset marks and use a couple of clamps to hold it firmly in place. This straight edge will act as a 'fence' to guide the circular saw and ensure a nice straight line. Place the circular saw on the plywood with the saw's base plate firmly against your fence – check that the left edge of the saw blade is exactly in line with the mark which you want to cut along.

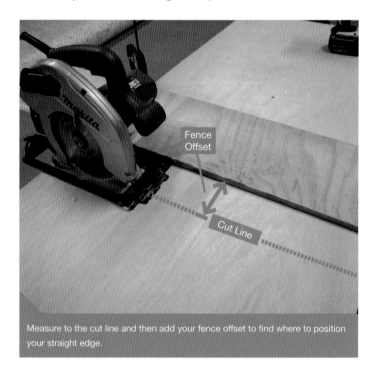

Fence Offset

Cut Line

Measure to the cut line and then add your fence offset to find where to position your straight edge.

Adjust the depth of the saw blade so that it goes through the board but no more, as shown here on the right.

5. Adjust the depth of the circular saw blade so it will go through the wood but not by much (this helps the saw run cleanly and means you don't need lots of clearance under the board).

6. Try to arrange the cable in such a way that it won't get snagged on the corner of the board when you're halfway along the cut. Be careful you don't cut through the cable (or anything else... like your fingers). Holding the saw's base plate against the fence, start the cut and, providing you're happy, continue the cut the whole length of the board.

7. You should have a reasonably clean cut, but depending on the wood and your blade you may need to sand the edge down a bit to get rid of splinters.

8. Re-measure the board and if all has gone well it should be correct. If it's slightly out you may need to refine your fence-offset measurement for your next cut. Over time you should get this process very slick and cut perfect straight edges every time, without ever having to draw a long line and follow it.

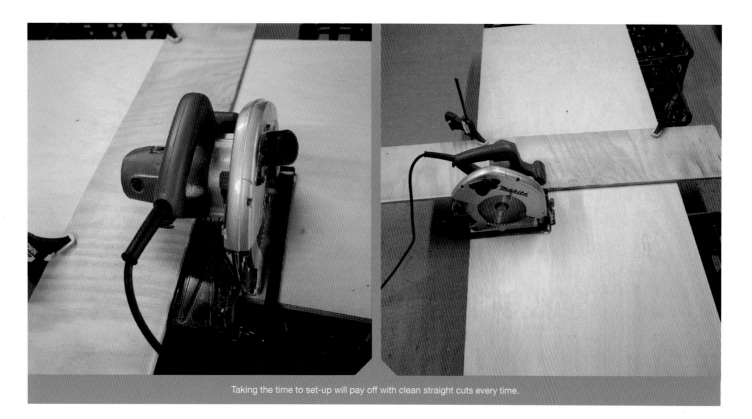

Taking the time to set-up will pay off with clean straight cuts every time.

# 17 Cutting Shapes with a Jigsaw

EASY / MODERATE
2/5

| PREREQUISITES | Selection of jigsaw bades |
|---|---|
| DO BEFORE | - - |
| COMBINE WITH | Making furniture, cutting bed boards, etc. |

A circular saw is great for cutting long straight lines from one edge of a board to the other. However, often you need to cut curves or cut out a shape in the middle of a board – the perfect tool for these jobs is a jigsaw. Jigsaws are also the tool of choice for cutting holes in the side of the van – for example for windows, water inlets, etc.

In order to cut a shape out of the centre of a piece of plywood:

1. Place the board face down on a level and well supported surface. Measure and mark out the hole to be cut.

2. On the inside / waste side of the shape being cut out, use a drill with an 8–10mm bit to cut a hole just big enough to fit the jigsaw blade through. You may want to drill a hole near each corner to make cutting the shape out easier.

A jigsaw is the tool of choice for jobs such as this.

Start the jigsaw cut by drilling a 8-10mm hole on the waste side of the cut line. (Make sure you keep the cable out of the way.)

This method is fine where you don't need to re-use the off-cut.

3. If there are long straight cuts to be made you can position a straight edge as a fence to guide the jigsaw, although even then it is tricky to avoid slight wavering of the blade. Sharp new blades help.

4. If you want to preserve the piece of wood being cut out – for example if it is to be re-used as a door for a cupboard – you can use a technique known as 'plunge cutting'. This is an alternative to drilling a hole to start the cut. To make a plunge cut, you hold the jigsaw firmly and vertically with the front of the guide plate resting on the board, start the blade running and carefully lower the jigsaw down until the blade is hitting your cut line. Continue lowering the saw down with a firm grip until the blade works its way through the wood. There is a knack to plunge cutting without make a mess of the board (or snapping the blades) – practice on off-cuts before risking the manoeuvre on an important piece. Some jigsaw blades have a shaped tip that is designed to make plunge cutting easier and if you are doing a lot these are worth a little extra. Always wear safety goggles when plunge cutting in case the blade snaps and pings towards your eyes.

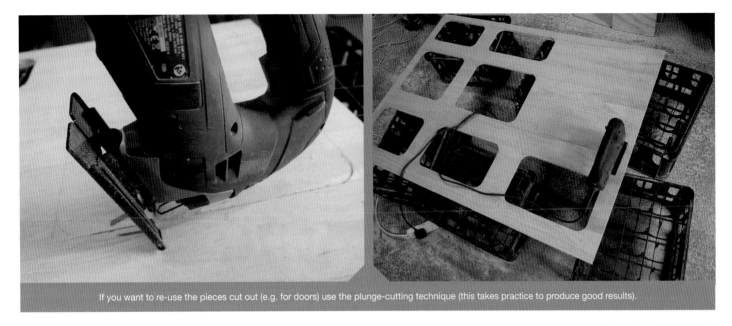

If you want to re-use the pieces cut out (e.g. for doors) use the plunge-cutting technique (this takes practice to produce good results).

## Notes on jigsaw blades

You will need a selection of blades for your jigsaw:

● Narrow fine toothed blades for thin plywood – these are great for cutting tight curves. Also known as 'scroll' bits.

● Medium toothed blades for wood for cutting clean straight edges. In general avoid large toothed 'fast' blades which will cut straight and fast through thicker boards but usually make more of a mess with splinters.

● Fine toothed blades for metal sheet for any cuts in the side of the vehicle. These also tend to work well for cutting plastic and fibreglass (e.g. shower trays).

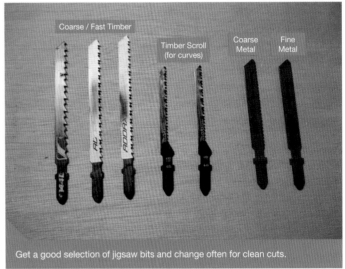

Get a good selection of jigsaw bits and change often for clean cuts.

There are many other different blades available – read the description on the packet (about material, thickness, speed, and shape of cut) carefully when buying them to make sure they suit your purposes. Note that most jigsaw blades cut on the up-stroke and therefore the ply should be face down when cutting, but some blades have the teeth reversed to cut on the down-stroke (often labelled 'R' or called worktop blades) and these should be used with the plywood face up.

## Notes on cutting plywood cleanly:

• Splintering occurs where the saw blade exits the wood.

• Circular saw + jigsaw – plywood face down.

• Handsaw + table saw – plywood face up.

• You can also add a sacrificial piece of wood to cut into, or use masking tape to protect the board.

## Notes on drilling holes cleanly:

• Splintering will occur when the drill bit exits, so drill into the wood with it face up.

• Drill through into a bit of scrap wood.

• For bigger holes and for hole saws - drill until almost through, with tip of drill bit showing through, then swap sides.

# 18 Scribing a Board to Fit

| PREREQUISITES | - - |
|---|---|
| DO BEFORE | - - |
| COMBINE WITH | **Making panels, constructing furniture** |

When confronted with the challenge of having to shape a board to fit neatly against a curved or irregular surface, the technique of scribing is an essential skill.

One way to get a board to fit against an awkward shape is to take a guess at the right shape, make a cut, hold it up, refine it, hold it up again, refine it some more, etc. Another way to do it is to use a bit of paper or thin card to 'crease it' into the shape, then cut the card along the crease to create a template. Sometimes these approaches actually work reasonably well.

However there is a better, more technical way of getting the right shape and that is to 'scribe' the board. Scribing is an age-old method which lets you transfer the shape you are trying to fit onto the piece of wood you are cutting. The basic method is as follows:

**1.** Line your board up against the edge it's the closest match to. If the board is tricky to hold like this either fix it in place or get a helper to hold it for you.

**2.** Use a compass with a pencil in it and set the width of the compass to the widest gap between the board and the surface to be fitted against.

**3.** Holding the board steady, draw the compass along the edge of the surface so that the pencil transfers the shape onto the piece of wood.

To scribe a board to fit, either use a compass or hold a pencil on a batten at the widest gap, then move the compass or batten up the side of the van marking the line on the board as you go.

Boards scribed and cut to fit.

The steps above are often all you need but depending on the situation you may need to modify them a little. One problem is when the gap is wider than the set of compasses you have – you can buy proper scribing tools to overcome this, but you can also just use an offcut piece of wood or a length of dowel and hold the pencil alongside it.

Another problem with scribing can be that you can't get the piece of wood into the right position because it's too large to fit until it's been cut – a classic chicken and egg situation. The way to handle this is to scribe the shape of one edge onto a smaller offcut of plywood, cut the shape out, and then use this as a template for one edge of your main board. The board should then fit into a position from where you can scribe the remaining edge shape onto it.

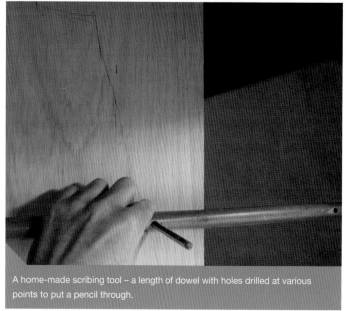

A home-made scribing tool – a length of dowel with holes drilled at various points to put a pencil through.

## Finishing Plywood Edges

When constructing furniture out of plywood, you inevitably end up with one edge of plywood visible at each joint. Some people like to be able to see the raw plywood edge and this can actually look quite good once sanded and varnished. Alternatively you can cover the edges in a variety of ways, some of which are shown in the images that follow. A common option in campervans is to use plastic T-Trim, but this requires routing a precise slot in the edge of the boards before knocking in the trim – tricky to do well for many self-builders and impossible without a router. Other options include iron-on edging tape which is straightforward and can look good and be trimmed with a sharp blade; or thicker edging strips which are more robust but harder to apply without professional edge-banding and trimming tools. There are also a variety of plastic and aluminium edge profiles available which slot over the ply and can help personalise your conversion aesthetic.

# Joining Boards Together

One of the most common tasks required is to join two pieces of plywood together at right angles. There are all sorts of complicated ways to do this – for example dovetail joints, dowling joints, biscuit joints, and many others. However, for the majority of DIY converters simplicity is the key and actually there are a few easy and good ways to join two boards together.

## Glue and Screw

The basic right angle joint is called a 'butt joint'. The simplest way to fix a butt joint is to use wood glue along both edges and then screw through one board into the other. In some circumstances this is OK, but there are a couple of problems with it: a) the screw heads will be visible; b) screwing into the edge of a bit of plywood often doesn't hold very well. If you are attaching a thin bit of ply onto a thicker piece this may be fine, and for this you could also use panel pins instead of screws. The technique works best in situations where you can screw (or pin) through into a softwood batten rather than into the edge of a bit of plywood. Screw heads can be covered using screw caps, and pin-heads can be hidden by punching them beneath the surface and then using some wood filler to hide the holes.

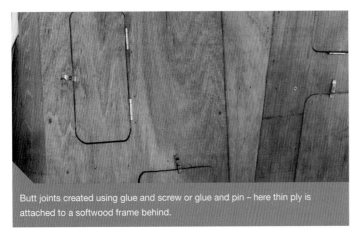

Butt joints created using glue and screw or glue and pin – here thin ply is attached to a softwood frame behind.

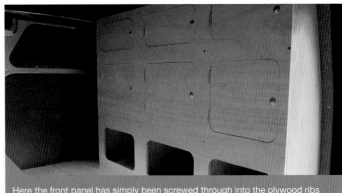

Here the front panel has simply been screwed through into the plywood ribs behind. Other fixing methods are usually more elegant, but this does the job.

## Furniture Blocks

Also known as fixit blocks, corner blocks, KD (Knock Down) blocks, assembly blocks, carcase fixing blocks, and numerous other names. These little plastic blocks sit on the inside of the join between the two boards and get screwed into each – they are relatively robust and reasonably foolproof. They come in lots of different colours to match your wood, although you should try to position them such that they aren't easily seen. Instead of furniture blocks you can also use right angled metal brackets or even small blocks or battens of hardwood timber with holes drilled in them.

The boards you are joining need to be thick enough for the screws to have enough to bite into – 12mm is probably the minimum, 15mm is better, 18mm is heavier than it needs to be. Try to use just the right screws to suit the combination of block and board – the screw should go as far as possible into the wood without sticking through the far side.

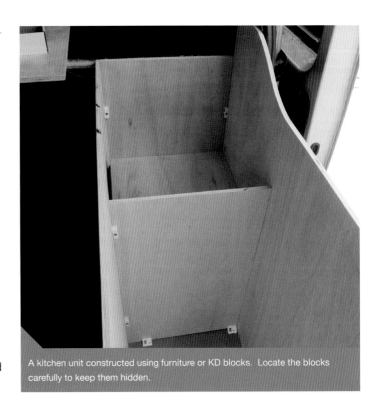

A kitchen unit constructed using furniture or KD blocks. Locate the blocks carefully to keep them hidden.

The best way to use these blocks is to fix them to one board first, screwing through the single hole so that the block can still rotate slightly. Ensure the block is flush with the edge of the board otherwise you will have a gap. Then bring the second board into place and screw through the remaining two holes in the block, creating a tight joint. If you've no intention of ever disassembling the joint, you can also glue the boards before screwing them together for additional strength and to reduce unwanted movement.

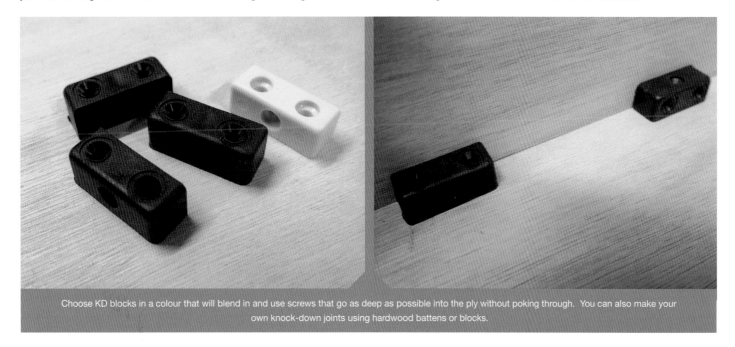

Choose KD blocks in a colour that will blend in and use screws that go as deep as possible into the ply without poking through. You can also make your own knock-down joints using hardwood battens or blocks.

# Pocket Hole Joinery

One of a number of more advanced ways to join two boards together is a technique known as pocket hole joinery. Ideally you need to buy a jig to use this technique with success and there are several good ones on the market (e.g. made by Kreg, Trend, UJK, and others). This will probably only seem like a good option to the perfectionists amongst you, but it is a satisfying and elegant way to make various joints.

The jig allows you to accurately drill angled holes in one piece of wood such that the tip of the screw will exit at the exact mid-point of the board's edge before entering the joining board to create a hidden and strong joint. You need to have a practice with the technique first and ensure you set the jig up correctly for the thickness of wood you're using. It works best on boards from 15mm upwards. At a push and with short screws you can just about use the technique on 12mm board as well.

The angled 'pockets' left on the inside face of the join can be covered using plastic pocket-hole caps or you can also make your own wooden (usually hardwood) plugs that can then be chiselled flush for a really nice finish. There are a number of good books on more advanced joinery and cabinet making and these are well worth a read if you out-grow the techniques described here.

There are a variety of more advanced and 'hidden' ways to join boards together. You can explore classic techniques such as dovetail joints or use approaches such as cam and dowel or pocket hole joinery.

A jig for pocket hole joinery.

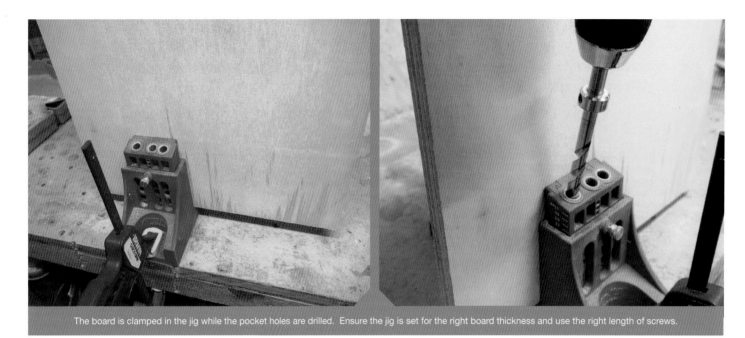

The board is clamped in the jig while the pocket holes are drilled. Ensure the jig is set for the right board thickness and use the right length of screws.

Portable pocket hole jigs can also be useful, and the technique can be put to good use in numerous situations.

A kitchen unit constructed using pocket hole joints. The holes can be covered up using either plastic caps or home-made hardwood plugs.

# Framing

An alternative to constructing units by joining two boards together, is to construct a frame out of softwood and then clad it in thinner (e.g. 3mm) plywood. If you use just the right thickness of softwood to achieve the strength you need, but no more, this can be a lightweight and cost-effective way to build. It is probably a bit more time consuming, and in some ways less elegant, which is probably why most converters will just connect thicker boards together. Your frame will rarely need to be built out of anything thicker than 2x1" (50x25mm) and you may well be able to get away with 'inch by inch' battens. You might have to create thinner battens yourself by ripping down lengths of 2x1" using a circular saw (or far easier by using a table saw if you have access to one). Combining this technique with solid 15mm boards can also be a good approach – using the thicker boards where they are needed and framing with thin ply everywhere else.

One easy way to build like this is to glue and clamp the framing stock onto the thin ply, and then join the pre-made panels together by screwing through the ply into the framing pieces.

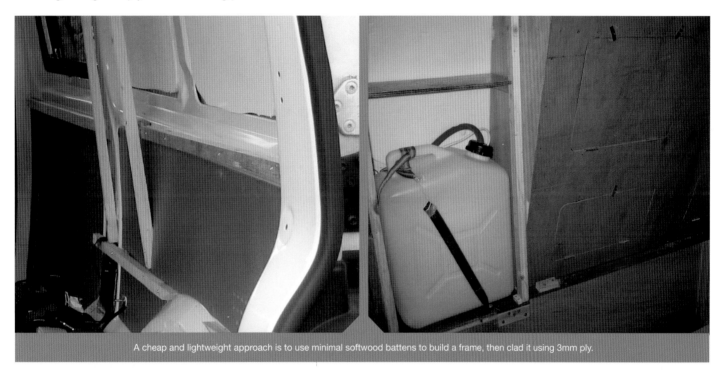

A cheap and lightweight approach is to use minimal softwood battens to build a frame, then clad it using 3mm ply.

Here a mix of 15mm furniture ply and softwood framing with matching 3mm ply has been used to good effect.
Note the board edges have had a slot routered in them to allow finishing with knock-in plastic T-trim.

# LIGHTWEIGHT FURNITURE PLY

**FREE ONLINE SAMPLE SERVICE**

→ Cuts cleanly and neatly

→ Tough, scratch resistant surfaces

→ Half the weight of MFC

→ Certified sustainable timber (PEFC ™)

→ 9 plys for better screw retention

Online at: **www.morland-uk.com**
Or call us: **01938 551 980**

www.morland-uk.com

# CONSTRUCTING FURNITURE

There are many well-travelled and much-loved campervans that have little more than a bed board in them, however some well constructed furniture units are a common feature of most good conversions. The previous chapter led through a whistle-stop tour of the various joinery skills that come in useful when tackling a campervan project; building on these core techniques, this chapter now takes a look at how to put it into practice and build some furniture for your conversion.

## Furniture Kits

Alongside talking through how to construct furniture yourself, it is worth pointing out the growing availability of professionally made campervan furniture. For instance you can buy a ready-made kitchen unit and in some cases all you need to do is screw or bolt it in place. In fact, some conversion companies have begun to outsource the furniture making so that all they have to do is pick the wood finish, order it, and fix the units in place. Perhaps not an approach for the purist, but an option to consider. If your design is unusual then this is unlikely to be a good option, but if you are following a well-trodden conversion path you might find that buying some pre-made furniture saves you significant time and might even end up saving you money.

Further to buying pre-made units, you can also buy entire furniture kits which may be a good approach for those of you who don't fancy doing the joinery themselves. Having mentioned that as an option, we will now go back to the purpose of this book which is to show you how you can do it yourself.

## Constructing Kitchen Units

A good kitchen unit will form the focal point of most conversions, so if you get this right you will be able to construct the rest of the living space around it. The length of the unit is usually constrained by its position in relation to your front and rear seating as well as the side door or the end of a fixed bed platform. You will need to take into account the various appliances you are installing and how they will fit in relation to the kitchen unit. In particular your sink / stove unit and perhaps a fridge or grill and oven will have to be chosen in conjunction with deciding on your unit's design. You have a choice between building the unit in isolation (in a workshop, or your living room) and then fixing it into the vehicle, or building the unit in-situ. For the DIY converter, there are several advantages to building in-situ and that is the approach described here. There are many variations to how such units are built, but the following describes some basic guidelines which can then be altered to suit your requirements.

# 19 Constructing a Basic Kitchen Unit

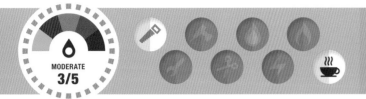

MODERATE
3/5

| PREREQUISITES | Flooring, Windows, Insulation, Panelling, Wiring |
| DO BEFORE | Other units |
| COMBINE WITH | Rear seat & bed design |

Start by establishing the exact location and dimensions of the unit - this will depend on the rest of your planned layout as well as any obstacles such as doors, windows, and wheel arches. In a domestic kitchen, the usual height of the units is 890mm off the floor, and then the 40mm worktop is placed on top of the carcases bringing the finished height up to 930mm. Often motorhome units will be a little lower than this so that they sit below the windows, but it is still a good measurement to bear in mind. Low roof campervans will need lower units as they will usually be used when sitting – once again, the bottom edge of the windows should provide a good guide.

1. Try making a very rough mock-up of the kitchen unit to get an idea of size and requirements, and to get a better feel for how the unit will be constructed. Cut five pieces of waste ply (or cardboard) roughly to size – these will be your back, front, sides, and a worktop. The side and front panels should be your target unit height minus the thickness of the worktop. The back panel can be the same height as the others with the worktop sitting on top, or you can choose to make the back extend up beyond the worktop as a splash-back. If the unit is sitting against the wall of the vehicle, you may decide to omit the rear panel altogether (in which case you will need to scribe the side panels to fit the shaped wall).

2. Start your real unit by refining the shape of the back board until you are happy with it and then securely fix it to the vehicle. You can fix it using self tapping screws straight into a strut, use rivet nuts with bolts, or use wood screws into timber battens previously fastened in place for this purpose. You can also use some furniture blocks to firmly secure the board to the floor.

3. With the back board fixed in place you can begin to build the unit onto it. The side panels can be fixed next at right angles to the back board using furniture blocks (or pocket holes etc). Any intermediate panels will need to be cut short enough to allow clearance under the sink and stove.

This rough mock-up was constructed in a short space of time using some unused 9mm ply. It is basically just a box – four bits of ply make the back, front and sides, plus an extra piece on top for the worktop.

A new unit being built to fit around a 50 litre compressor fridge. The back board has been cut to size, shaped, and fixed to a hollow strut on the van using self tapping screws. The left and middle panels are cut to width and joined with the back board using furniture blocks.

**4.** Now you can see the unit taking shape, you can decide what you want in the way of doors and shelves. Mark out the shapes of the doors on the front panel and carefully cut these out. If you do this using a plunge cut with your jigsaw to start (as described in the Joinery Skills chapter), you will be able to retain the pieces cut out and make the doors out of them later. It is useful to number the back of the board and the cut-outs so that you know which goes where.

**5.** Next you can fit the front panel into place. This is a different approach from domestic kitchen cabinet construction where the front of the cabinet is open until the door is added. At this point check that the unit is sitting perfectly square and fix the side and front panels in place to the floor once you are happy.

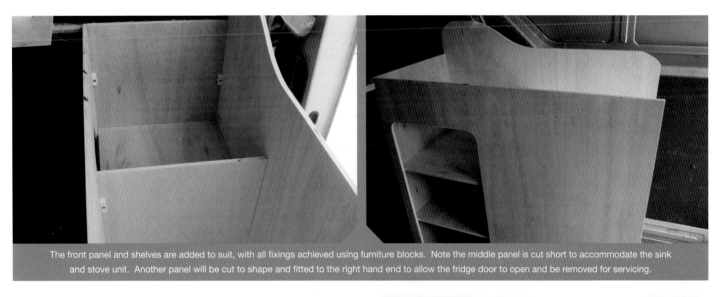

The front panel and shelves are added to suit, with all fixings achieved using furniture blocks. Note the middle panel is cut short to accommodate the sink and stove unit. Another panel will be cut to shape and fitted to the right hand end to allow the fridge door to open and be removed for servicing.

**6.** Add shelves in as required – fixing them in with more furniture blocks works well as it all helps the rigidity of the structure. The shelves will also further help 'square up' the unit.

**7.** Place your worktop on top of the unit and prepare to fit your sink and stove (more on that later).

The loose worktop cut roughly to size before being shaped and prior to sink/stove installation (described later).

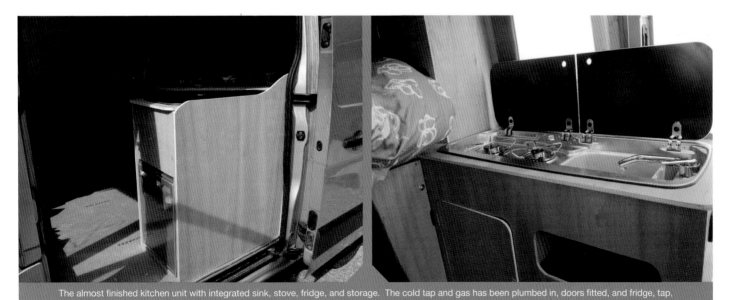

The almost finished kitchen unit with integrated sink, stove, fridge, and storage. The cold tap and gas has been plumbed in, doors fitted, and fridge, tap, and light switches wired up. The unit is then varnished for protection.

# 20 Advanced Kitchen Units

ADVANCED
4/5

| PREREQUISITES | Flooring, Windows, Insulation, Panelling, Wiring |
|---|---|
| DO BEFORE | Other units |
| COMBINE WITH | Rear seat & bed design |

There is no single design of kitchen unit that will suit every conversion, and of course part of the fun of these projects is to create something that suits your custom requirements that will also stand out from the crowd. The more advanced example shown below demonstrates some of the techniques discussed previously and in the Joinery Skills chapter, and highlights that the only things stopping you from creating your own customised kitchen unit are a little bit of imagination and the willingness to give it a go.

A kitchen unit in 15mm lightweight furniture ply starting to take shape with rear panel cut to shape, intermediate panels fixed using pocket hole joinery, and services for water and gas installed.

Fitting the worktop with hole prepared ready for the sink-stove combo unit to be installed.

An alternative to standard jointing techniques, these right angle corner profiles create a nice finish in places where the joins will be particularly visible.

The unit almost complete with stove installed, shelves fixed in place, with only the doors left to hang.

The fridge and food unit built to match the kitchen unit. Note the plywood edges have been finished here using iron-on 22mm edging strip trimmed to size with a Stanley blade.

# A Note on Timber Choice

When constructing campervan furniture, it is important to strike a balance between structural robustness and keeping control of the weight. Using boards of 15mm is ideal for most purposes. 18mm boards will certainly be very strong and have ample width to screw into etc., however they are overkill for most purposes and add unnecessary weight to your vehicle. Using thinner boards such as 12mm is possible and these will still offer a reasonable level of structural rigidity while obviously weighing and costing less, however there are a few problems with using 12mm ply for unit construction:

- The screws don't have much to bite into and you have to find exactly the right length of screw to go in as far as possible without poking out the other side.

- Most items such as hinges, catches, door handles, etc. available for the campervan market are designed with 15mm ply in mind. Therefore if 12mm ply is used you will have to add 3mm ply shims behind hinges etc. in order for them to fit properly – a disproportionate amount of additional effort.

One weight-efficient technique is to combine matching 15mm and 3mm furniture board. The 15mm is used where required – e.g. for walls or where both sides are visible – and everywhere else 2 x 1 inch softwood framing is used with 3mm facing ply over the top (see more in Joinery Skills chapter).

The finished unit making its first cup of tea.

# 21 Fitting a Sink-Stove Combo Unit

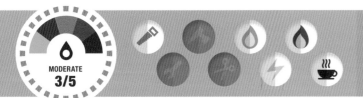

**MODERATE 3/5**

| PREREQUISITES | Construct base kitchen unit |
|---|---|
| DO BEFORE | Gas & Plumbing Installation |
| COMBINE WITH | - - |

Once you have constructed the carcase of the kitchen unit, the next step is to fit a worktop and your sink and / or stove into it. You can choose to just use a bit of hardwood or marine plywood for the worktop – most of it will be getting cut out anyway to make way for the stove unit. Alternatively there are factory edge-banded worktops (15mm thick) available in various sizes and these are certainly a good choice if you are after a professional finish. Fitting a sink-stove combo unit into the worktop is fairly straight-forward:

1. The worktop (simple 12mm ply in this case) is cut to size in preparation for the sink / stove unit.

2. Lay the stove unit upside down on-top of the worktop and draw round it with a pencil. Remove the stove and mark another line an inch or so inside the first line – the exact shape of the hole depends on the unit and if available use a template and follow the manufacturer's instructions.

3. Cut out the shape using a jigsaw. Try the stove unit in the hole and make adjustments as required.

4. Place the unit onto the worktop (the right way up). There should be a rubber strip sitting under the lip of the unit to create a good seal – this can be supplemented using sealant if required.

5. The worktop can now be fixed into the unit if it hasn't been already. Depending on the stove unit it is sometimes easier to fix the worktop in place first.

6 Plumb in the gas, tap, and sink waste. Wire up the tap if using a micro-switch. Keep all the pipes and cable neat using clips and make sure there is plenty of clearance under the stove burners.

![A newly cut worktop waiting for the sink stove to be installed.]

A newly cut worktop waiting for the sink stove to be installed.

Draw round the sink stove - note that you will have to reverse the worktop otherwise your shape will be the wrong way round.

![The worktop and the edges should be varnished or treated so that it doesn't delaminate when it inevitably gets wet.]

The worktop and the edges should be varnished or treated so that it doesn't delaminate when it inevitably gets wet.

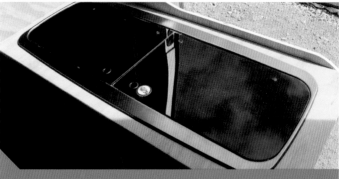

If the unit has metal clips, attach these and tighten them up. Some units are fixed with screws going through rubber washers from the top into the worktop.

# Squeaks & Rattles

No matter what you decide to construct in your van, you should constantly have 'squeaks and rattles' in the back of your mind. Unfortunately, eliminating all such unwanted noises is a big ask, especially when driving on rough and windy roads. However, paying a little attention to the issue during the conversion phase should make for a quieter and more pleasant driving experience. There are two main culprits, both related to each other:

● Rubbing – whenever there is movement between two solid objects there is a risk of them rubbing against each other and making a noise. Key culprits are bits of plywood rubbing against bits of PVC, plastic, or metal. Poorly fitted plywood joints will also squeak as the two bits of ply move against each other.

● Rattling – the rule of the road is that anything remotely loose will rattle. Key culprits are stoves, plates and cutlery, fridge shelves, loose doors, etc.

Firstly, everything should be as securely fastened together as you can manage – units should be constructed in such a way that you can push them firmly without them budging. Each time you attach bits of timber together remind yourself that they will be subjected to years of movement in the back of the vehicle. Use both glue and screws to create secure joints and use shelves attached all around to give units more rigidity. Where appropriate ensure there are bits of carpet in between likely squeaking candidates – i.e. where a timber unit attaches to a metal strut, or where a plywood wall touches a PVC board.

To some extent rattles need to be identified and tackled once on the road, but start with some basics: use dish-towels to pad stove grills, cut little bits of foam to store between plates, wrap cutlery in a towel, create cardboard divides between mugs and glasses, make carpet wedges to ensure doors don't move, and so on. And when all else fails, and it almost always does… don't beat yourself up too much about it, just turn the music up loud and enjoy the scenery!

A well constructed kitchen unit has as much attention paid to eliminating squeaks and rattles as it does to how it looks. Note the superior finish of the factory edge-banded worktop.

# 22 Constructing a Rear Storage Unit

| PREREQUISITES | Panelling & Bed platform |
|---|---|
| DO BEFORE | - - |
| COMBINE WITH | Other furniture |

EASY / MODERATE
2/5

If there's one thing you can't have too much of in a campervan it's storage – installing cupboards and cubbyholes wherever you can fit them in is the only way to keep the place half-tidy. In particular, installing cupboard space capable of stowing away shoes, jackets, clothes, extra food, etc., is a great addition to any campervan. There are an unending number of ways to construct cupboards, so the rear storage unit described here is but one example.

1. Start by working out what the unit will be attached to – it doesn't need lots of fixing points but ideally you should find a minimum of four good solid points to attach the unit to the vehicle.

2. Work out the width, length, and height of the unit and cut rectangles of ply for each bulkhead – in this case 4 pieces were needed: the two end pieces plus two intermediate walls.

3. Carefully scribe each board to fit against both the vehicle side wall and the ceiling (see more info on scribing in the Joinery Skills chapter).

A large space at the side of a fixed bed – perfect for a rear storage unit.

Four ribs have been individually scribed and cut to fit in place.

4. Once the side panels are shaped and positioned as required, install two rows of 2 x 1" softwood battens which will hold the shelves. The battens can be shaped with a diagonal at the front edge to create a neater finish. Glue and screw the side battens onto the ply. In this case the rear battens are screwed through into the vehicle wall struts, and this becomes the principle structural fixing method.

5. Cut six shelves to fit over the battens. Screw the shelves into the battens both at the sides and the back. Once this step is complete the unit is now solidly fixed into the vehicle and should be robust enough to withstand the rigours of driving – sudden braking, potholes, bendy roads, etc.

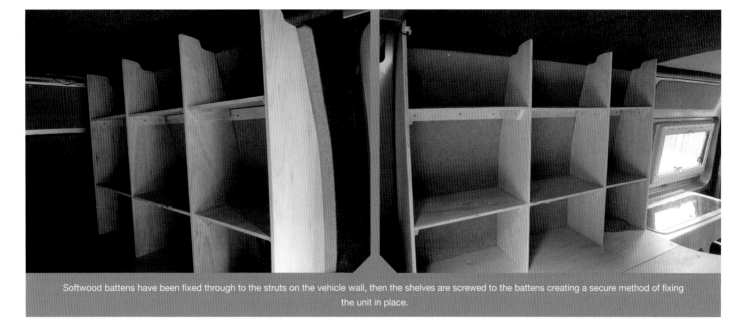

Softwood battens have been fixed through to the struts on the vehicle wall, then the shelves are screwed to the battens creating a secure method of fixing the unit in place.

**6.** Cut a single large sheet of ply to act as the front panel. Carefully mark out openings to match the shelves. Leaving a reasonable lip at the bottom and sides is quite useful for holding items inside the cupboard, particularly if doors won't be added. If you start the jigsaw off using plunge cuts (see Joinery chapter) you will be able to reuse the piece cut out to make the doors. In the case of this rear unit, doors were to be installed for the top six openings, but the bottom three holes were to be left open as the mattress would negate the need for doors.

**7.** Attach the front panel to the unit carcase. Due to time pressure, in this case it was simply glued and screwed through into the ply – this is the quickest method, but a more elegant method allowing the fixings to be hidden is to attach furniture blocks to the panel at strategic points and then screw these into the side ribs.

**8.** Sand down all the door edges and fit push button catches. Then attach hinges to the front panel of the unit and then hold the doors in place and screw the hinges on.

**9.** Varnish or paint the unit as required, then fill it with your worldly belongings and get on the road.

The front panel attached to the ribs, with doors installed together with hinges and push-button catches. The bottom three openings have been left without doors as the mattress will largely cover them (but still allow access).

# 23 Constructing an Overhead Locker

| PREREQUISITES | Panelling |
|---|---|
| DO BEFORE | - - |
| COMBINE WITH | Other finishing touches |

**ADVANCED 4/5**

Overhead lockers are one of the trickier joinery tasks in a campervan. There are multiple problems to contend with, such as what will hold the unit up, how to attach the doors, and deciding whether it's worth the hassle. If you have tackled everything else so far though, an overhead locker will add some valuable extra storage for such items as books and maps, or perhaps more food and kitchen equipment. As with most other tasks in this book, there are numerous ways to skin the cat, but the steps that follow illustrate one example method. Note that a professional converter or cabinet maker would often construct the locker in a workshop and then install it (or install a factory made unit), but for the uninitiated constructing the unit in isolation is probably more difficult, and will also usually use more timber so may well result in a heavier construction. Building in-situ is a useful approach for the self builder, particular for one-off custom projects and where the design 'evolves' rather than being a fully formed vision at the outset. As a simpler alternative to constructing a complete overhead locker, you could also consider installing a shelf with either a high lip or even a net to stop items falling off.

**1.** Before the unit is installed, identify a number of good quality fixing points – the bottom shelf can run between the bathroom side wall and the front cab pelmet board. To add further support along its length a hardwood batten can be secured at the back of the bottom shelf and attached to the horizontal wall strut above the window. The two dividing side panels can be positioned in line with the ceiling struts so that they provide support to the front of the locker from above.

**2.** The long bottom shelf can be cut and secured in place, then the two side panels can be scribed to fit and firmly fixed in, using pocket holes and hardwood battens or furniture blocks could also be used. At this point the unit is structurally integrated with the vehicle.

The overhead locker being constructed in situ.

The vertical ribs have been lined up with the ceiling struts (in line with the join in the ceiling panels) in order to provide robust fixing points. Hardwood battens screwed into the horizontal metal strut behind are providing additional structural fixing points at the back of the locker.

**3.** A top rail can be attached with locker hinges, and these are good in that they will hold the doors up against the ceiling while open. However, locker hinges can be unnecessarily powerful in this setting, so sometimes using a one-piece front panel instead can be preferable.

**4.** The front panel can be attached to the carcase using pocket holes hidden inside or a similar jointing technique. The two doors should be carefully sanded and conventional hinges and catches installed.

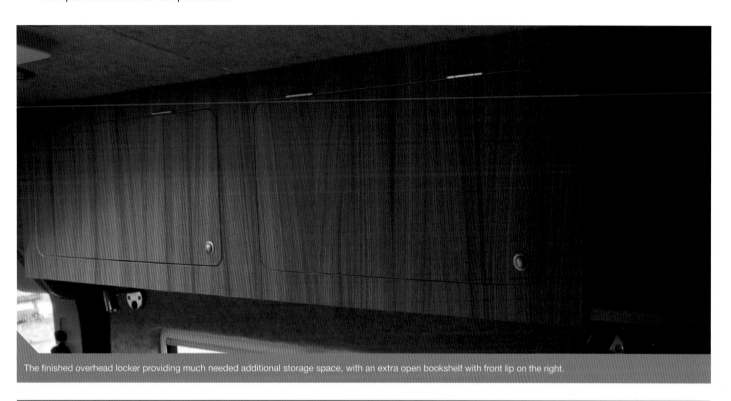

The finished overhead locker providing much needed additional storage space, with an extra open bookshelf with front lip on the right.

# Doors, Hinges, & Catches

The easiest approach to cupboard doors is to get rid of them altogether – sometimes an opening onto a shelf with a reasonable lip or up-stand can be just as useful for stuffing things into.  Fitting doors is quite time consuming, and the hinges etc. can be quite fiddly.  If you are going to install doors, there are two main ways to consider:

● The first 'side-hung' door method is similar to that found in a domestic kitchen unit.  Here the carcase is completely open at the front, and the door hinges are attached directly onto the side panel.  Have a look in your home kitchen and look at how the doors are attached to the units.

● The second 'cubbyhole' method is to attach a front panel to the unit, with door holes cut out of it.  The hinges are then attached to the front panel rather than the side panel.  With this method, one option is to re-use the bits of wood you cut out of the panel so that the doors sit flush inside the opening.  Alternatively, you can make doors that are bigger than the opening and mount them raised on-top of the front panel – this approach is frequently seen in campervan furniture but tends to be less efficient at using pieces of wood, and also potentially means the grain or pattern of the wood won't match up.

There isn't a right and wrong way – both methods can be used to excellent effect in a campervan and often the two methods are seen in use side by side.  The side-mounting approach is possibly a little less hassle with the hinges, and the doors are simpler rectangles of ply that make up the entire front of the unit.  The front panel cubbyhole approach is perhaps better in a campervan setting because the front panel can be made to provide a large overlap which does a good job at holding things in place on the shelves.

Although there are lots of different catch mechanisms that you could use to keep the doors closed, the push-button type catches have become fairly ubiquitous in campervan construction.  They are popular for a reason – they are easy to install (with a little practice on some off-cuts) and do a good job of locking the door shut while driving.  Alternatives such as magnetic catches have a habit of swinging open the first time you go round a tight bend.

Spending time getting the doors, hinges, and catches right helps create a professional finish.  These button lock catches do a great job of keeping doors shut while travelling.  Both of these doors are flush-mounted but one is side-hung (as with a domestic kitchen unit) while the other is cubbyhole-mounted onto the front panel directly.  Here iron-on edging tape has been used to cover exposed cut edges.

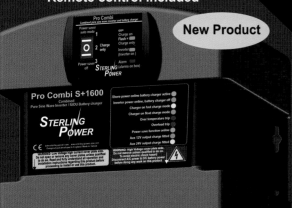

# ELECTRICS, BATTERIES, LIGHTS, & WIRING

If you want comfort when parked up in a campervan or motorhome, you need electricity… simple as that.  Having power lets you live on the road just as you would at home – turn the lights on, listen to music, watch TV – and more important than those things, electricity also powers items such as water pumps, heater fans, fridge compressors, water heaters, etc. (often in combination with gas).

Campervan electrics can be powered from two different primary sources – either from batteries (usually 12Volt), or from mains power (230Volts in the UK and Europe).  In general the items you install in your campervan should be designed to run on a 12V system (more on this later).

If you are parked up somewhere that you can 'hook up' to the mains, then you can use as much power as you care to (with limitations depending on the source, and you will probably have to pay for it).  If you are parked up in the middle of nowhere you won't have access to the mains so you need to rely on battery power.  There are also various other ways to get electricity such as generators, solar panels, and wind turbines, although an in-depth discussion of these items is beyond the scope of this book.  Modern vehicles are equipped with powerful alternators capable of generating large amounts of power in a short period of time, so you are actually travelling with the means to replenish your batteries on a regular basis (so long as you don't run out of fuel).

———

"If you want comfort when parked up in a campervan or motorhome, you need electricity… simple as that."

———

# Leisure Batteries

If you run your electrical items directly off the vehicle starter battery, then at some point you'll run your starter battery down to the point where you can't start the engine in the morning; either that or you will constantly be living in fear of using up too much electricity and will end up reading by the light of head-torch rather than risk needing a jump start the next day. The solution to this problem is to add a second battery to the vehicle, reserved for use when parked up.

There are two types of vehicle battery – starter batteries and 'second' batteries (second batteries are also known as 'leisure' and 'deep cycle' batteries). Starter batteries are designed to supply large amounts of power in short bursts – specifically to start the engine; traditionally, starter batteries are not designed to get regularly run down – they function best when the engine starts first time and the alternator then tops them straight back up. Leisure batteries on the other hand are designed to function well when you run them down time after time – this is why they are called 'deep-cycle'. Leisure batteries can in an emergency be used to start an engine, but they are primarily designed for extended use by lower power users – for instance by the sorts of appliance you find in campervans.

You've presumably already got a starter battery in your campervan – now you need to add a second, deep-cycle, leisure battery. Your starter battery will be used to start the engine, your second battery will be used to power your appliances (water pump, heater fan, lights, laptop, etc.) while you're parked up. In this way you can happily forget about how much power you're using and know that you'll still be able to start the engine after your long weekend at the beach. Of course you do still need a way of re-charging the leisure battery, so the ideal arrangement involves a system where your van's alternator charges both batteries while you're driving, but only your leisure battery is drawn on whenever the engine isn't running. Similarly, only the starter battery should be drawn on when the engine is started.

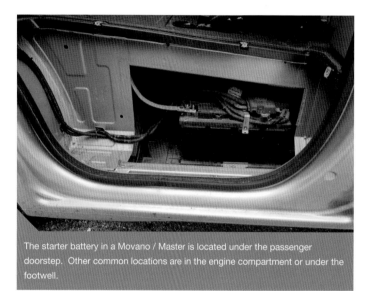

The starter battery in a Movano / Master is located under the passenger doorstep. Other common locations are in the engine compartment or under the footwell.

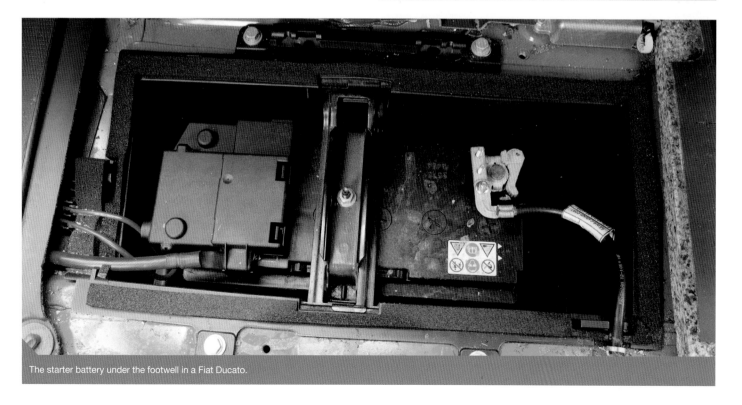

The starter battery under the footwell in a Fiat Ducato.

# 24 Installing a Leisure Battery

| PREREQUISITES | - - |
| DO BEFORE | - - |
| COMBINE WITH | Wiring |

**EASY / MODERATE**
**2/5**

Firstly, find a good place to store your second battery. First choice is in the engine compartment but there often just isn't space. Vehicle manufacturers often allocate a space intended for a second battery – for example a second battery tray in the engine compartment, under the passenger seat, or in a foot-well – and it's worth trying to find out where that position is for your particular vehicle. Ideally you should have the leisure battery as close as possible to the starter battery and alternator (making charging more efficient and cutting down on cable routing).

You also need to think of safety – most batteries give out hydrogen when they charge and can potentially leak acid or even blow up (rarely). So if you need to site the battery inside the van due to lack of space in the engine compartment, you'll need to create a boxed in area keeping the battery isolated from pretty much everything else. In particular, do NOT put the battery right next to the gas! – definitely asking for trouble. Most batteries come with a tube that allows you to vent any hydrogen produced during charging to the outside of the vehicle. You also need to fix the battery firmly in place – use an old battery tray from a scrap-yard, fashion something using timber battens, bolts and large washers or a strong bit of webbing – an opportunity to be inventive!

A 90Ah sealed lead acid leisure battery fitted neatly under the drivers seat in a Transit Connect.

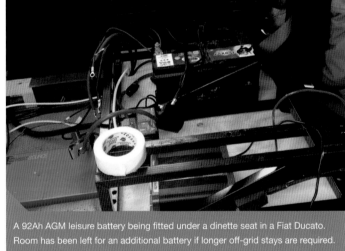

A 92Ah AGM leisure battery being fitted under a dinette seat in a Fiat Ducato. Room has been left for an additional battery if longer off-grid stays are required.

## Battery Size

One important consideration when installing your vehicle electrics is what size of battery your conversion will need. Battery size is measured in Amp-hours (Ah) which can be thought of as showing how many hours the battery could power a 1Amp appliance. For many people this will not require too much thought – if your campervan has a limited number of electrics and you are only likely to be parked up for a night or two then most batteries will serve your purpose fine. A single leisure battery around the 95 to 120Ah size range is a good balance between providing a fair amount of power without taking up too much space or adding too much weight.

If you are planning extended spells parked up in between driving, or if you have a long list of electric appliances with greedy power requirements, then you may need to consider adding more battery power. In fact a general rule of thumb is that you should have twice the amount of Amp-hours than you actually need. You should be able to make a list of all the electrical items you will be using, and their rating. Then estimate how many days you want to be able to park up for in between drives (and therefore in between charges) and then work out how many hours each item will run for and therefore the number of Amp-hours required.

**Example:**

A mid-sized campervan wanting to park up without driving for three days with the following electrical requirements:

| Appliance | Rating (Amps) | Estimated daily usage (hrs) |
|---|---|---|
| Lights | 1 | 5 |
| Heater (gas heater with small electric fan) | 1.5 | 3 |

| | |
|---|---|
| Total Daily energy requirements | = (1 x 5) + (1.5 x 3) = 9.5 Amps / day |
| Number of days between charging | = 3 |
| **Total Amp-hours required** | = 3 x 9.5 = 28.5 |
| **Recommended Min Battery Size** | **= 28.5 x 2 = 57 Amp-hours** |

As you can see from the example above, a reasonably small leisure battery of 70 or 90Ah would be sufficient and would probably also allow for running other small items such as water pumps and phone chargers. However, adding in a small compressor fridge, running continuously (24hrs a day) at 1.7Amps changes the requirements dramatically:

| | |
|---|---|
| Total Daily energy requirements | = (1 x 5) + (1.5 x 3) + (1.7 x 24) = 50.3 |
| Number of days between charging | = 3 |
| **Total Amp-hours required** | = 3 x 50.3 = 150.9 |
| **Recommended Min Battery Size** | **= 150.9 x 2 = 301.8 Amp-hours** |

The latter example would need at least two large leisure batteries connected together, or the addition of some other power source such as a solar panel, or a compromise such as accepting that the fridge can only be used sparingly. The other thing you can plan to do is run the engine for a while when parked up to recharge the battery, but you will need to make sure you have enough fuel for that (plus it isn't the most environmentally friendly thing to do). There are multiple ways to tackle this type of conundrum, but coming up with a reasonable idea of your requirements and their implications is a good place to start.

Don't get too carried away – additional battery capacity comes hand in hand with increased cost, space requirements, and a significant weight penalty. You also need to remember that all of those batteries need to be charged! If your power requirements are large, consider adding a solar panel to your system rather than creating an endless array of batteries. Of course the other way to get round this is to park up somewhere you can hook-up to the mains (more on that later).

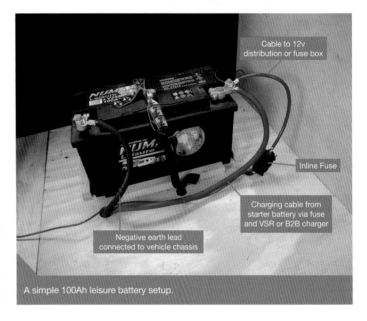

Cable to 12v distribution or fuse box

Inline Fuse

Charging cable from starter battery via fuse and VSR or B2B charger

Negative earth lead connected to vehicle chassis

A simple 100Ah leisure battery setup.

**Safety warning - all examples on these pages have been simplified to aid readability. Actual details will depend on the specifics of your installation and for a more in-depth discussion you should consult other sources or an auto-electrician.**

# Battery Bank Wiring

It is possible to get really big single leisure batteries but they rapidly get very unwieldy so if you need lots of battery power, connecting two or three together is a better approach. A battery bank is constructed by connecting the batteries together in parallel – this results in retaining the same voltage (i.e. 12V) but adding the capacities together. Two 115Ah batteries connected together in parallel will give you a capacity of 230Ah. To connect in parallel you connect positive to positive and negative to negative. You should try to use matching batteries for the best results. Do not make the mistake of connecting in series (positive to negative) which would double the voltage (i.e. to 24V) and leave the capacity unchanged.

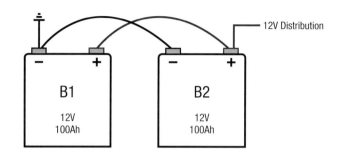

## Simple Battery Bank

**Parallel Wiring**
**Result : 12V 200Ah**

If you are planning a bigger battery bank containing more than two or three batteries you should read up on battery bank balancing and other issues which are beyond the scope of this book.

# Battery Type

There are three main different types of leisure battery worth considering, each with its own pros and cons.

- Lead-Acid – the traditional favourite for both starter and leisure batteries. These batteries have been around for a long time (over 150 years) and are good at supplying large currents in bursts such as when cranking an engine. They are relatively low cost. They require periodic topping up of the de-ionised water which serves as the electrolyte. Some are sold as 'maintenance free' which (in theory) shouldn't require topping up, or at least less frequently. Make sure you get a battery that is specifically labelled as being for leisure or 'deep cycle' use. These will give off hydrogen when charging and ideally this should be vented to outside the living space via a tube.

- AGM – Absorbent Glass Mat batteries use an electrolyte soaked glass-fibre mat in between the battery cells. The electrolyte won't spill out so in some cases these can be used in any orientation (take the manufacturers advice on this). They are sealed and don't 'gas' in the same way as normal lead-acids do. They are genuinely maintenance free and no topping up is required (or possible). They are more expensive than normal lead-acid batteries but in theory should cope with more recharging cycles (so long as the charge voltage is limited as per the manufacturer's guidance). There are also Gel batteries that are sealed too but they don't offer significant advantages over AGM. Both lead-acid and AGM batteries should be reassuringly heavy as this tends to also be a signal of quality.

- Lithium Ion – These batteries are still fairly uncommon in the campervan market but the technology has been improving rapidly in recent years, partly due to the electric car market pumping research money at the industry. Although they are expensive, they do offer advantages such as being lighter weight and offering longer life-spans. There have been safety risks associated with lithium ion batteries and care must be taken with charging. Be careful when doing straight Amp-hour cost comparisons: you should be able to get away with a smaller capacity lithium ion since they can be regularly discharged to 80%, whereas lead-acid and AGM batteries should only be discharged to 50%.

A selection of bits and pieces for a campervan electrical system – only add in what you need as the costs can quickly add up.

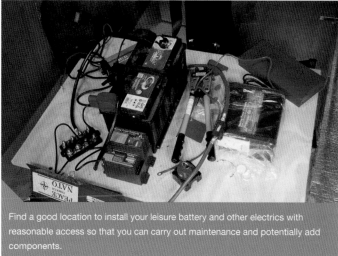
Find a good location to install your leisure battery and other electrics with reasonable access so that you can carry out maintenance and potentially add components.

# 25 Disconnecting the Battery

| | |
|---|---|
| MODERATE 3/5 | PREREQUISITES - - |
| | DO BEFORE - - |
| | COMBINE WITH Removing seats, installing charging systems, etc. |

For tasks such as making charging system connections or removing seats (which can trigger airbags), the first thing you need to do is disconnect the battery. This avoids giving yourself a shock and helps prevent potential damage caused while doing the work.

Disconnecting the battery is very straightforward – you need a socket set with the right size socket, open the bonnet, find the battery, take the cover off it if there is one, undo the negative terminal and tuck the earth lead well away from anywhere where it could accidentally touch either terminal. Reverse this procedure to re-connect it, all the time being very careful not to touch both terminals at once.

- Be careful when undoing a terminal with a socket wrench that you don't twist it round and hit the other terminal.

- Connecting the positive terminal to anything metal while the negative earth lead is still connected will result in a shock.

- If you are disconnecting the battery you may need a code to put into your radio or alarm after reconnecting it.

Note that on some modern vehicles the manufacturers, in their wisdom, have made getting at the negative terminal extremely tricky. If this is the case in your van, it is still possible to disconnect the battery by disconnecting the positive terminal instead of the negative – be especially careful when doing this that you don't accidentally hit any metal with the wrench as you will receive a shock.

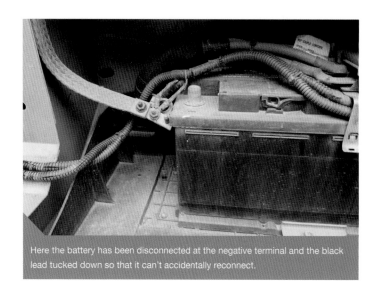
Here the battery has been disconnected at the negative terminal and the black lead tucked down so that it can't accidentally reconnect.

# 12V Distribution & Circuits

Once you have installed a leisure battery, you are now ready to do your wiring. The core of the standard system is to run a cable from the leisure battery to a fuse box. It is good practice to place an inline 'master' fuse on this cable – the cable and fuse should be capable of carrying the maximum foreseeable load. A nice optional addition is to also install an isolation switch on this cable which makes it easy to turn off the entire living area electrics – handy if the vehicle won't be used for a while for instance.

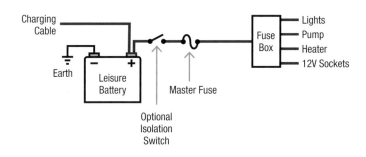

## 12v Distribution

Sometimes taming the wiring in a conversion project can be daunting, but persevere and it will begin to make sense.

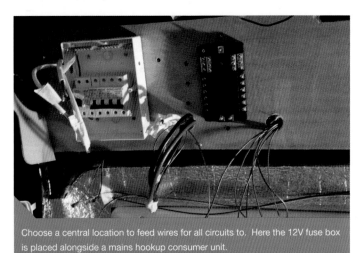

Choose a central location to feed wires for all circuits to. Here the 12V fuse box is placed alongside a mains hookup consumer unit.

The fuse box (also known as a distribution box) allows you to split your electrical appliances into a number of different circuits, each using appropriately sized cable and protected by the correct sized fuse. Many campervans will only need a few wiring circuits – for instance lights, water pump, heater – while bigger conversion projects could have ten or more and may even have more than one fuse box.

| Circuit | Fuse Rating * |
|---|---|
| Lights | 5A |
| Heater | 5A |
| Fridge | 15A |
| Pump | 10A (pressure pump) |
| Sockets | 15A |
| Water Heater | 10A |

\* Fuse ratings are examples only and should be adjusted to suit your own appliance ratings.

| Common Symbols in Diagrams | | | |
|---|---|---|---|
| ⊙ | Alternator | ⏚ | Earth (Vehicle Chassis) |
| ∿ | Fuse | ☼ | Lights / LED |
| ⟋ | Switch | | |

Different fuse and cable ratings for the various circuits.

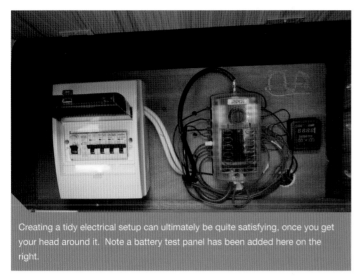

Creating a tidy electrical setup can ultimately be quite satisfying, once you get your head around it. Note a battery test panel has been added here on the right.

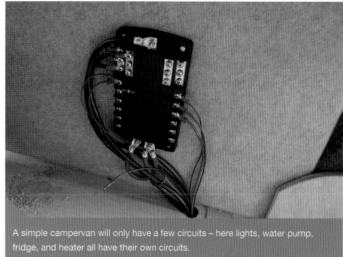

A simple campervan will only have a few circuits – here lights, water pump, fridge, and heater all have their own circuits.

# Cable

The cable to use when wiring campervans is 12V flexible automotive cable. The more power running along the cable, the thicker it should be. Thicker cable has less resistance and therefore will carry the current with less voltage drop. If a cable is too thin for the load it is carrying, it will heat up and could be a fire risk. All cables should be protected by a fuse that will blow well before the cable would get too hot. The longer the length of cable is, the more voltage drop becomes an issue and the thicker the cable should be to compensate for this.

Vehicle manufacturers creating large wiring looms containing thousands of metres of cable will use precise calculations to ensure they are using the thinnest (and therefore the lightest and cheapest) cables they can get away with. However, a conversion is unlikely to use an excessive amount of cable, so you can make life easy on yourself by over-specifying the cables you use – that way you don't have to worry about calculating exact currents and acceptable voltage drops.

Automotive cable is measured in a few different ways that can be quite confusing. The easiest way to buy it is from enlightened retailers that give their cable current ratings instead of telling you how many strands there are or what the cross-sectional area is. A cable's current rating is less scientific, but a far more user-friendly description. Using red cable for the live feed and black for the earth run keeps things simple.

| Application | Suggested Cable Sizing |
| --- | --- |
| Battery to battery link cable | 35Amps if using a B2B charger (depends on output of charger). If linking batteries directly via a relay, the cable needs to be the same spec. as that connecting alternator to starter battery (e.g. 150Amps, could even be more). |
| Earth Cable | Usually sold as 'earth cable' so just use that. It needs to be thick enough to carry the max load including charging. |
| Battery to Fuse Box | Big enough to carry your max living space load (e.g. add fuse ratings on your fuse box together). |
| Lights, heater fan, submersible pump, other small items | 8Amps |
| Pressure water pump, water heater | 17Amps |
| Fridge, Sockets | 27Amps |

For those who want to know, the full breakdown of a cable specification given as "28/0.30mm, 2mm$^2$, 17.5Amp" is as follows: 28 strands of 0.30mm diameter, 2mm$^2$ cross sectional area, 17.5Amp continuous current carrying capacity. There is plenty of information online about calculating voltage drops etc. if you are interested, but don't get bogged down!

# Appliance Ratings and Fuses

Every electrical appliance has its own rating telling you either how much power it uses in Watts, or how much current it will draw in Amps (sometimes both). If you have one figure but not the other, you can use the equation:

**Current (Amps) = Power (Watts) / Voltage (V)**
For example, a 1.5Watt LED light will use 1.5W / 12V = 0.125Amps.

If you have a number of items on a circuit, you need to add their power requirements together to come up with the total load – for example if there are five 2Amp appliances on a circuit, the total current draw when they are all on will be 5 x 2 = 10Amps. With this information, you should be able to work out how many amps each of your circuits will carry. Once you have worked this out, you should choose a fuse that will blow if a significantly higher current than expected appears on the circuit. The fuse is present to protect the cable – in other words if something goes wrong on your circuit, you want the fuse to blow well before any other problems occur (such as the appliance or cable heating up causing a fire). In the example above, where the total anticipated load is 10Amps, the fuse should be higher - say 12 or 15Amps - and the cable should be rated higher still - 17Amp cable will be plenty.

# Earth Points

In most vehicles the negative terminal of the battery is earthed to the vehicle chassis. Because of this, you don't need to run earth wires from appliances all the way back to the negative terminal, you just need to attach them to the chassis somewhere. Vehicles usually have a number of factory designated 'earthing points' (bolts with good connections to the chassis that are designed to have earth cables attached to them) and if you can find where these are it is good to use them.

You can also create your own earthing points wherever you need them – the key requirement is there needs to be a good connection to the metal chassis. Find a spot where you can place a bolt through part of the metal structure of the vehicle and scrape away all the paint in order to ensure a good connection. Crimp a ring terminal onto the end of your earth cables, thread them onto the bolt and tighten the nut with washer up so that the terminals are nicely connected to the chassis.

You don't need to run individual earth cables for every appliance – you can just connect them together as and when it proves convenient. The only thing to ensure is that the earth cables are rated sufficiently to carry the loads routed along them.

An ad-hoc earthing point with the paint removed. Where possible use formal earthing points provided by the vehicle manufacturer.

A bus-bar can be useful in more complicated conversions – here it allows numerous thick cables to connect into the battery in a tidy and efficient way.

# Crimping & Terminals

The main technique for connecting cables together in a conversion is by using crimp terminals. The terminals come in a variety of types but the most useful are insulated spade and ring terminals. To keep things simple they come in three sizes – red (small), blue (medium), and yellow (big). Getting a selection pack at the start of your project will get you off to a good start. Ring terminals (often un-insulated) are available in multiple bigger sizes for use with battery and charging cables etc.

# 26 Crimping a Terminal

You will need a pair of wire strippers and a crimping tool. The standard crimping tools are cheap and effective and have the red, blue, and yellow sizes marked on them.

1. Cut the cable to size and carefully strip a small bit of insulation off the end – around 5mm is usually plenty. Twist the cable so that all the individual strands are held together.

2. Hold the terminal loosely in the crimpers and thread the stripped cable into it. The stripped cable should be in good contact with the metal of the terminal, and it should be the right size for the cable – if it's too loose use a smaller sized terminal.

3. Use the crimp tools to securely squash the terminal onto the cable. You should aim to crimp each terminal twice – once to squash the metal onto the stripped wire, and another to squash the plastic onto the insulated cable which helps relieve strain on the joint. You need to squeeze the crimps fairly tightly in order to create a firm crimp – use both hands to squeeze the crimps if you need to.

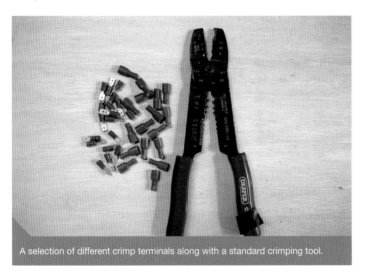

A selection of different crimp terminals along with a standard crimping tool.

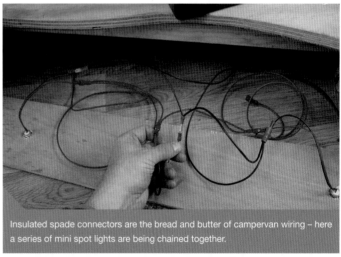

Insulated spade connectors are the bread and butter of campervan wiring – here a series of mini spot lights are being chained together.

Crimp each terminal twice and use the correct size for the cable being used

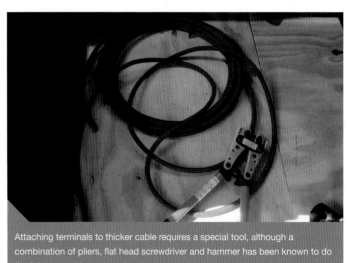

Attaching terminals to thicker cable requires a special tool, although a combination of pliers, flat head screwdriver and hammer has been known to do the job too.

# Lights

Good lighting is one of the key elements to creating a great looking campervan. Getting this right can make a huge difference to any conversion and really lift the space. There are a large variety of different types of 12V lights – spotlights, reading lights, and strip lights, to name a few. All lights should be LED based as these are far more efficient than older alternatives.

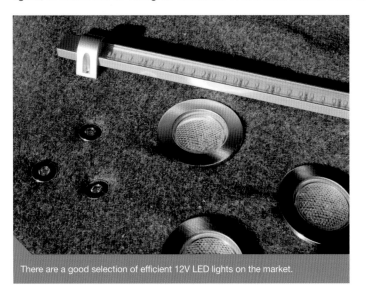

There are a good selection of efficient 12V LED lights on the market.

Recessed spot or down-lights do a great job of lighting your living space.

# 27 Wiring Lights

EASY / MODERATE
2/5

| PREREQUISITES | First fix wiring, panels fixed |
|---|---|
| DO BEFORE | - - |
| COMBINE WITH | - - |

The wiring for lights is straightforward.

1. Run a red cable from a fuse in your fuse box to one of the terminals in a switch.

2. Then run another red cable from the other terminal in the switch to the light.

3. Run a black cable from the light to an earth point or connect into an existing earth cable.

For the majority of LED lights using 8Amp cable will be plenty (thinner would usually be fine too), and depending on how many lights are on the circuit a fuse of 5Amps or less will be fine, but add up the ratings of all the lights to give you a figure for your particular installation.

## Light Wiring

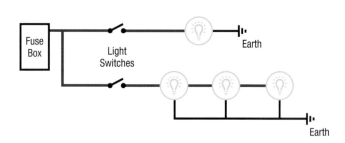

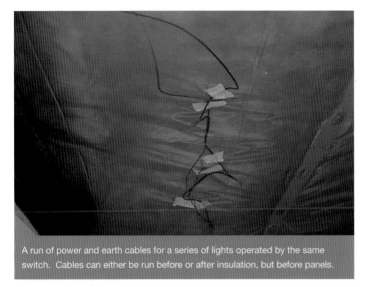

A run of power and earth cables for a series of lights operated by the same switch. Cables can either be run before or after insulation, but before panels.

A single light switch next to double mains sockets.

Spade connectors make connecting lights up an easy job.

If your light has a switch integrated in it (e.g. a reading light) then the wiring is even easier – run one cable from the fuse to the light, and another cable to an earth point. If you want multiple lights to be operated from the same switch, you need to wire them in parallel – i.e. run a red cable from the switch to the first light, crimp this together with a second red cable and run that to the next light, and so on until you reach the last light in the chain; the earth cable for multiple lights does the same – it runs in a chain from the first light to each other light in turn and then to an earth point.

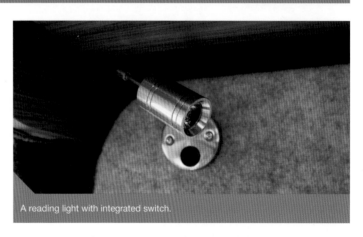

A reading light with integrated switch.

Sometimes little touches make a big difference and clever use of lighting can really lift a conversion.

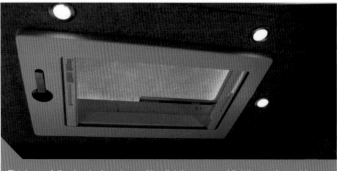

Think carefully about where to position lighting as good lighting makes a big difference to van life.

# victron energy
## BLUE POWER

The automotive market comprises a broad range of applications requiring a reliable power supply. In vehicles such as fire engines, ambulances and police cars a human life may depend on an autonomous system. That is also true for adventure vehicles visiting remote places. In all such instances it is vital that systems function flawlessly. Victron Energy offers you such solutions, ensuring safety through energy freedom and independence.

Energy. Anytime. Anywhere.

The Victron Connect App lets you get live status info and configure Victron Smart products with built-in bluetooth support.

Victron Remote Management (VRM) allows remote monitoring all over the world.

Watch instruction videos at: www.youtube.com/user/VictronEnergyBV
Find stockists at: www.victronenergy.com/where-to-buy

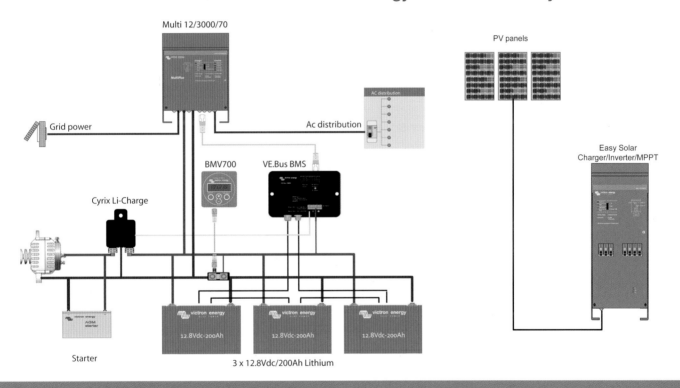

# MAINS POWER, HOOKUPS & INVERTERS

If you want to be able to use a lot of electricity in your vehicle, or for a lengthy time between running the engine, the best way is to park somewhere that you can plug the campervan into the mains. Once you're plugged into the mains you have an endless supply of power and can use as much or as little as you like (within the limits of the supply and your fuse box). With mains power, appliances such as electric water heaters, microwaves, large fridges, electric blankets, kettles, satellite TVs, etc., all become fair game for the comfort seeking traveller.

The majority of campsites offer pitches with electric hookup points, where you pay a little more in the nightly fee for the privilege. Sometimes hookups are also metered or token-fed so that you pay for the amount you use. Provided you have a long enough cable, and a willing provider, you can plug in anywhere you can find a power socket – outside a friend's house, alongside a holiday cottage, or in a hotel car park to name a few potential options.

**Safety warning – mains power (230V) is highly dangerous, potentially deadly, if used or installed incorrectly. You should only attempt the wiring of 230V systems in a vehicle if you are competent enough to do so – exactly as within a house. Mains systems should be tested and certified by a qualified electrician – if you plan to do some of the wiring yourself you should talk it through with the electrician who will sign it off before you start.**

There are three key components of a mains hookup system – a mains battery charger, a consumer unit, and the hookup socket.

## Mains Hookup Wiring

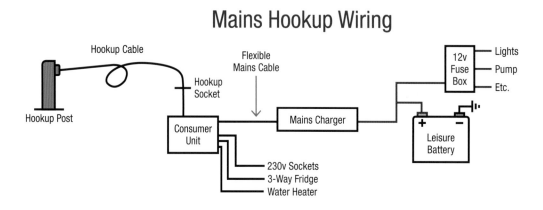

# Mains Battery Charger

A mains battery charger serves two functions – the most obvious is that it allows you to recharge your leisure battery (and potentially your starter battery as well). The more important reason for having a mains charger is that it also acts as a transformer, converting the 230V AC power to 12V DC which allows you to use the rest of your 12V electrics as normal. All your 12V lights, water pump, etc. continue to be powered as normal, blissfully unaware that you are hooked up to the mains.

The mains battery charger keeps the leisure battery topped up while on hookup allowing you to use all your 12V electrics as much as you like.

A mains battery charger next to the consumer unit.

# Mains Consumer Unit

The consumer unit is exactly the same as you will find in your house, only usually with far fewer circuits on it. The power comes into the vehicle via the hookup socket, and from there a cable goes to the consumer unit. The consumer unit is basically a fuse box which has a number of circuits on it. Common circuits might be:

- Fridge
- Charger
- Sockets
- Water Heater

The consumer unit usually has one RCD to detect and protect against faults on any of its circuits, plus each circuit is protected with an MCB, the modern equivalent of a fuse, of the right rating. (RCD – Residual Current Device; MCB – Miniature Current Breaker).

The consumer unit is a small version of the one in your house. It distributes mains power to a number of circuits, each with their own protection device.

# 28 Installing a Hookup Socket

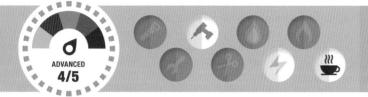

| PREREQUISITES | - - |
|---|---|
| DO BEFORE | Insulation, panels, furniture |
| COMBINE WITH | - - |

**ADVANCED 4/5**

You usually need to cut a hole in the side of the van to install a hookup socket, though sometimes it is possible to cheat by finding somewhere to mount the socket externally (e.g. on the side of a bumper or similar) and then route the cable into the vehicle. The socket is wired on the inside via a cable to the consumer unit. The socket allows you to plug a hookup cable into it, with the other end of the cable plugged into a campsite hookup pillar or similar.

1. Locate a suitable place for the socket – ideally reasonably close to the consumer unit, and somewhere it won't get in the way of other features of the conversion. If panels and insulation are in the way you'll have to take them off (so ideally install this prior to insulating). Remember that when hooked up you will have a cable trailing from the socket outside the van which can form a trip hazard if in the wrong place.

2. Carefully measure and mark the hole to be cut. Masking tape the whole area to avoid scratching the paint. Drill a hole to start with then use a jigsaw with fine metal blade to cut out the shape. Treat the cut metal edges with anti-rust primer.

3. Install the socket in the hole, ensuring it is well sealed with mastic. Sockets are usually bolted together – one part inside the van, the other outside, with the vehicle's skin sandwiched in between.

The hookup socket is installed in the side of the vehicle.

The internal side of the mains hookup socket – the cable is wired to the socket and then goes to the consumer unit.

A typical hookup post at a campsite. Carrying a good length of hookup cable with a couple of adapter plugs gives you plenty of flexibility.

## Mains Cable

All mains cable used in a vehicle should be flexible rather than the stiff solid core varieties often used in domestic homes. Stiff cable is likely to work its way loose with all the movement experienced when driving a campervan on rough roads. The cable sizing should be chosen according to the requirements of the circuit.

## Hookup Limitations

In practice, the amount of power you can use when on a hookup is limited to the rating of the hookup point. Hookup points are usually protected by a miniature circuit breaker (MCB) and 16Amps is a common size, though some campsite facilities may be lower. A 16Amp 230V supply limits you to 3.68kW of power at one time – if you go above this you will trip the MCB and in some cases you may need to get the campsite to reset it for you. If you really go for it you might even manage to trip your neighbours' hookups as well, so try to avoid overloading your system while they're watching their favourite soap opera.

## Inverters

When you can't plug into a mains hookup, it is still possible to use mains powered appliances – for this you need an inverter. Batteries supply DC (Direct Current) power while mains supply is AC (Alternating Current). Most electrical items you have in your house are designed to run on 230V so won't work on a 12V circuit without the addition of an 'inverter'. An inverter takes 12V DC power from the battery and changes it into 230V AC – you can then either plug a household plug directly into the inverter, or run a cable (usually via an RCD plug) from the inverter to some 3 pin sockets which can be used as they would be in your house.

Installing an inverter allows you to use mains power while off-grid and away from mains hookup.

Be aware that using an inverter with limited battery power carries efficiency penalties, so use it sparingly. Items such as laptops already run on DC power (albeit often at voltages other than 12V), so rather than using an inverter to change your DC power to AC, only for it to then be transformed back into DC, it is more efficient to get a 12V charging cable for them. If the appliance you want to use is solely for van-use (e.g. a microwave), then consider getting a 12V model instead of using a mains version with an inverter. An interesting exception to this may be fridges – testing recently carried out by Sterling Power indicated that using a 230V compressor fridge with an inverter had the same power requirements as the 12V equivalent. Alongside efficiency differences between 12V and 230V motors, this finding is partly testament to how efficient modern inverters have become, with current takes having dropped from 2Amps down to a nimble 0.5Amps on recent models.

**Safety warning – inverters convert relatively safe 12V power into potentially deadly 230V power, so tread carefully and get an electrician involved if required.**

Since inverters are quite high power consumers, it often makes sense to run a dedicated cable to them from the battery with an appropriate in-line fuse, rather than running them off a fuse box circuit. Inverters come in a range of sizes, from relatively low power units right up to beefy workhorses – you should buy the inverter to suit your intended use... get one powerful enough to cope with the appliances you want to use but you don't need more than that. Combi charger / inverters are also available. A few items such as microwaves and bread-makers might only run on a 'pure sine wave' inverter – these are more expensive than the more standard 'quasi / modified sine wave' inverters. Most items will be fine on a quasi-sine inverter but if you plan to plug something unusual into it do a little research to check before buying. There are also square wave inverters but these are less common these days.

# 29 Fitting Multi-source Sockets

| PREREQUISITES | Mains hookup, inverter, sockets |
| --- | --- |
| DO BEFORE | - - |
| COMBINE WITH | Wiring, consumer unit & socket installation |

**ADVANCED 4/5**

If you are installing 230V sockets and planning to alternate between being on mains hookup and off-grid inverter (or generator) use, it is possible to arrange your wiring so that your sockets can be used no matter where the power supply is coming from. In order to achieve this you need to install a multi-way selector switch upstream of the sockets. With this arrangement you then need to turn the switch to select the power source before using the sockets – e.g. 0 – sockets off; 1 – mains hookup; 2 – inverter; 3 – generator. The alternative to this is to install separate sockets for the different power supplies – e.g. you might install a single socket for inverter use while all the others will only work when on hookup.

Including both 12V and mains sockets offers maximum versatility.

Installing mains sockets that can be powered both from the consumer unit when on hookup and from the inverter when off-grid requires a multi-way switch. The alternative is one set of sockets for the inverter, and another for use on hookup.

# BATTERY CHARGING

In simple terms, your vehicle's alternator charges your starter battery whenever you're driving. The aim is to connect your leisure battery up so that it will get charged when driving as well. If all else was equal, a big cable running from the positive terminal of the starter battery to the positive terminal of the leisure battery would be pretty much all you'd need to get the alternator to charge the second battery. Unfortunately it's not quite as simple as that, because doing this would connect both batteries together, all the time.

## Split Charging

What you need to achieve is to connect the batteries together only while driving so that you protect each battery from getting used at the wrong time. When you park up and stop the engine, the two batteries should be isolated from each other so that you can use your living space appliances – lights, fridge, TV, etc. – without draining the starter battery. When the vehicle is being started, only the starter battery should be in use. Only once you are driving should the two batteries be linked together so that the alternator charges both starter and leisure batteries. This setup is known as 'split charging'.

> "Unfortunately it's not quite as simple as that… When you park up and stop the engine, the two batteries should be isolated from each other."

## Split Charging Overview

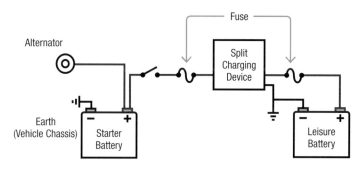

In days gone by, there was a relatively simple solution to this problem – known as a 'split charge relay'. However, the more modern the vehicle, the more complex the wiring and electronics, and the more powerful the alternator. This means that on most modern vehicles (from approximately year 2000 onwards) the old DIY solution becomes difficult: it's much harder to find the right wires to get the required ignition-switched feed, and because modern alternators are much more powerful the relay and cables used need to be far more heavy duty. There is also an increasing trend towards 'intelligently managed' charging systems, especially on Euro 6 compliant vehicles from around 2014 onwards, which makes things even more complicated. Cobbling together an 'old-school' split charge relay system on top of a complex modern wiring setup will not only be tricky to achieve, it is also unlikely to work as you intended it to.

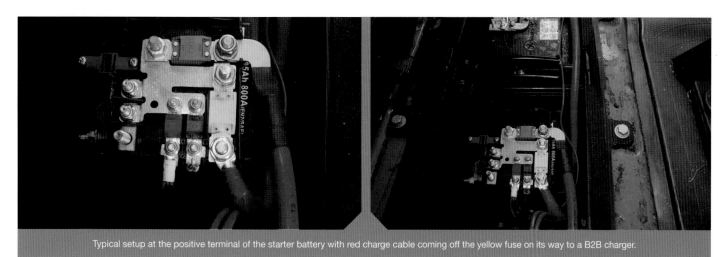

Typical setup at the positive terminal of the starter battery with red charge cable coming off the yellow fuse on its way to a B2B charger.

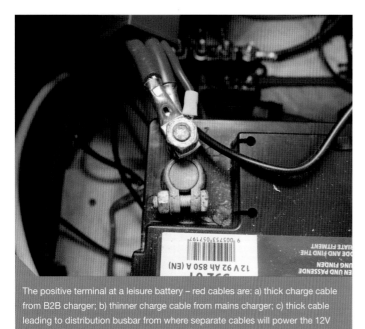

The positive terminal at a leisure battery – red cables are: a) thick charge cable from B2B charger; b) thinner charge cable from mains charger; c) thick cable leading to distribution busbar from where separate cables will power the 12V fuse box, and an inverter (both via inline fuses).

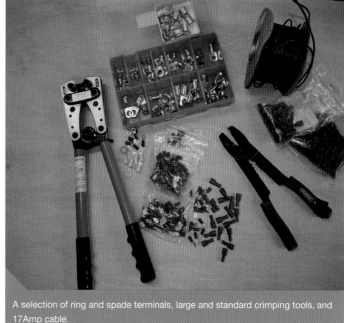

A selection of ring and spade terminals, large and standard crimping tools, and 17Amp cable.

# Euro 5/6, Regenerative Braking, and Voltage Limiting

The swift march of progress often leaves casualties in its wake, and it seems that simple battery charging solutions for DIY converters is one such example. As vehicles have become fancier, and as part of the drive to reduce the environmental damage caused by vehicles, something has also been lost for would-be converters… simplicity.

Increasingly stringent European Emission Standards culminated in the introduction of the Euro 5 standard (in 2009) and then the Euro 6 standard (in 2014). These standards have pushed manufacturers to make their vehicles more efficient and less polluting. One way to achieve better miles per gallon and reduce emissions is for the engine to do less work, and the ways that manufacturers have found to do this have implications for charging our leisure batteries.

## Common Efficiency Measures in Euro 6 vehicles:

- Previously wasted kinetic energy is now captured from braking and used to recharge the battery – this is known as regenerative braking or SRC (Smart Regenerative Charging).

- Alternators now load the engine less frequently. Rather than continually keeping the starter battery fully charged, it is now allowed to partially discharge so that there is space for 'free' electricity to be stored when it is generated (i.e. during braking).

Of course this is good news for the environment, but the implications for battery charging are that we can no longer rely on the alternator passing a nice high voltage to the starter battery whenever we are driving; and if there isn't a high voltage at the starter battery, we'll struggle to charge our leisure battery. The flip side of this voltage limiting, is that during short regenerative charging periods the voltage being sent to the battery can shoot up to a level that may be damaging to leisure batteries that weren't designed to handle such high charging voltages.

"…we can no longer rely on the alternator passing a nice high voltage to the starter battery whenever we are driving…"

One way to establish the extent of the predicament in your vehicle is to get a simple voltage metre and plug it into the 12V socket on your dashboard then as you're driving along have a look at how the voltage varies. If you get anything other than a reasonably constant and high voltage (e.g. 14+Volts) then you probably have a smart charging system. In a vehicle with regenerative braking, you will see the voltage remain low (e.g. 12.2Volts or similar) for prolonged periods of time, followed by short periods of high voltage (potentially 15+Volts).

Modern battery to battery (B2B) chargers aim to tackle this problem, and some models are designed to have integrated 'intelligence' to allow them to work out when the vehicle is running or not. B2B chargers are also designed to charge the leisure battery as efficiently as possible and are able to keep charging despite low voltages, as well as protect against high voltages. In some cases B2B chargers will still need to be triggered by an ignition switched source rather than by voltage sensing (more on this below).

Install a battery gauge so that you can easily monitor the voltage of both starter and leisure battery – this helps you understand how well your system is performing.

An attractive long-term solution is for the vehicle manufacturers to provide converters with a good mechanism allowing them to interface (ideally with ease and at a reasonable cost) with their complex systems, however we will probably be waiting a long time for such an enlightened approach and in the meantime you must carefully consider the options below and accept that this particular aspect of vehicle conversions is just not as simple as it once was.

# Split Charge Options

There are actually multiple different ways to achieve split charging, but the following section explores the main two split charge options that self builders should consider for modern vehicles, to help you home in on your ideal battery charging solution.

## Option 1 – Battery to Battery Charger

The sophisticated approach to linking the two batteries together is to use a battery to battery (B2B) charger. B2B chargers monitor the state of both batteries and control the voltage levels so that they charge in the most efficient way. B2B chargers still need something to trigger them to turn on and off and many rely on an internal voltage sensing relay for this purpose.

One of the big potential advantages of B2B chargers is that they can work regardless of any complex voltage management going on. These chargers are getting more intelligent all the time – when set up to switch on and off purely by sensing voltage (known as 'auto mode'), the B2B's software will make educated guesses about what the current state of the vehicle is. A more certain mechanism is for them to be controlled via ignition-switching, but as already discussed the wiring for that can be awkward.

### Split Charging with B2B Charger

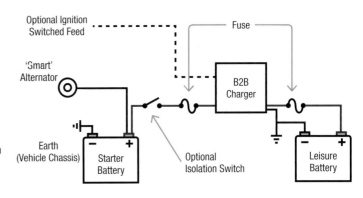

Notes: Cable, fuses, & isolation switch rated according to B2B Charger rating.
e.g. 30A B2B Charger = 50A cable 40A fuses.

The thing a B2B charger can do, that other options can't, is draw current from the starter battery and 'ramp it up' to a higher voltage to send to the leisure battery – so even in vehicles where regenerative braking and voltage limiting is happening, the B2B charger can continue to provide a good charging service to your leisure battery. B2B chargers can also protect the leisure battery against damaging high voltages which are often seen in Euro 6 vehicles during regenerative braking events.

If you have a large leisure battery or a battery bank, then it is even more important that you recharge it in the most efficient way possible, and B2B chargers are the only real option if this is the case for you.

A battery to battery charger alongside isolation switches, fuse box, consumer unit, and bus bar / earthing bar.

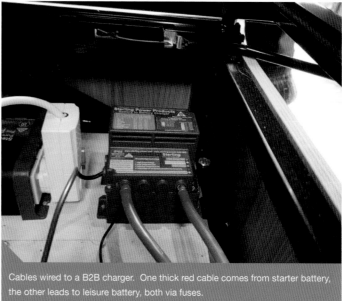

Cables wired to a B2B charger. One thick red cable comes from starter battery, the other leads to leisure battery, both via fuses.

# Option 2 – Voltage Sensing Relay

Note – this option should only be considered for vehicles without regenerative braking and smart charging. A less sophisticated (though also a bit less expensive) way to link the two batteries together is via a voltage sensing relay (VSR). A VSR is an electronic switch that is triggered to turn on when the voltage rises above a pre-defined level. When the alternator is charging the starter battery, the VSR will sense that the voltage has gone up and switch on to allow the current to flow through to charge the leisure battery. When the engine is turned off, the alternator will stop charging and the voltage will drop. When the VSR senses the voltage dropping past a certain point the relay will switch off, thus isolating the two batteries from each other.

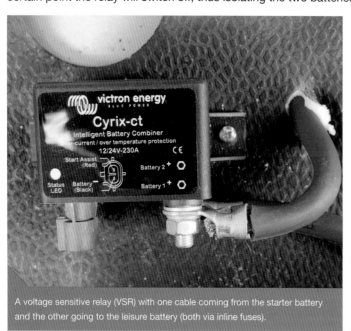

A voltage sensitive relay (VSR) with one cable coming from the starter battery and the other going to the leisure battery (both via inline fuses).

## Split Charging Using VSR

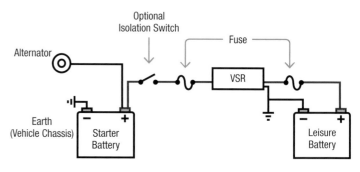

Notes: VSR, cable, fuses and switch choice must be based on alternator rating.
e.g. Alternator 150A. Fuses 180A. Cable, Switch, & VSR 200A+.

The major advantage of using a VSR over the old-school approach of an ignition switched relay is that you don't need to tap into any vehicle wiring – the VSR only needs a thick new cable coming from the vehicle battery and turns on and off based on the voltage on that cable. This makes the wiring required for a VSR far simpler than for an ignition switched system. Your VSR will need to be powerful enough to handle the current generated by your alternator, and inline fuses (mounted in 'Mega' fuse holders) should be included in the system to protect against unexpected power surges.

## Disadvantages of VSRs:

- They are completely reliant on sensing the voltage, which in some cases won't work as intended – particularly in Euro 6 vehicles built from approximately 2014 onwards, where 'intelligent' management of charging is going on.

- A VSR is either on or off – it won't control and adjust the charge sent to the leisure battery so does not charge the leisure battery in the most efficient way. A system using a VSR may not manage to fully charge the leisure battery, and it may also allow damagingly high voltages through to your leisure battery, particularly if regenerative braking is in operation.

If you have a vehicle with big leisure batteries, battery banks, regenerative braking or smart charging, a VSR is unlikely to be a good solution.

# Smart Charging Case Study

One recent conversion project on a 2016 Transit Connect found the following. A volt meter plugged into the 12V socket on the dashboard showed that regenerative charging and voltage limiting was indeed happening. The pattern was difficult to pin-point exactly, but in essence after starting the vehicle the alternator would bring the voltage up to a high charging level for a short period (e.g. 14.8V), but then the voltage would rapidly drop down to a level insufficient for conventional charging (e.g. 12.2V). The voltage would rise again during significant braking events such as descending hills and then drop again quickly.

# Disabling Smart Charging

Manufacturers of Euro 6 vehicles sometimes provide a mechanism whereby smart or regenerative charging can be temporarily switched off in favour of a 'conventional' charging mode. For instance, in a Transit Connect a wire is located inside the glove-box that enables the smart charging to be switched on and off as required. With the smart charging switched off the voltage meter will show a far more continuous alternator charging regime. At first glance this may seem an attractive glimmer of hope for converters, however caution is required – switching smart charging off in your vehicle undermines the efficiencies and Euro 6 stature of the vehicle, so shouldn't be done unless recommended by the manufacturer. If you are going to these lengths anyway, you may be better advised to fit a B2B charger, make it ignition switched if required, and leave your smart charging enabled.

# Notes on Alternators

There is a continuing trend towards ever more powerful alternators with most modern panel vans now containing alternators rated at least at 120Amps, with 140 - 200Amps also now being fairly common. In fact this represents an excellent power supply that you are carrying around with you – more than powerful enough to be used in conjunction with a good inverter to allow you to run hairdryers, power tools, microwaves, etc. when parked up at the beach. When coupled with a good B2B charger, these powerful alternators are also capable of recharging your leisure batteries in an efficient way, and in a relatively short period of time. The only thing with using the alternator in this way is that it uses up diesel, so it doesn't entirely solve the conundrum of prolonged off-grid living.

# Ignition Switched Feeds

Once upon a time it was relatively easy to find the wires coming out of the back of a vehicle's alternator and use a 'Scotchlok' snap connector to tap into the charge warning light (typically on the alternator's D+ terminal). This technique gave you a wire that you could then use as an ignition switched feed to trigger a split charge relay on and off to control your battery isolation and charging. When the engine is on, the wire becomes live and switches the relay on, connecting the batteries together. When the engine turns off, the ignition switched wire goes dead, the relay goes off, and the batteries are separated. That technique is still possible on older vehicles but all but obsolete on modern vehicles.

The principle of an ignition switched feed is still a good one, but it is far trickier to achieve in modern vehicles without expert help. You need to find a wire that becomes live only while the engine is running. Be careful not to use a wire that becomes live before the engine actually starts as then your batteries will be linked while the engine is being cranked (i.e. don't use something that comes live on the first couple of clicks of the ignition key but before the engine starts). Unfortunately engines and vehicle electrics have become so elaborate now that it is all but impossible to provide any sort of general advice or technique to find an ignition switched feed. If you don't have the skills to track this down yourself you may need to enlist help from an experienced auto-electrician.

If this wiring under the steering column brings you out in sweats, you probably need to enlist help if you need an ignition switched source.

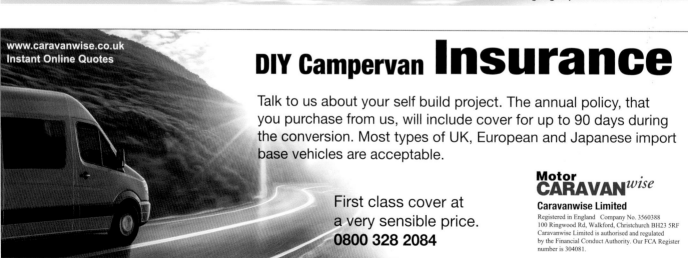

# WINDOWS & ROOFLIGHTS

Living in a house without any windows wouldn't be that much fun, and campervans and motorhomes are no different. Of course there are some windows in the cab area of the vehicle already, but it adds a lot to a campervan if you can let some daylight into the living space as well.

You might manage to find a vehicle to convert that already has windows where you want them, however it is also eminently possible to add windows into pretty much any vehicle. The basic process involves cutting a hole in the vehicle and fixing the window in place. At first glance this may not be a task you are willing to take on yourself, and if not there are many conversion and window fitting companies who can do the work for you. However, with some basic DIY skills and a chunk of courage fitting a new window into a vehicle is entirely achievable.

## Window Types

There are a number of different types of windows, all of which are suitable for campervan conversions:

- **Bonded windows** are the sort of windows you see factory-fitted on most new-style vans after around the year 2000. The bonded style windows generally give a bigger field of vision, and tend to look more modern and flashy. Most of these windows are single glazed panes of glass stuck (i.e. bonded) onto the metal of the van – the only thing holding them on is glue (i.e. there isn't any rubber, clamps, or screws actually holding them in).

- **Framed windows** come in engineered units with good thermal performance (most are double glazed acrylic) and often include built in blinds and mosquito nets. These windows are a great addition to a conversion, not least due to their insulating properties. They look quite different to bonded windows so part of the choice may depend what style you like the look of.

- **Rubber-mounted windows** are single glazed windows that are held in place by a thick band of rubber that slots over the metal skin of the vehicle. These windows are a more 'old-school' type and most van manufacturers no longer factory-fit rubber-mounted windows. Because rubber-mounted windows are declining in popularity compared to bonded windows, they are not necessarily a cheaper option anymore. Having said that, they are still good and appropriate windows to use in a camper conversion – particularly in older style vehicles where they may well look more in-keeping than a modern alternative might.

There are also a few other window variations – for instance **Top Hung** windows which, as the name suggests, hang from a bar mounted above the opening

# 30 Window Installation

| PREREQUISITES | Indoor space or good weather forecast |
|---|---|
| DO BEFORE | Insulation, panelling, flooring |
| COMBINE WITH | Rooflights, hookup sockets, other structural changes |

There are more detailed instructions to follow, but the basic steps of fitting a new window in a vehicle are always the same:

1. Pick the window location and size.

2. Buy the window (plus rubber / bonding kit as required).

3. Remove any panels, insulation etc.

4. Remove any stiffening struts.

5. Carefully! Measure, mark, and cut the hole.

6. Depending on window type, prepare for fixing into hole.

7. Fit window.

8. Seal it if required.

9. Complete the conversion and go on holiday!

## Recommended Tools

Since you are cutting a hole in the side of the vehicle, it's a good idea to ensure you have everything prepared and to hand before starting. You may well want to pick a good weather window and / or have a wet weather back up plan (e.g. get the van inside a garage or rig up a tarp or awning to work under). Some of the main tools you will need are as follows:

- An angle grinder.

- A jigsaw with plenty of metal cutting blades (you will probably break quite a few).

- Plenty of masking tape (some wide tape is useful).

- A flat file and a good sharp knife.

- Sealant gun plus sealant and bonding (if applicable).

- (Optional) Some big bits of cardboard for templates.

- Some paint / primer to protect the bare metal.

- (Optional but useful) A helper – if you can find an experienced one who has done it before, even better.

An angle grinder in use cutting a strut.

Make sure you have the right tools to hand before starting.

# Preparation & Removing Struts

Most panel vans are designed with obvious places where windows should go – there are usually window shaped sections in the panels where they would have put windows if the panel van had been a combi or minibus version.

Obviously you need to be able to get at the outer skin of the vehicle, so take off any ply panels and insulation etc. Often you will find a metal strut going up the middle of the window shape – these are designed to add stiffness to the panel and stop the side of the van acting like a wobble board when driving. Before cutting the hole, you are going to have to remove this strut. This may differ from van to van, but the easiest way for most DIYers is to use an angle grinder with a metal cutting disc to cut the top and bottom of the strut and then use a knife if required to slice away anything sticking the strut to the metal. Be super careful with the angle grinder – you only want to cut through the strut and NOT the side of the van. You should also pay careful attention to where the filings from the angle grinder go – they are capable of wrecking seat fabric or even windscreens (true story) so place strategic dust sheets or bits of plywood to protect and contain. You should have a fire extinguisher on hand in the unlikely event of the sparks from the grinder setting fire to something.

There is a school of thought that says to do the window on the sliding or rear door first. The idea being that if you do muck it up first time (which you won't) then it would in theory be easier to get a replacement door than a whole new integrated side panel. Not really a theory the author would like to test out.

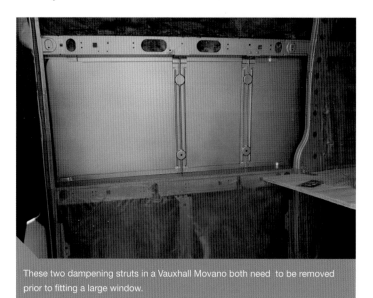

These two dampening struts in a Vauxhall Movano both need to be removed prior to fitting a large window.

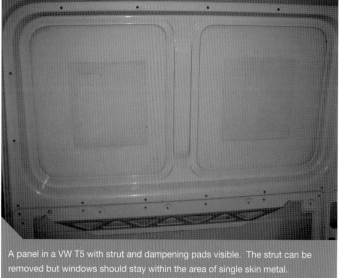

A panel in a VW T5 with strut and dampening pads visible. The strut can be removed but windows should stay within the area of single skin metal.

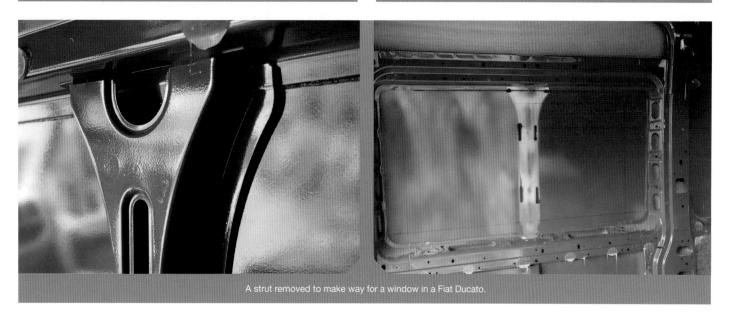

A strut removed to make way for a window in a Fiat Ducato.

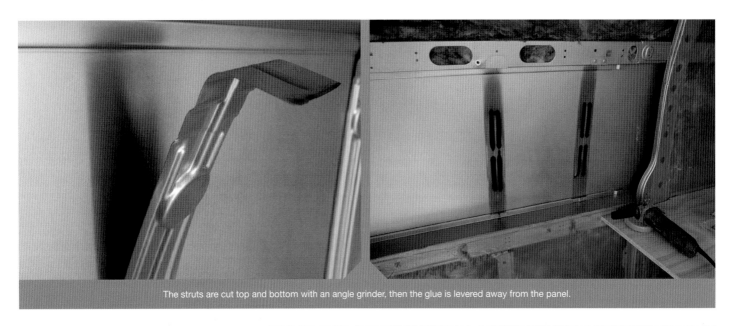

The struts are cut top and bottom with an angle grinder, then the glue is levered away from the panel.

Take care when angle grinding as the filings can easily damage chair fabric, dashboards, and even windscreens. Don't set fire to the dustsheets though!

# Marking Out

Before you can mark the shape to cut out, the first thing you need to do is find a reference point so that you can get the window in the right position – this can be tricky but take your time. If you need to you can drill a small pilot hole well within where the hole will be (i.e. in the waste material) and use this as a reference point to measure from. When choosing window size and location bear in mind aspects such as kitchen unit heights (an opening window is handy near the stove), as well as passenger seat positioning.

It is easiest to cut the hole from the outside, so once you have a rough idea where the window is going stick a liberal amount of wide masking tape around the area. The shape you will be cutting out can then be marked onto the masking tape. Use a straight edge to mark the lines and remember to get the right curves at the corners to match the window being installed (use a compass if required). Don't try to use a spirit level to get the window horizontal or vertical (the van may not be parked level) – it is more important for the window position to match with the vehicle's lines.

The hole size will vary for different kinds of window and most windows should come with instructions giving you more detail of the exact size the hole should be. For bonded windows the window needs to stick to the van metal, so the hole for the window should be smaller than the window – there is usually a large blacked out area which is intended to overlap with the vehicle and take the glue. For rubber mounted windows, the hole should be slightly larger than the window to allow room for the rubber mounting strip (usually just over 5mm extra all the way around but double check this is right for your windows) – too tight and you'll struggle to get the window into the rubber, too loose and it'll fall out. Framed windows work by clamping the front and back of a frame over the skin of the vehicle, so the hole will be larger than the glass but smaller than the edge of the frame (check the instructions with your specific windows for the exact hole size).

A panel without a window... yet. A daunting prospect for first-time window installers but the end result will be worth it.

A good wide layer of masking tape is added first in roughly the right place, then measure carefully and mark out your cut line.

# Templates

Sometimes it can be useful, especially for first timers, to create a template out of a big piece of cardboard. For example for a rubber mounted window, place the window pane flat on the cardboard and draw around it carefully. Move the window somewhere where you're not going to break it, then check that the length and width of your drawing matches the stated dimensions of the window pane. You should then make adjustments to the template, for instance by adding a 5-7mm border all around (if rubber mounted), or as per the instructions that came with the window. Now cut the template out with a sharp knife (remember not to wreck your living room carpet at this point!).

If you are confident you can transfer the measurements directly onto the van, but a template can help out the first couple of times. If nothing else, sticking the template to the side of the van gives you a good idea of what the window will look like. Remember at every point that this is a precision operation. The template and cut lines must be exactly the size you want them to be – draw precise lines, and measure at every opportunity.

# Cutting the Hole

This isn't all that technically difficult, but it does involve a fair degree of confidence to cut a big hole in the side of your pride and joy. It's not really a question of "what happens if I get it wrong", but more "whatever you do – don't get this wrong!".

Check your measurements on the internal side – normally the lines should sit inside the double skin of the van so that you are only cutting through a single thickness of metal. If you are using a template, blu-tak it to the panel and draw around it – once again, this is a precision task. Measure and double measure the shape you've drawn and prepare yourself mentally for what you're about to do. If you're using a jigsaw to cut the hole, drill a start hole inside the scrap area of panel. You may want to drill more than one hole – for instance one at the end of each straight edge – to make jigsaw logistics easier.

Cut along your guideline as exactly as possible with the jigsaw. A tip is to hold a straight edge to help guide the jigsaw and stop it wavering too much. Make the effort to get good jigsaw blades – fine ones for cutting thin metal (depending on your vehicle). It's quite possible to go through packets of blades if the ones used aren't quite right and keep breaking. Just cut slowly, the rounded corners take extra concentration but a (good quality) jigsaw is a surprisingly user friendly tool. Change blades often to keep the cut clean.

> "It's not really a question of 'what happens if I get it wrong', but more 'whatever you do – don't get this wrong!'."

You can cut from inside or out, but cutting from outside is recommended as it gives you more room to work. Make sure you've adequately protected the van's paintwork from the jigsaw (i.e. lots of masking tape, particularly outside the lines, and particularly if you need to run the jigsaw plate over any ridges etc). A great tip here is that while you're cutting the hole, after every foot or so of cut put some wide masking tape over the new cut – the masking tape stops the loose bit of metal panel vibrating too much and should hold the panel in place as you make the last cut.

And 'Voila' – you should have cut out a nice window-shaped piece of metal from the side of your van.

File down any rough edges, measure the hole again (though if it's too big, you'll either need a bigger window or you're on your own), clean and dry the edge and treat the metal with an anti rust primer paint.

Take a deep breath and triple check before drilling the first hole to allow your jigsaw blade in.

Carefully cut the shape out with your jigsaw using fine metal blades.

No return! One way or another, you now need to fit a window in the hole.

File and treat / prime the newly cut edges. Clean up all metal filings from in and outside the vehicle.

Use plenty of masking tape to protect the paintwork from the jigsaw base plate. Taping a protective sheet over the panels also helps protect against rusty filings.

Carefully mark out, drill starter holes, then cut along the lines. Pay attention to adding curves at corners if required.

A newly cut opening just waiting for a window to be fitted.

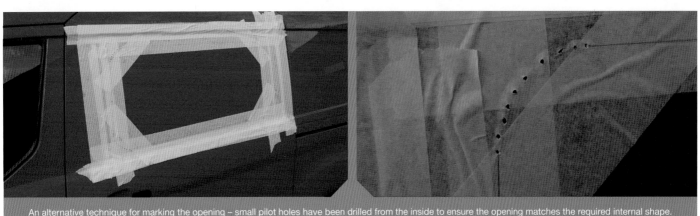

An alternative technique for marking the opening – small pilot holes have been drilled from the inside to ensure the opening matches the required internal shape.

# Framed Windows

Framed windows will in general be thicker than the panel on your van, so you need to build a timber sub-frame around the inside of the hole you've cut. The timber sub-frame ends up sandwiched between the inner and outer window frame, and as the screws are tightened the outside of the window will be pulled tightly against the outside of the van. Choose the thickness of wood for your sub-frame to match the requirements of the window – usually some 2 x 1" or similar, or some strips of plywood will do the job. Cut the bits of wood to size and stick them onto the metal around the hole on the inside using high temperature adhesive or similar, and you are ready to fit the window. If the side of the vehicle has a slight curve, you can cut the timber into several segments to allow them to sit flat.

Run a thick bead of sealant (e.g. Sikaflex 221 adhesive sealant) around the inside of the outer frame, and then have a helper hold the window in place while you go inside to fix the inner frame. Attach the inner frame to the outer using screws and tighten the whole thing together. To protect the window, leave the protective film on until you're completely finished.

One advantage of framed windows is that they leave the thickness of the window frame to accommodate insulating and lining your van, so it is much easier to get a good interior finish than with bonded or rubber sealed windows. Of course the fact that these are double glazed is a big selling point for high quality conversions, especially if you have spent time and money doing a good job on insulating the rest of the vehicle.

A softwood frame is glued around the inside of the opening. Using several segments or adding a series of partial cuts allows the frame to curve slightly at the sides.

Offer up the window to the opening before fixing in place.

Screw the inner frame to the outer, sandwiching the battens in the middle.

Add a good bead of sealant around the edge before getting a helper to hold the framed window in place.

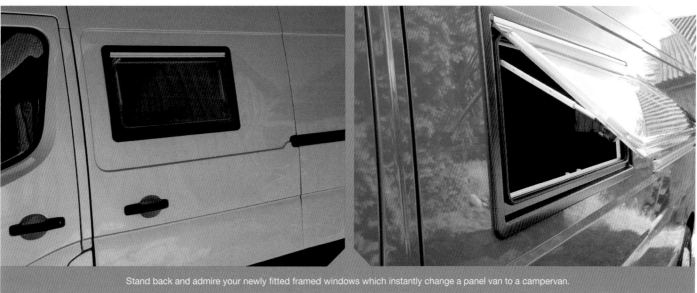

Stand back and admire your newly fitted framed windows which instantly change a panel van to a campervan.

Carefully insulate, carpet, and panel around the framed window for a cozy and professional looking finish.

# Bonded Windows

Fitting bonded windows is relatively straightforward, provided you've got all your measurements right so far. The best approach is to buy a 'bonding kit' with your window which usually consists of a tube of bonding adhesive sealant, a length of rubber trim to fit over the exposed metal edge, and often a couple of chemical wipes – one to clean the surfaces, and one to prime the black surface on the window. Some bonding kits will also include a primer which is applied prior to the sealant.

Ensure the metal is clean and sealed with anti-rust primer so that no bare metal is visible. Then fit the rubber trim onto the cut edge – this will be visible on the inside so keep it as neat as possible. Be careful the trim doesn't sit too proud on the outside as it will hamper the window sticking to the vehicle correctly.

Factory fitted bonded windows.

Have a 'dry run' first, then once you are sure you're ready to fit the window, consistently apply a thick bead of the bonding sealant all around the window hole. Now, carefully, put the window over the hole and push it onto the sealant ensuring that there are no gaps and the window sits flush on the surface of the metal. It is a good idea to have a friend help you with this. Once stuck on, put masking tape along the edges of the window to help hold it in place while the sealant dries. Clean up any squeeze out of sealant on the in or outside of the window and leave to dry. You will need to wait a couple of hours before moving the van – longer if it's very cold.

A DIY fitted bonded window in a VW T4.

A bonded window along with smart decals in a VW T5.

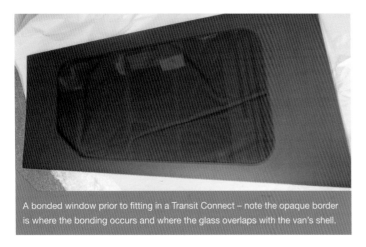
A bonded window prior to fitting in a Transit Connect – note the opaque border is where the bonding occurs and where the glass overlaps with the van's shell.

After the hole is cut, filed, and treated, a rubber trim is slotted over the edge.

A thick bead of bonding sealant is applied round the edge either to the window or the van. Some fitters place the bead directly alongside the black trim for a better seal.

A satisfying end result. Wait for a couple of hours before driving the vehicle.

A small sliding bonded window with closed cell foam & foil insulation on the inside.

Professional window fitters apply the sealant to a replacement windscreen and demonstrate what a neat bead of bonding should look like.

# Rubber Mounted Windows

When buying the window, check it comes with the correct rubber mounting strip, ideally as part of a kit which includes the little rubber bead insertion tool that makes this job easy.

Once you've cut the hole and filed and primed the edge, you can slot the thick strip of rubber onto the outer skin of the vehicle – this gives you your frame for the glass. You need to cut the rubber to the right length – try and make it slightly longer so that you end up with a really neat butt joint. To help prevent leaks, the rubber joint should be at the base of the window rather than at the top.

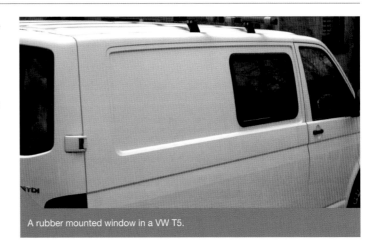

A rubber mounted window in a VW T5.

Once the rubber frame is in place you need to slot the pane of glass into it – professionals make this look super easy, but the first time you do it it's probably going to seem pretty hard work – try and make sure you've got a friend there to help you hold things and work the glass into place. If you've cut your hole too small, you may struggle to get the glass in... but if the hole is too big it will go in too easily and may fall out. Some use a technique with a bit of string inside the rubber that then gets pulled out to pull the rubber over the window.

You're nearly there... but now you need to secure the window in place. The exact details vary but there is usually a thin bead of rubber that gets inserted into a slot in the thicker rubber mount. It makes this job far easier if you have got hold of a beading tool. Use the tool to feed the bead into the slot in the rubber frame. This pushes the thick rubber frame out, creating a more secure window seal. A bucket of warm soapy water also helps to keep the rubber more pliable and aids feeding the bead in.

If necessary, it is also possible to put sealant under the rubber mount, though ideally the rubber is well fitted enough to not need it. You can push the nozzle up and under the rubber frame, squeezing a thin, and as equal as possible, amount round the whole frame.

## Final Steps

Cutting any metal in your van will generate thousands of tiny metal filings. These little bits of metal get everywhere and will rust over time if left in or on the vehicle. Vacuum, brush and vacuum again to try and get rid of as many as possible. This is one of the key reasons why it is good to do any drilling or cutting first, while the van is still a shell as it is easier to get at all the little nooks and crannies and clean out any filings. If you have managed to catch most of them in a dustsheet then even better. Once cupboards and floors are fitted this is pretty impossible and you will miss some, only to find a nice pile of rusted metal if you come to lift up the floor in a few years time. You also need to religiously clean filings off the outside of the vehicle.

If you have got this far, well done! Fewer and fewer people take on this task themselves – it is daunting but also pretty satisfying.

———

"If you have got this far, well done! Fewer and fewer people take on this task themselves – it is daunting but also pretty satisfying."

———

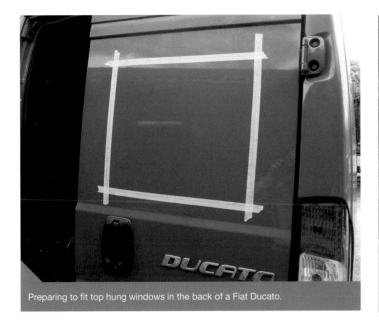

Preparing to fit top hung windows in the back of a Fiat Ducato.

Using masking tape to protect the panel and hold the loose sheet still while cutting.

Adding a plywood panel and separate blinds to a rear window.

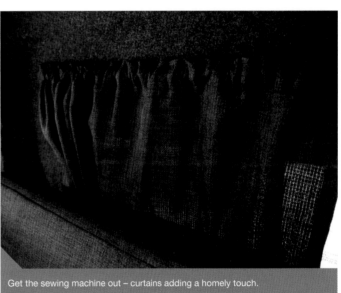

Get the sewing machine out – curtains adding a homely touch.

Top hung rear windows and a great view in a Fiat Ducato.

# 31 Fitting Rooflights

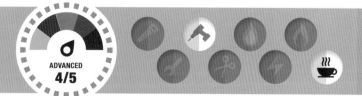

| PREREQUISITES | Safe working platform, good weather forecast |
|---|---|
| DO BEFORE | Insulation, panelling, flooring |
| COMBINE WITH | Window installation, other structural changes |

ADVANCED 4/5

Rooflights add a great deal to the living space of a campervan – not just the benefits of having light flooding in, but also a great way to ventilate moisture out of the vehicle. Fitting a rooflight is a lot like fitting a window. Fitting a ceiling fan, or an air con unit is also a similar exercise. It goes without saying that cutting holes in the ceiling is not for the faint hearted and it is essential that the fixture is perfectly sealed so that rain can't get in.

Many rooflights are designed for the caravan and coach-built motorhome market where roofs are generally flat. In contrast, the roof of a panel van is often ribbed in some way which makes getting a water tight seal even trickier.

Most rooflights are constructed in the same way as framed windows discussed earlier – in other words they are often (not always) double glazed acrylic units with integrated blinds and fly-screens. The fitting process is almost the same as fitting a framed window – position, measure, and cut the hole, prime the bare metal, construct a timber frame of the right thickness, add sealant and then connect the inner and outer frames together with screws. The following are some additional considerations specific to rooflights and other roof furniture:

- Some vehicles have special areas in the ceiling which are designed for cut-outs – these areas are usually flat and if they fit your needs then this will be the best place to put your rooflight.

- Access to the roof while fitting a rooflight can be tricky, particularly in large vehicles. Spend a bit of time constructing a good safe working platform for yourself as this will make the job a lot easier.

- If fitting onto a ribbed area of the ceiling, think carefully about how you will achieve a water tight seal prior to committing yourself. You may be able to source a tailor made solution to this problem in the form of a shaped frame that fits into the ribs... if not, you may need to try to make something equivalent yourself. Whatever materials you use they will get regular soakings, so pick carefully and make sure things are fully treated and sealed before being exposed to the elements. Marine plywood accompanied by plenty of adhesive sealant may be one good material to use for this purpose.

- Bear in mind that anything you install in the roof is likely to get in the way of a roofrack, so you may need to ask yourself what your priorities are.

- Pay close attention to cleaning up all metal filings – both inside and on the roof.

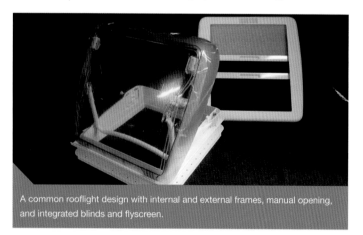

A common rooflight design with internal and external frames, manual opening, and integrated blinds and flyscreen.

As with cutting window holes, use masking tape to mark out and protect the roof before getting your jigsaw out.

Most rooflights are designed to sit on a flat surface, so you may need to source (or make) an adapting frame to cope with ribbed roofs.

Once the hole is cut, check the light fits nicely before building a frame.

A softwood frame is constructed on the inside and brackets fix the rooflight down.

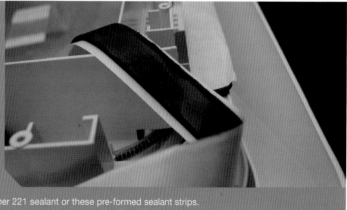
The rooflight needs to be fully watertight - use either 221 sealant or these pre-formed sealant strips.

Take some time to setup a good solid working platform.

A rooflight installed above the living space, with carpeted panels sitting underneath the internal frame.

A rooflight installed above a shower room creates both good lighting and ventilation, while retaining privacy.

# Fixed High-top & Pop-top Roofs

Fitting a pop-top or a fixed high-top is a fantastic way to turn a low-roof van into a high-roof van. The work involved here is a major change to the vehicle and is really beyond the scope of this book. The basic techniques are similar to windows and rooflights in that you are marking and cutting a hole, and then installing the new roof. However, this job is ideally done by those who have been trained to do it. It requires at least two people and is preferably done in a workshop large enough to get the vehicle inside. You may well find that buying the roof and fitting yourself won't actually save much money as installation is often included in the pricing structure.

The classic pop-top roof has the major advantage that when driving around you retain a low-roof vehicle – more aerodynamic, better handling round windy roads, easier to fit under height barriers at beach parking areas, and for some the aesthetics will also be important. However, pop-tops have the disadvantage that every time you park up you have the hassle of putting the roof up, and then need to collapse it before setting off again. Pop-tops are also generally less warm and insulated, and more 'tent-like' than their fixed high-top cousins, although some pop-tops are surprisingly robust and cosy.

A fixed high-top adds a permanent standing height roof to your low-roof campervan. If considering a fixed high-top you could choose to just get an original high-roof vehicle instead, but often people find that they don't wish to be limited in their base vehicle choice, and that they may need slightly more height than the normal high-roof vehicle model offers. Another advantage of a fixed high-top van is that there can be a permanent bed space built in that doesn't need to be dismantled for each move.

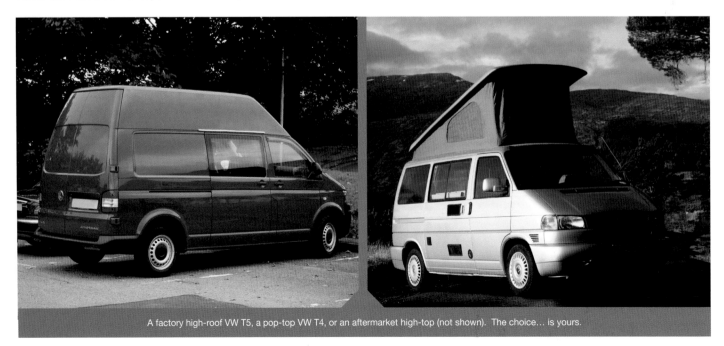

A factory high-roof VW T5, a pop-top VW T4, or an aftermarket high-top (not shown). The choice... is yours.

# HEATING

Even if you only intend to go away in your van to warm countries and in the summer, fitting a good heater is still highly recommended. It's amazing how cold it can get in a van at 3am, and amazingly satisfying to be able to flick a heater on with your big toe without even getting out of bed. If you have aspirations of being warm in your campervan, you should also focus on good insulation and window insulation mats (both covered elsewhere in the book).

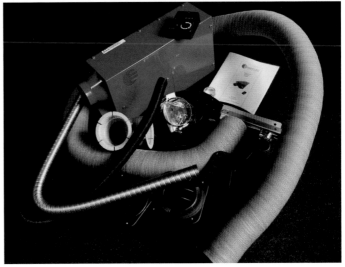

> "It's amazing how cold it can get in a van at 3am, and amazingly satisfying to be able to flick a heater on with your big toe without even getting out of bed."

## Types of Heater

The only heaters recommended for campervans and motorhomes are 'room-sealed' which means that all of the combustion gases produced are vented to the outside of the van – an important safety attribute if you wish to wake up in the morning. These heaters are also usually 'blown air heaters' which just means that air from inside the van is sucked in to the heater, heated up, and then blown back out into the living space – usually through one or more ducts. Many caravans and bigger motorhomes will use radiant heaters that may or may not also have a blown air component – these can be powerful and good solutions but may also take too much space in a small vehicle.

Open convection type heaters where the combustion occurs inside the space to be heated should not be used in confined spaces and having one on while you're asleep is not safe! Likewise using your gas stove to heat the van up is OK as a side effect while cooking, but naked flames and campervans never mix well and remember that combustion gases are being given off as long as the stove is on – acceptable for short periods with good ventilation, but bad news for anything other than that. Other heating options have also been used – such as using a simple electric fan heater or infrared heater while on electric hookup, or even an electric blanket plugged into your leisure battery via an inverter – however, these are inefficient and clunky solutions that fall a long way short of the ideal.

Popular options are room sealed blown air heaters fuelled by gas or diesel with an electric fan.

A radiant caravan heater can be a powerful option in bigger vehicles and some also incorporate blown air ducting.

# Gas or Diesel?

There are two main options for fuelling heaters: gas or diesel. Both gas and diesel heaters are in widespread use and although pros and cons are often quoted, in fact both are excellent options for campervan conversions. Proponents of diesel heaters will tell you that a principle advantage is that the fuel is available everywhere and it's always going to be pretty easy (and essential anyway) to fill back up with diesel. If you also install a diesel stove you may be able to dispense with the need for gas altogether. Using diesel as your single fuel source removes the need to find space for gas cylinders, addresses gas installation and safety concerns, and frees you from the potential frustrations of changing cylinders abroad. There is a common perception that diesel heaters are more efficient and powerful and gas heaters are quieter, but really it depends on the heater model in question so those generalisations aren't necessarily correct.

One downside of diesel heaters is that tapping into the vehicle's diesel supply (especially on newer vehicles) can be tricky and some heater manufacturers discourage DIY installation… but then you aren't supposed to install gas plumbing yourself either. If you are a more confident mechanic than a plumber, or vice-versa, then this may sway your decision between gas or diesel heating. Be conscious of warranty issues: a new or nearly new vehicle's warranty may be affected if you accidentally damage the main fuel supply, and some heater manufacturer's warranties won't cover DIY installation – if you are in any doubt you can seek help from an authorized dealer for the heater in question.

Gas fuelled blown-air heaters are very popular – the majority of campervans need gas anyway for their stoves, so it makes a lot of sense to power your heater from the same canister (though obviously you will use more gas and therefore might need to carry more if using it to both cook and heat). There is also the option of installing an underfloor refillable LPG gas tank (described later) and this is a great space-saving solution which shares some of the convenience advantages of using diesel. Probably the most powerful argument for gas heaters instead of diesel is that you don't want your heater to burn through your diesel when you are running low. If you are staying in the van when it is cold and have the heater on at night, there is always the danger that you run out of fuel; running out of gas is fine – you might get a bit cold and have to swap bottles or find a replacement canister in the morning – but running out of diesel is bad news and this could leave you stranded unable to start the vehicle. To avoid this pitfall, take precautions such as ensuring the fuel hose will always leave a reserve amount in the tank.

# Altitude & Temperature

Diesel heaters tend to work without issue up to around 1200-1500metres high. Above this height they may need a special 'altitude kit' or some level of adjustment. In cold temperatures, diesel heaters should work so long as your engine does – diesel in cold regions contains anti-freezing additives and this will usually keep your heater running down to around -30°C. Although most gas heaters will run off both butane and propane, the use of butane in cold weather scenarios isn't advisable as it will stop working below around 5°C. There is more on this issue in the Gas chapter, suffice to say here you should use Propane bottles instead of Butane (i.e. red not blue for Calor). LPG tends to be a mix of gases so should be fine in cold weather, especially if it is a 'winter mix'.

# Diesel Heating & Cooking from one product

**wallas®**
**XC Duo**

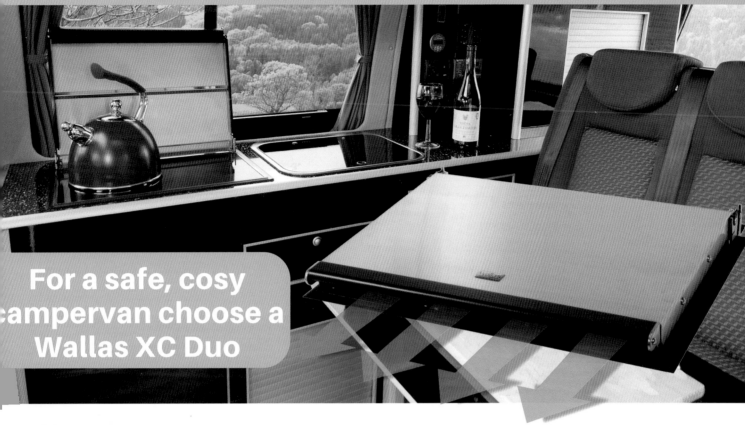

**For a safe, cosy campervan choose a Wallas XC Duo**

**Gas Free**
No open flame, safe campervan

**Operates on diesel**
direct from campervan fuel tank

**Thermostat Control**
Cosy & warm campervan

**No gas / bottles**
Extra storage in campervan

**Very quiet**
Peaceful campervan

**Room sealed combustion**
Balanced flue system, exhausts to the outside of the campervan

**Uses very little battery power**
Cooking & heating in campervan for longer

**Dry Campervan**
Does not create condensation like gas cooking

**www.campervanheating.co.uk**
**Tel: 01663 734800**

# Installing Diesel Heaters

Most of the steps involved in installing a diesel heater are relatively similar to installing a gas heater as described later in the chapter – e.g. air intake and exhaust pipes through the floor, 12V wiring and thermostat, and hot air ducting. The big difference is you will need to tap into the vehicle's diesel supply (or install a separate diesel tank, which is another option). This is a task for those who are confident with vehicle mechanics – if that doesn't apply to you it is worth getting a professional to do the installation for you, or at least help with the fuel supply aspect of it. You will need good access under the vehicle so use of a ramp or at least a trolley jack and axle stands are essential.

This is only a quick overview to give you a flavour of what is involved – some (not all) diesel heater manufacturer's discourage DIY installation and the details will depend on the vehicle and heater (or stove) in question. It makes sense to wait until you are reasonably low on fuel before starting so that you don't end up with diesel everywhere. Start by removing any protective shielding from around the fuel tank so that you can undo the fuel tank support straps. Support the fuel tank with your trolley jack (be careful where you place the jack so as not to damage the tank or the sender unit), undo the straps, and lower the tank. This gives you access to the diesel 'sender unit'. Disconnect the vehicle's fuel hoses and wiring and remove the unit. Alter the sender as required to introduce your new fuel pick-up pipe (specific to your vehicle). The new fuel line is attached to the pick-up pipe and then routed neatly under your vehicle to the new appliance. The fuel tank is then raised and secured back in place and the installation of the rest of the heater can continue.

The diesel tank is lowered to give access to the fuel pipes and sender unit. More installation info at www.campervanheating.co.uk.

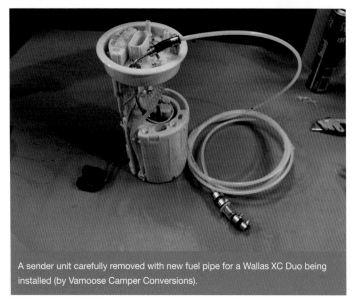

A sender unit carefully removed with new fuel pipe for a Wallas XC Duo being installed (by Vamoose Camper Conversions).

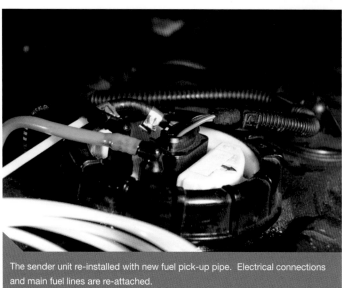

The sender unit re-installed with new fuel pick-up pipe. Electrical connections and main fuel lines are re-attached.

# 32 Installing a Blown-air Gas Heater

| | |
|---|---|
| **PREREQUISITES** | - - |
| **DO BEFORE** | Flooring |
| **COMBINE WITH** | - - |

MODERATE
3/5

Here the installation of a blown-air room-sealed LPG heater is covered. The heater's output rating of 2000W (2kW) is a similar sort of output to an average electric fan heater. This type of heater is one of the simpler heaters to install and provides enough heat for small to mid size conversions even when used in winter. More powerful models are a good option for larger vehicles (e.g. long or extra long wheelbase Ducatos, Sprinters etc). There are also models available that are mountable under-floor, and yet others that act as integrated heaters and water heaters. The following should of course be read in conjunction with the specific instructions for the heater you are installing.

## Summary:

- Step 1 – Locate where you will mount the heater.

- Step 2 – Drill holes for the combustion air intake and exhaust.

- Step 3 – Fix heater to floor and attach combustion pipes.

- Step 4 – Run piping and fit the internal heating vents.

- Step 5 – Plumb into gas.

- Step 6 – Fit thermostat and wire electrics.

## 1. Locate where to mount the heater

You need to have a bit of a think in advance about where the heater will be located. It involves drilling a couple of holes through the floor of the van which it is best to do early on (before all the units and floor are in place) making it easy to clear up all the metal filings you will generate. Obviously you need to check underneath the van to ensure your location is well clear of things like fuel tanks, brake cables etc. If there is plywood or other flooring where the heater is being installed it is usually best to remove or cut out a section to allow the heater to be installed directly on the metal van floor.

Choose a location for the heater where it will be boxed in but still semi-accessible should it need servicing at a later date (under bcd boxes or seating platforms are often good locations). Note that in an ideal world the heater should not be in the same space as your battery or other electrics. Have a think about where you plan to have your heat ducting and outlets – try not to put the outlets somewhere they will often be blocked by bags, shoes, etc. You need to ensure there will be room for the heat ducting pipe which protrudes from one end of the heater – do a dummy run with everything attached and positioned first before drilling any holes.

Installing a blown air heater under a seating platform is a common and space-efficient solution.

## 2. Drill holes for the combustion air intake and exhaust

You need to drill two holes in the floor of your van for the combustion exhaust and air intake pipes. These pipes come out of the bottom of the heater and need to go to the outside of the van. Take the chance to double check your positioning. A room sealed heater like this needs a source of oxygen and a vent for the combustion gases which is separate and "sealed off" from the inside of the van.

When drilling the holes through your van floor remember:

- Be careful about what you are drilling into – check underneath the van first. Drilling holes into the fuel tank by accident is an embarrassing problem to take to your garage!

- The combustion air intake has to be positioned where it will be able to draw up clean air i.e. not near the van exhaust or the heater exhaust pipe.

Start by drilling a pilot hole with a small (e.g. 3mm) metal drill bit. Assuming you are happy the hole is in the right place, you can either use a hole saw of the right diameter, or use your biggest metal drill bit and then widen it out using a round file.

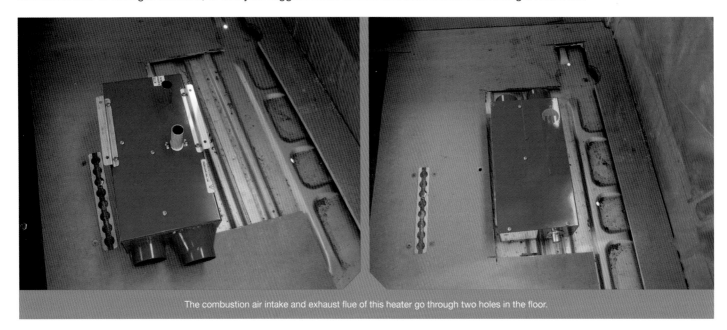

The combustion air intake and exhaust flue of this heater go through two holes in the floor.

## 3. Fix heater to floor and attach combustion pipes

Once you've created the holes for the intake & exhaust, you can fix the heater down using the mounting brackets and some self tapping screws. Use anti-rusting paint (e.g. Hammerite) on bare metal at every opportunity and really make sure you get rid of all the metal filings produced.

Once the heater is in place, you need to fit the under-van pipes and cut them to size. Ideally the combustion gas vent should be taken to the edge of the vehicle and attached with a stainless steel p-clip. The combustion air intake should be located in such a way that it is going to get a clean supply of air – i.e. away from the combustion gas pipe and the vehicle exhaust. Try to ensure that both pipes have a fall or downward slope to help avoid any build up of condensation or debris.

Exhaust gases are directed to the edge of the vehicle, away from the combustion air intake.

## 4. Run piping and fit the internal heating vents

You then need to run the internal ducting and the intake and hot air vent grills. The heater will pull fresh cold air from the interior of the van in through the air intake grill, warm it through the heater and then pump it back out into the van via the ducting as nice hot air. The norm is to put the intake and primary hot air vent in the side of the unit or box which surrounds the heater. If you feel the need you can have more than one hot air outlet by introducing Y junctions in the ducting. Multiple outlets can be useful in a big conversion, especially if there is more than one room, but many vans don't really need more than one outlet.

The vents are best installed in a piece of plywood by cutting a round hole of the right size – either using a hole saw or use a compass to draw the circle and cut it out with a jigsaw with a fine blade. The ducts are secured to the vents and the heater using jubilee clips.

It makes sense to position the cold air intake slightly away from the hot air outlet if possible, and pick your vent locations carefully so they aren't going to have things dumped in front of them all the time. Although having a vent beside your feet might seem a nice idea, you may well find your feet getting too hot before the rest of the van warms up. It's also worth remembering that warm air rises.

Hot air ducting, gas connections, power and thermostat wiring.

Cool air intake and hot air outlets can be placed where they won't get blocked.

## 5. Plumb into gas

Gas plumbing is dealt with in a separate chapter, and this should only be done by those who have the qualifications and / or competence to do so safely. However, a gas hose or pipe should be led to the heater and connected in.

## 6. Fit thermostat and wire electrics

You need to pick a convenient spot for the thermostat which controls the heater going on and off – the usual is to place it in a position similar to where you'll be sitting in the van, away from drafts, windows, and stoves, and somewhere fairly central where you can easily reach it from your seat / bed / etc. Being able to reach the thermostat from the bed without having to get up is definitely a big advantage on a cold night.

Finally you need to wire the heater up to the leisure battery (via the fuse box – see Electrics chapter), and wire the thermostat and heater together. The wiring for this type of heater is a straightforward task and explained in the instructions.

Now all you need to do is finish the rest of your conversion, take to the road, and wait for your first cold night to bask in the satisfying glow of your lovely warm van!

Thermostats should be placed in easy reach of both living space and bedroom. Next page - A larger heater installation with dual hot air ducts.

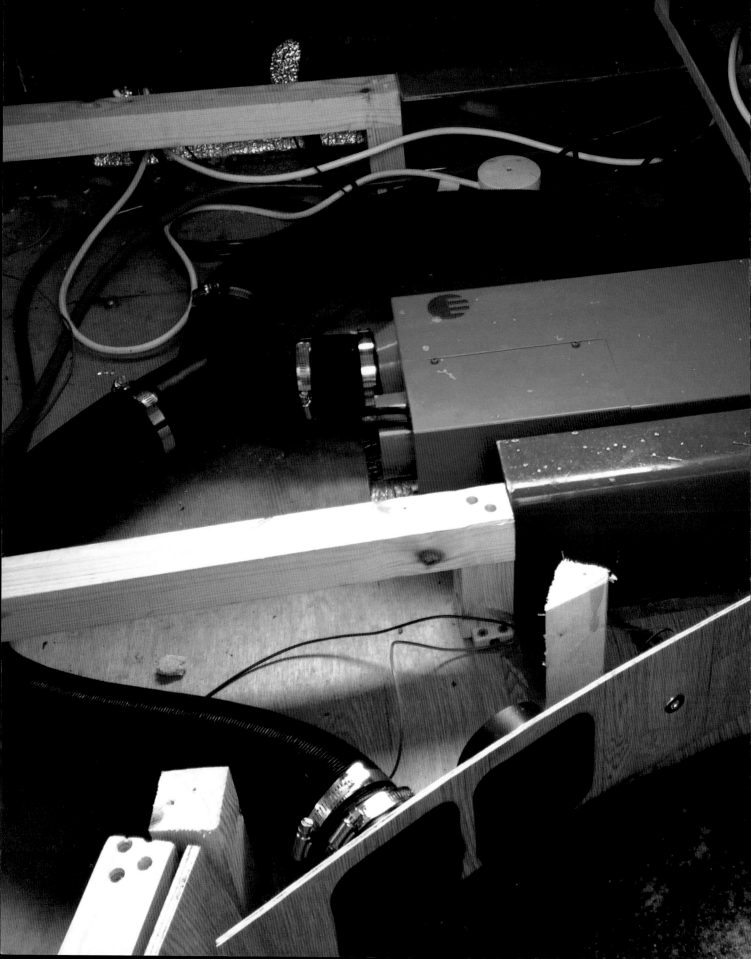

# GAS

The discussions on vehicle electrics elsewhere in this book illustrate that, unless you are plugged into a mains hookup, electricity as a power source is in short supply. Ever since the early days of campervans there has been a requirement for an efficient and highly portable fuel capable of powering all the accoutrements of comfort on the road – namely stoves for cooking, heaters to keep you warm, and sometimes also items such as water heaters and fridges. Bottled gas has always been an excellent match for these requirements, and as a result there are few campervans driving around that do not have some form of gas installation.

The simplest gas installation consists of a small gas bottle connected via rubber gas hose to a stove – in other words a glorified camping stove. For many budding campervan converters this arrangement will be more than adequate for their needs, and for some there will be merit in using a portable camping stove that has the big advantage that you can then use it outside on nice days. However, as conversions get more elaborate, the list of gas appliances often grows and the gas installation needs to become more sophisticated.

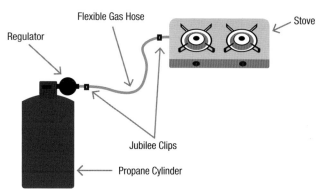

## Basic Gas System

Flexible Gas Hose

Regulator

Stove

Jubilee Clips

Propane Cylinder

## Who can install gas?

Safety warning – Poorly installed and maintained gas plumbing and appliances can cause explosions, fires, and silent killers such as Carbon Monoxide poisoning. Therefore the simple answer to 'who can legally work on gas installations in campervans' is that you need to be a Gas Safe Register (GSR) certified engineer with the correct endorsements. The "Caravan – LAV" endorsement (LAV = Leisure Accommodation Vehicle) is a specific category of work that GSR engineers should be qualified for in order to work on campervan and motorhome gas installations. Note that GSR was previously called CORGI.

In other words, if you stick to the letter of the law, you are going to have to find a certified gas engineer to do your gas plumbing for you. There is a slight loophole to the above rules in that you are also legally allowed to work on gas installations (in a non-paid setting) if you are 'competent'… however, that is not carte blanche for all budding DIY enthusiasts to get stuck in because 'competent' in this case has been further defined to mean that you should be trained and capable to the same standard as would be required by GSR, so unfortunately this apparent loophole does not apply to the vast majority of would be converters.

It seems fair to point out that, while good safety regulation has an important role to play, there is also a disparity between the current legislation and common practices on the ground. Many, many DIY converters have successfully tackled their gas installations themselves. Perhaps simpler DIY installations (e.g. involving a gas bottle, a rubber hose, and a stove) are easier to justify than more complex ones utilising copper pipe and multiple appliances. Ultimately it is up for the reader to decide whether they are capable of undertaking this task safely, and whether they are happy to do so given the current safety legislation. A good middle ground, and the one most recommended by this book, is to carry out as much of the work as possible yourself but enlist a GSR engineer to make all final connections and test the installation prior to use.

"Carry out as much of the work as possible yourself but enlist a GSR engineer to make the connections and test the installation."

# Go Gasless?

In fact it is possible to have a fully functional campervan without using gas. Diesel heaters (and water heaters) are not only available but are high quality alternatives compared to their gas fuelled cousins. Diesel stoves are also available though they tend to have a reputation for being costly and complicated alternatives to gas. The 3-way absorption fridge is commonly installed so that it can be used on gas when off-grid, but compressor fridges consume far less electricity so can be good options, provided you aren't solely reliant on limited battery power. Clever use of powerful alternators, battery to battery chargers, inverters, solar panels or wind turbines, mains hookups, and other electrical technology can complete your power requirements and allow you to circumvent the problems associated with gas installations.

# LPG, Butane, and Propane

LPG stands for Liquid Petroleum Gas – both Propane and Butane are types of LPG. When LPG is sold at a petrol station pump it is usually a mixture of Propane and Butane – the exact mix varies but often there is more propane in winter and a higher butane proportion in summer.

The use of butane in cold weather scenarios isn't advisable as it will stop working below around 5°C. Often you will hear people say that their gas has frozen, but in fact the freezing point of butane is -140°C and the freezing point of propane is -188°C. LPG (butane and propane) is stored in canisters in compressed liquid form, and the regulator controls the escape of the liquid out of the bottle – as it escapes it expands and boils (i.e. turns from a liquid into a gas or vaporizes). When it gets cold (under around 5°C) Butane will stop vaporizing effectively because it is too close to its boiling point of -1°C. Propane is far better suited to cold usage as its boiling point is -42°C so it will continue to vaporize out of the cylinder effectively down to -30°C and probably a little lower.

If you have an under-floor LPG tank it will probably be fine in cold weather but be aware that if you have filled it during the summer it may well contain a high proportion of butane and therefore have a lower tolerance to cold weather. If you are having problems you will need to use up the gas and refill with a 'winter mix' containing a higher propane ratio.

# Gas Cylinders

The normal way for gas to be sold is by taking your empty cylinder to a dealer, and exchanging it for a full one. In order to obtain your first cylinder you have to pay a deposit on it (also called a 'cylinder refill agreement'). If you ever get to the point where you no longer need the cylinder you should be able to take it back and receive the deposit, though the amount decreases as time passes and you will need to have retained the contract document. In the UK, Calor cylinders are the most widely available with many local shops, petrol stations, and campsites selling them. There are competitors to Calor and they all produce cylinders which will work with the same regulator. However, in most places you won't be able to swap a Calor cylinder for one of another make (and vice versa) without paying a new deposit.

If you are travelling to the rest of Europe the situation gets a little more complicated – gas is widely available almost everywhere, but you probably won't be able to exchange your UK bottle. The worst case scenario is that you might have to take your current regulator off and swap it for one that's compatible with the new bottle (not the end of the world, but hassle none-the-less). Another annoying problem is if the only replacement bottle you can source won't fit in the space you have allocated. For these reasons the ideal approach is to get full bottles before you leave and try to take enough to last the duration of your trip.

One good approach is to carry a small back-up solution, such as the Campingaz 907 butane cylinder (2.75kg capacity) in case you get caught short (but make sure you have a regulator or adapter to fit it into your system). One big advantage of Campingaz is its wide availability across Europe, and elsewhere.

Cylinders come in a number of different sizes and they are measured by the weight of the liquefied gas inside them.

## Calor propane cylinder sizes

| Cylinder size (Capacity) | Height | Diameter | Off-take / Content ** | Full weight (approx) |
|---|---|---|---|---|
| 3.9kg | 340mm | 240mm | 7.5kW / 55kW | 8-10.5kg |
| 6kg | 495mm | 256mm | 11kW / 84kW | 15-17kg |
| 6kg CalorLite* | 487mm | 246mm | 11kW / 84kW | 10.5kg |
| 13kg | 580mm | 315mm | 15kW / 182kW | 25-35kg |

* A nice feature of the CalorLite 6kg bottle (apart from the weight saving) is that it has an integrated gauge showing how much gas is left.

** The Off-take number is the recommended maximum amount of gas available at one time – i.e. if you have all your gas appliances running at once your cylinder off-take needs to be enough to handle it.  The second number in kilowatts is the approximate amount of power available in total – this should let you work out how long a bottle will last if you guess how much you'll use each appliance.

There are a number of larger sizes that are unlikely to be suitable for campervan use.

# Regulators

Most appliances designed for use in campervans will operate on either propane or butane (or an LPG mix), but you will need to install the right regulator.  Regulators do what the name suggests – they regulate the gas as it vaporizes out of the bottle.  Since 2003, the supply pressure for gas has been standardised across Europe at 30mbar (if you have an older campervan it may still use a butane regulator at 28mbar, or propane at 37mbar).  Propane regulators usually screw into the valve on the bottle with an anti-clockwise thread (i.e. they screw on and off in the opposite direction to most other threads).

One common regulator setup is for the regulator to be mounted on a wall, for instance at the back of a gas locker.  There is then a length of flexible hose (known as a pigtail) that connects the cylinder to the regulator.  The advantage of this arrangement is that rather than having to change regulator to accommodate different cylinders, you can carry several different pigtails to cater for different cylinder types.

"Propane is far better suited to use in cold weather as its boiling point is -42°C compared to -1°C for Butane."

# Gas Plumbing

Unfortunately, detailed gas plumbing is beyond the scope of this book and the regulations say you shouldn't be doing your own gas plumbing anyway unless you're already competent (i.e. a trained gas engineer). The simplest gas plumbing involves flexible rubber LPG hose connected to nozzles using jubilee clips. In fact connecting a rubber hose to a regulator or a stove is a straight-forward process:

1. Boil a kettle and fill a cup with hot water.

2. Thread the jubilee clip onto the hose.

3. Dunk the hose into the hot water for 20seconds or so.

4. Push the hose all the way onto the nozzle.

5. Wait for the hose to cool so you don't damage it and then tighten the jubilee clip.

6. Check for leaks – e.g. by putting some washing up liquid over the joint and checking for small bubbles.

In a simple gas installation where everything is close together, you may only have a gas bottle, a regulator, a stove, plus maybe a heater. The plumbing in this instance could all be done using flexible hose, with a Y or T connector on the hose soon after the regulator to split the gas feed between the two appliances. In theory flexible gas hose should be replaced every five years, or at least inspected for signs of decay or damage.

Warming up a flexible gas hose in warm water before pushing it onto a stove connection.

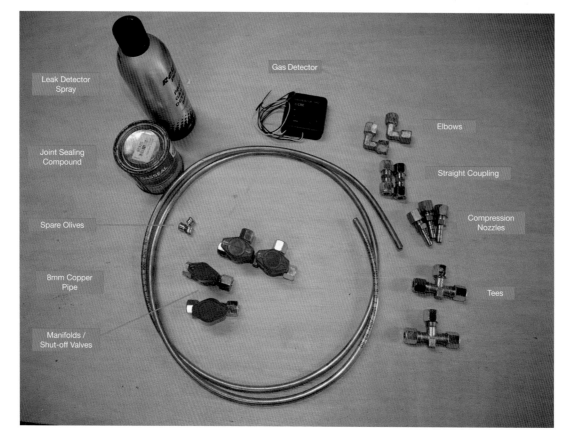

In a more complex gas installation, 8mm copper gas pipe must be used. Each appliance should have its own manifold or cut-off valve. Appliances which may need to be moved for servicing (e.g. fridges) will need to have 'tails' of flexible hose linked into the copper plumbing. The copper pipe can be bent into curves using pipe benders and cut using a pipe cutter. Various connections are available including tees, elbows, pipe-hose adapters, etc.

You should consider installing a Carbon Monoxide alarm and possibly also a gas alarm (to detect leaks). Locating a fire extinguisher near an exit is also a sensible precaution. When travelling you should turn the gas off at the bottle, and in particular at petrol stations and on ferries.

_____

"Always install a Carbon Monoxide alarm and keep a fire extinguisher near an exit."

_____

A more complex gas and plumbing setup. Here the supply comes from an underfloor LPG tank to the regulator. Then a number of isolation manifolds feed stove, water heater, heater, and 3-way fridge.

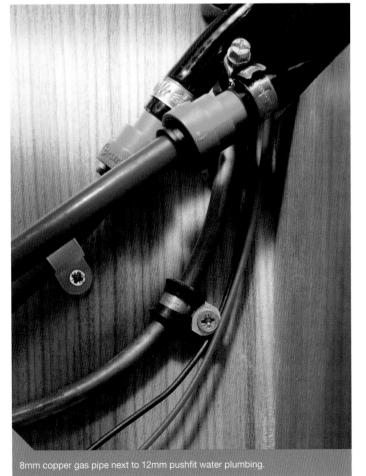

8mm copper gas pipe next to 12mm pushfit water plumbing.

A gas pressure test being performed.

# 33 Constructing a Gas Locker

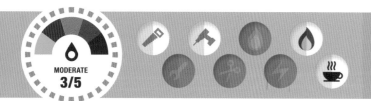

MODERATE
3/5

| PREREQUISITES | - - |
| DO BEFORE | - - |
| COMBINE WITH | **Constructing furniture** |

Gas bottles should be stored in sealed lockers designed for the purpose. There should be vent holes in the floor under the gas locker to allow any leaking gas to escape (LPG is heavier than air). Your gas bottles should NOT be located anywhere that a spark could be generated – for example do not put your gas bottle in the same space as your battery. You should install robust straps in your gas locker to hold the cylinders firmly in place, even when driving on rough ground. You can buy purpose made metal gas lockers, which are the belt and braces approach, but building out of timber is also common.

A basic gas bottle setup with a 6kg propane bottle. This isn't a formal gas locker but still does a good job of keeping the bottle secure and in a reasonably safe location.

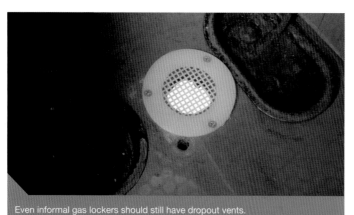

Even informal gas lockers should still have dropout vents.

A high standard (though non-metal) gas locker.

A home-made but well-constructed gas locker.

A good example of straps and drop-out vents in a high quality gas locker.

## Advanced Gas System

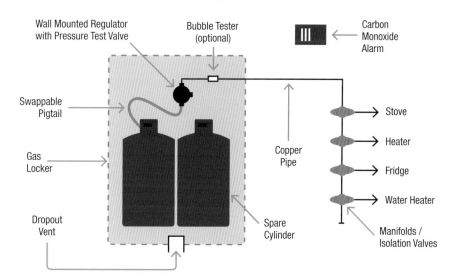

Wall Mounted Regulator with Pressure Test Valve

Bubble Tester (optional)

Carbon Monoxide Alarm

Swappable Pigtail

Gas Locker

Copper Pipe

Stove

Heater

Fridge

Water Heater

Dropout Vent

Spare Cylinder

Manifolds / Isolation Valves

# 34 Installing Under-floor LPG Tanks

ADVANCED 4/5

| PREREQUISITES | - - |
| DO BEFORE | Flooring |
| COMBINE WITH | Underfloor water tanks, heater installation |

Rather than deal with gas bottles that need to be periodically exchanged, a more sophisticated solution is to install an under-floor LPG tank which is refillable at petrol stations. Note that not all petrol stations carry LPG, so although the service is widely available geographically (and availability is steadily improving) you may have to search a little to find the right station in your area. One advantage of an under-floor tank is that it frees up space inside and you can potentially install quite a large tank and fill it up when the opportunity arises, well before it hits empty. This differs from canisters where you need to wait until they are empty before exchanging them.

Installing an LPG tank is relatively straight-forward and involves drilling holes in the floor for brackets and straps that hold the tank. The tanks are heavy, so installing one without the van on a ramp is possible but awkward. As with the rest of gas plumbing, an engineer should be enlisted to make the connections but you can do some ground-work routing pipes, mounting the tank, installing the inlet, etc. yourself.

Installing an LPG filler inlet is very similar to installing a mains hookup socket or water filler inlet – mark and cut the hole, and fit the valve flush to the vehicle using plenty of sealant. The pipe inside the vehicle will usually travel from the inlet down through the floor of the vehicle – you should route this pipe inside a larger sealed conduit (e.g. a length of waste water hose or similar) so that any gas will drop through the floor.

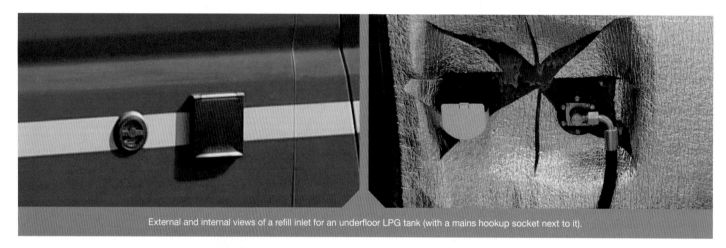
External and internal views of a refill inlet for an underfloor LPG tank (with a mains hookup socket next to it).

An underfloor LPG tank.

"Installing an under-floor LPG tank frees up space inside and lets you refill whenever the opportunity arises."

# Filling LPG Tanks

Filling an LPG tank for the first time is quite daunting – it is well worth going online and watching a video of how to do it before taking the plunge. There are a couple of different systems in use so it is worth reading up on these and the adapters available prior to making a big trip.

One slightly disconcerting feature when refilling is a slight puff of gas usually escapes when disconnecting – this is normal and you will soon get used to it. There have been incidents of people being stopped from refilling LPG tanks abroad, but this tends to be when the filler inlet has been installed inside the vehicle - if you install the inlet correctly on the side of the vehicle you are unlikely to experience problems.

LPG refilling station.

# KITCHENS & FRIDGES

Perhaps the ultimate in self-sufficiency when on the road is being able to prepare food for yourself wherever and whenever you choose. What better way to warm up for a surf or a chilly dog walk than to boil up some water and have a cuppa? Drive your loved one somewhere nice, cook up a meal, crack open the wine, watch the sunset, then wake up at the beach for a fry-up. The simplest of campervans have a bed and not much else, but there is no question that adding kitchen facilities makes the experience far more enjoyable.

The kitchen doesn't need to take up loads of space – the basics consist of storage for food, pans & utensils, a stove or hob, and a sink. Optional extras include ovens, grills, microwaves, 12V kettles, and fridges.

## Stoves

Gas campervan stoves come in all shapes and sizes, from small single burner stoves to three or four ring stoves suitable for travelling chefs and foodies. Diesel stoves (and stove-heater combis) are also available but are currently less widely used in the campervan world. The most popular stove models have two or three burners as this allows you to cook a wide variety of food without taking up too much space. One option is to carry a portable camping stove, and while this is perhaps a less sophisticated option, these have the advantage of being usable outside as well as saving on installation faff.

There are numerous sink-stove combination units on the market that both look great and save considerable space. There is more info on constructing kitchen units and fitting stoves and sinks in the chapter on furniture construction.

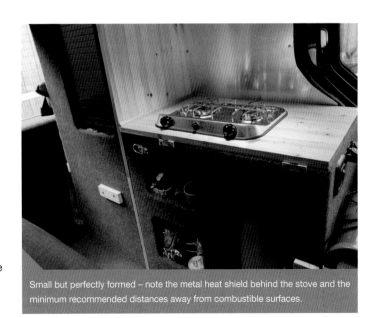

Small but perfectly formed – note the metal heat shield behind the stove and the minimum recommended distances away from combustible surfaces.

# Sinks

The simplest solution to a sink in a campervan is not to have one – you can make do pretty well with bottles (or containers) of water and a washing up bowl that gets tipped outside whenever you need to.  Having said that, adding a sink in doesn't take up much space, is fairly easy to do, and does add significantly to the liveability of the vehicle.

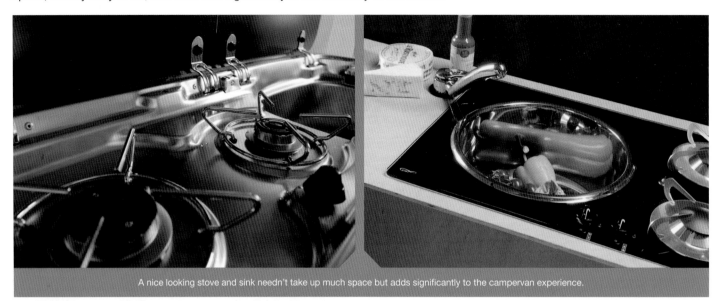

A nice looking stove and sink needn't take up much space but adds significantly to the campervan experience.

Small ovens, microwaves, and even full size cookers are all options for travelling gourmets.

Storage can be as simple as a food crate or a simple cupboard, or you can create drawers and storage racks for every last item.

# Fridges

Let's face it – most of us want a campervan so that we can go somewhere sunny and hot. However, having arrived at your dream destination and tackled the immediate problems such as finding your swimming stuff and the sunscreen, the realisation slowly but surely creeps in that you have no way of keeping the milk, cheese, meat, or beer cold. In some ways this is even more important than a sink and stove – having a way to keep a few essential items cold (and therefore fresh) makes van life substantially more civilised and frees you up to spend several days or longer in between visiting the shops.

There are two different types of fridge to consider – compressor fridges and absorption fridges, both of which come in a range of sizes and both of which have various pros and cons associated with them. There is also the low-budget, simple option of a cool box.

## Cool Boxes

If you are looking for the simplest, lowest cost way to keep a few things cold while travelling, a cool box may well be your preferred option. If all you are doing is day trips from your house, then a non-powered cool box with cold packs placed in it at the start of the day from your home freezer may suffice. However, for overnight trips and longer you will need a 12V plug-in model. Ideally you should wire up your electrics so that you have a 12V socket (powered by the leisure battery) next to where you will store the box, though you could also plug it in on the dashboard and only have it on while driving. One of the nice attractions of the cool box solution is its portability, so if you want to wander down to the beach for a picnic you can just unplug it and take it with you.

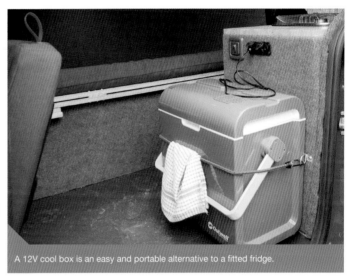
A 12V cool box is an easy and portable alternative to a fitted fridge.

## Compressor Fridges

The great thing about installing a 12V compressor fridge is that all you need to get it working is a 12V connection – wire it up and stick the beers in. They don't need any gas vents cut in the side of the van or other complicated installation procedures, although unlike a cool box they do need to be fitted into a unit. Compressor fridges (like their domestic cousins) use a compressor to circulate the refrigerant – unfortunately compressors make a noise, and you will usually hear it coming on at night.

You could also choose to use a domestic 230V compressor fridge, paired with an inverter – recent tests have suggested that with a modern inverter this can be just as power efficient as using a more expensive 12V model (see more notes on this in the electrical chapters). Of course individual models will vary, and this approach probably makes the most sense when you plan to be on mains hookup for the majority of the time (or if you already own a suitable 230V fridge).

A 50 litre compressor fridge.

# Absorption Fridges

Absorption fridges are also called three-way fridges because they can work on 12V, gas, or mains. The idea is to run them on 12V while driving, gas when parked up off-grid, and mains while on hookup. Instead of using a compressor, they use heat to circulate the refrigerant chemicals, and because there aren't any other moving parts they are almost silent in operation. You need to fit vents in the side of the van for this type of fridge. Cutting holes for the vents isn't too hard, but installation is significantly more involved than for a compressor fridge. Three-way fridges also need to be wired up to both 12V and mains wiring, as well as plumbed into the gas.

Although they are a fair bit harder to fit, absorption fridges are often used in campervans and motorhomes because they're quieter than compressor fridges, plus it's good to be able to run them off the gas so that you don't run out of power. Being able to run the fridge off the gas instead of the battery is particularly important if you plan to park up for any length of time off-grid. The flip side is that absorption fridges are far more power-hungry when running on electricity, so they aren't a good option if you don't want to use gas and are looking for battery efficiency.

# Fridge Pros and Cons

Both types of fridge are in wide use in campervans and motorhomes. It is possible to get a range of sizes in both types even though there's a perception that absorption fridges are better for larger conversions and vice versa. There are pros and cons to both types of fridge. It used to be that you had to be parked really flat for a 3-way (absorption) fridge to work but they've come on a lot in the last few years so this is not such an issue any more. The main reasons to install an absorption fridge is if you want silent operation and you want to run it on gas – if you are reliant on a 12V power supply you will likely need either solar power or to be driving regularly to recharge the battery. Note that when running on electric an absorption fridge will use significantly more power than a compressor fridge. The amount of noise made by the different types of fridges varies: compressor fridges do make more noise than absorption fridges and if you are a light sleeper this may be a concern.

In terms of the size of the fridge, a small 50 litre is a nice compact size but still big enough for a couple of days worth of meat, veg, milk, beers, etc. If you're carrying more people or want to last for more than a couple of days between going to the shop, you probably want to be looking at 80 litres or bigger. Campervan fridges do go bigger as well and may be what you need if you really have to feed a lot of people or are planning prolonged trips away from shops. However, the larger the fridge capacity the more space it will take up inside the van, and of course the more power-hungry it will be.

---

"12V cool boxes are simple, cheap, and portable, but less good at cooling. Compressor fridges are easy to install and power efficient. 3-way fridges are complicated to install, but offer quiet operation and have flexible powering."

---

# 35 Fitting a 3-way Fridge

**PREREQUISITES**   Multi-stage process
**DO BEFORE**   - -
**COMBINE WITH**   Cutting holes in the van, constructing kitchen unit

Fitting an absorption (3-way) fridge is not for the faint hearted. The task involves a range of skills from cutting holes in the side of the vehicle, to 12V and mains wiring, gas plumbing, not to mention constructing the unit for the fridge to sit in. You should enlist professional help from a gas engineer and electrician as required. Although it's a fairly involved task, there is no question these fridges add a lot to a conversion and they go a long way to freeing you up to go further and for longer away from civilisation. The skills needed to construct the unit are covered elsewhere, while the other basic steps are as follows:

1. Carefully work out the location that the fridge will be installed in. The fridge installation instructions should show in detail the dimensions of the unit as well as acceptable positions for vents. The vents need to be away from opening windows and take care they won't snag on any sliding door paraphernalia. There will need to be a sealed gap at the back of the fridge and you will need access to the top for wiring and gas connections.

2. Using similar techniques to those described in the window fitting chapter, cut holes for the vents, and treat the bare edges. Fit the vent frames but leave the actual vent out for now to allow access to the back of the fridge. The usual vent frames are attached using multiple short stainless steel self-tapping screws – hold the frame up to the van, use a thin marker to mark all the screw holes and then drill pilot holes for each screw. Use good sealant when fitting the vent to keep the rain out.

3. Construct the unit to house the fridge. The fridges are quite heavy, so if mounting them higher than floor level they will need to sit on a robust platform. The sides of the unit should create a snug fit with the fridge, while at the rear follow the manufacturer's guidance for the size of gap that must be left.

Holes cut for fridge vents, water filler, and water heater.

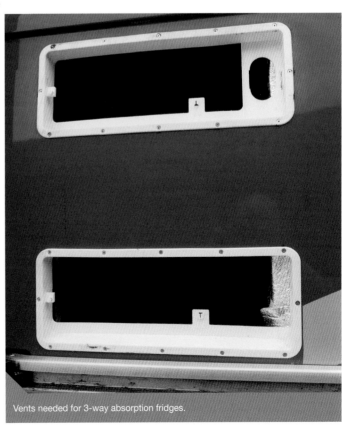
Vents needed for 3-way absorption fridges.

4. Create a sealed rear compartment. The exhaust fumes produced when running the fridge on gas are usually vented out through one side of the upper cooling vent, however if the wind is blowing a certain way there is a risk that those gases can slip back in through the vent (a flawed design really, but one that pervades the market). The air used for combustion should also be drawn from outside rather than from the living space. Therefore a crucial fitting concept is achieving a 'draught proof installation' – in other words you must ensure that the ventilation space at the back of the fridge is sealed off from the rest of the living area, and especially the sleeping area. The seal is best achieved using a flexible foam sealing strip, attached at the back of the unit for the fridge to butt up against. As a precaution a carbon monoxide alarm should also always be fitted.

5. Prepare the 12V and 230V supply cables as well as the gas plumbing (using a gas engineer as required).

6. Lift the fridge into position, ensuring the seal at the back is correct. Follow the manufacturer's guidance to screw the fridge into the sides of the unit. Connect the electrics and gas up.

Preparing the unit to take the fridge – the rubber foam seal at the back is needed to achieve a draught-proof installation.

The fridge fitted into the unit butted up to the seal at the back. This prevents cold draughts and gas exhaust fumes blowing back into the living space.

Pay close attention to safety – use fire retardant materials at the back of the fridge and follow the manufacturer's instructions to correctly route exhaust flues.

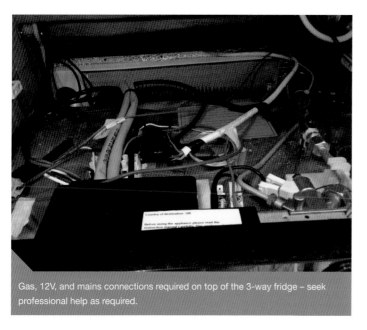

Gas, 12V, and mains connections required on top of the 3-way fridge – seek professional help as required.

7. Pay careful attention to how the gas flue is routed at the back of the fridge – ensure the flue has an upward slope to prevent the build up of condensate.

8. Place a removable shelf over the top of the fridge, ensuring a good seal is created to complete the isolation of the venting compartment. A heat deflector should also be installed at the top of the recess so that the heat is always directed out through the top vent.

9. Finally, if required, swap which side the fridge door hinges on and optionally add a décor panel to the front to match the rest of your units.

Once the fridge is commissioned, waste no time in filling it with tasty food, wine, and beer, and hitting the road for a test trip.

# Fridge Relay

Ideally the 12V supply should only be used while driving as otherwise an absorption fridge will rapidly drain the battery. You can rely on remembering to manually switch the 12V supply off in favour of gas, but since we're all flawed you are bound to forget at some point. Instead of relying on your memory, you can instead install an automatic system so that the 12V feed to the fridge is only live while the engine is running – as with split charging for your leisure battery, this can be achieved using either an ignition switched relay or a voltage sensing relay (except in vehicles with smart regenerative charging).

The controls on a 3-way fridge provide a choice between battery, mains, or gas operation.

The newly installed fridge being put to good use and adding significantly to any conversion.

# WATER & PLUMBING

After electricity and gas, water is the next most important service to install in a campervan. Thankfully, installing a simple water system is straightforward, cheap, and doesn't require any complicated skills. Best of all, water installations aren't governed by any regulations stopping you from doing it yourself.

# 36 Installing a Basic Water System

| | | | |
|---|---|---|---|
| **MODERATE 3/5** | | **PREREQUISITES** | Wiring |
| | | **DO BEFORE** | - - |
| | | **COMBINE WITH** | Constructing kitchen unit & furniture |

The simplest running water system consists of a tank, a submersible pump, a length of hose, a couple of jubilee clips, a micro-switch tap, and a 12V connection. The tank for a basic system like this could just be a simple container or plastic jerry can. A submersible pump is capable of sucking water out of the tank and sending it to a tap at the other end of the vehicle, however if you can locate the tank reasonably close to the tap then so much the better. You should make sure you have a plan for refilling the tank, but this could be as simple as carrying the tank to the nearest tap, filling it, and putting it back in the van. Or you could leave the tank in-situ and fill it using smaller bottles or a hose.

The hose should be half inch (approx 13mm) flexible water hose. If you need to you can warm the end of the hose up in a cup of hot water before pushing it onto the nozzles of the pump and tap.

The arrangement at the lid of the water tank is worthy of some thought. The submersible pump is attached to the hose and also has a cable going to it – this assembly is dropped into the tank. The ideal arrangement has the hose and cable passing through the lid of the tank in such a way that it is sealed when closed to stop water spilling out every time you brake, but you should also be able to unscrew the lid freely to allow filling, without winding the hose and cable assembly around with it.

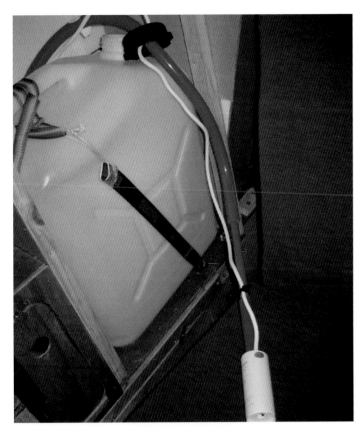

# Basic Water Sytem

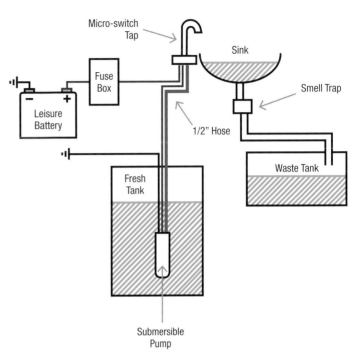

Micro-switch Tap

Sink

Fuse Box

Leisure Battery

Smell Trap

1/2" Hose

Fresh Tank

Waste Tank

Submersible Pump

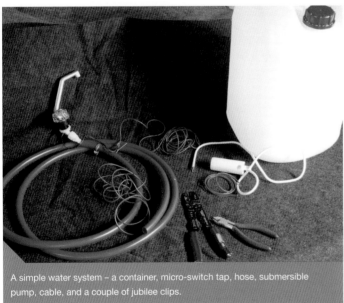

A simple water system – a container, micro-switch tap, hose, submersible pump, cable, and a couple of jubilee clips.

Connecting a submersible pump. Note the clear cap creates a seal on the container to stop the water spilling out, while the screw on cap can rotate freely.

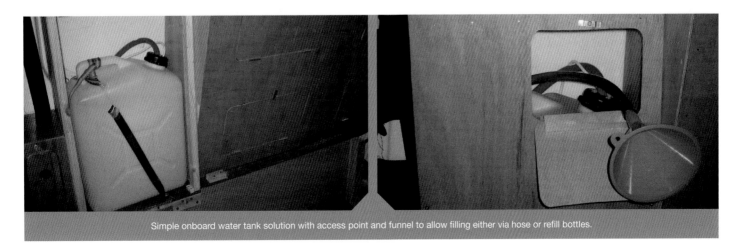

Simple onboard water tank solution with access point and funnel to allow filling either via hose or refill bottles.

# 37 Installing a Complex Water System

| PREREQUISITES | Wiring |
|---|---|
| DO BEFORE | - - |
| COMBINE WITH | Constructing furniture & kitchen unit |

MODERATE
3/5

Once your conversion ambitions start to grow, you may start to consider adding items such as hot water and a bathroom including a sink, a toilet, and a shower. You might even have a dog or bike cleaning hose, or an outdoor shower on your wish-list. All of these things are possible, but they will require a more complicated water system than that discussed previously. You will need a larger fresh water tank, a pressure pump rather than a submersible one, and you should use 12mm push-fit pipe instead of flexible hose. You will need to plan how to effectively drain-down the system, and consider where everything is going to be located. That said, even fairly complex motorhome water systems are achievable by novices so don't be too put off.

A good place to start designing your water system is to list the various water consumers you plan to have – for example:

- Kitchen sink
- Bathroom sink
- Shower
- Toilet
- Hot Water Boiler
- Outdoor hose or shower

If you plan to have hot water (discussed in more detail later), you will need to run a cold feed to the boiler and then hot pipes from the boiler to the various consumers. The toilet will only need a cold feed and some have their own separate flush tanks in which case they won't be connected to the rest of your water system.

Since every conversion is different, there is no single correct way to plan your system. Instead, the remainder of this chapter discusses the various aspects of water systems so that you can pick and choose the parts that suit your requirements.

"Conversions with multiple taps should be paired
with a pressure pump system."

## Draining Down

It is important to be able to drain down the system – either during cold weather while the vehicle isn't in use, or if you need to do work on the system for instance to replace a worn tap etc. Including isolation valves / taps for each distinct part of the water system also makes working on part of a system possible without needing to drain the whole lot. In a basic system the drain down provision doesn't need to be complicated – you can run the pump dry and then empty the water container outside. In more complex systems, you should plumb in at least one drain down point – these should be positioned at the lowest points in the system. The drain down point can be as simple as a shut-off valve with a pipe leading through the floor – switch the pump off (or remove its fuse), open the valve, then open all the taps and the system should empty.

Think carefully about your drain down points – is there anything that will prevent all the water in the system being drained? For example, a poorly sited non-return valve will hold the water in the system. You also need to be able to drain and clean the water tank, so ensure there is provision for this.

# Advanced Water System

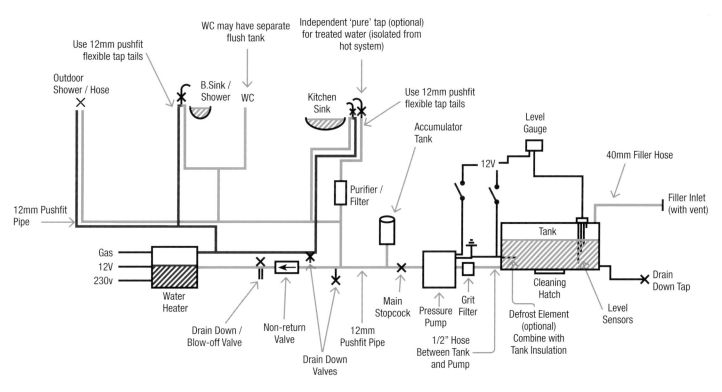

Use 12mm pushfit flexible tap tails

WC may have separate flush tank

Independent 'pure' tap (optional) for treated water (isolated from hot system)

Outdoor Shower / Hose

B.Sink / Shower

WC

Kitchen Sink

Use 12mm pushfit flexible tap tails

Accumulator Tank

Level Gauge

12V

40mm Filler Hose

Filler Inlet (with vent)

12mm Pushfit Pipe

Purifier / Filter

Tank

Gas

12V

230v

Water Heater

Drain Down / Blow-off Valve

Non-return Valve

Drain Down Valves

12mm Pushfit Pipe

Main Stopcock

Pressure Pump

Grit Filter

1/2" Hose Between Tank and Pump

Cleaning Hatch

Defrost Element (optional) Combine with Tank Insulation

Level Sensors

Drain Down Tap

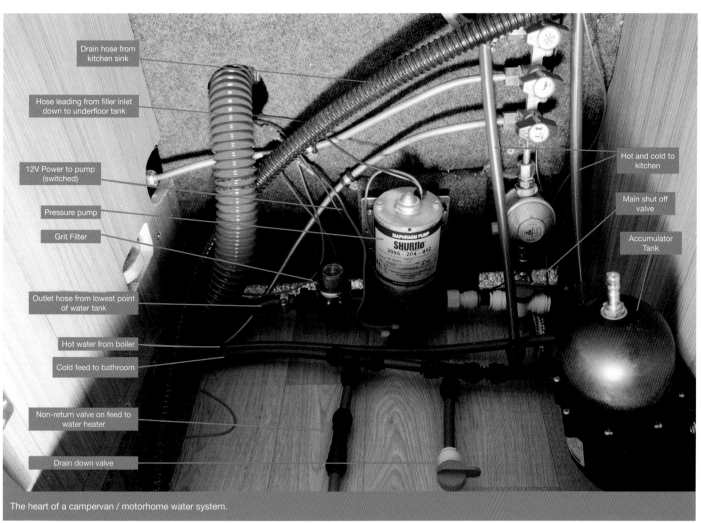

Drain hose from kitchen sink

Hose leading from filler inlet down to underfloor tank

12V Power to pump (switched)

Pressure pump

Grit Filter

Outlet hose from lowest point of water tank

Hot water from boiler

Cold feed to bathroom

Non-return valve on feed to water heater

Drain down valve

Hot and cold to kitchen

Main shut off valve

Accumulator Tank

SHURflo
DIAPHRAGM PUMP
2095 · 204 · 412

The heart of a campervan / motorhome water system.

# Pumps

There are two main types of water pump for use in campervans – submersible pumps and pressure pumps. Pressure pumps are also known as diaphragm pumps. As a rule of thumb, use a submersible pump in a basic system (usually with a small tank and a single tap) and use a pressure pump for a more complex system which will often have more than one tap and perhaps a shower.

Submersible pumps are attached to a hose and lowered into the water tank. They are usually switched on and off by a micro-switch integrated inside the tap. When the tap is turned on, the switch is triggered which in turn activates the pump. When the tap is turned off, the switch is disconnected and the pump goes off.

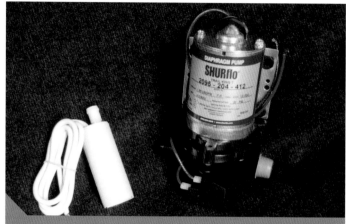

A small submersible pump next to a pressure pump – usually a pressure pump is warranted once the system grows beyond a single sink.

Pressure pumps sit on their own outside the tank. The pump is attached via a hose going to the lowest point on the tank. Instead of being switched on and off by a switch in the tap, this pump is usually triggered by a pressure switch (often integrated into the pump). The pressure switch triggers when it senses any drop in pressure in the system – so if any tap in the system is turned on, the pressure drops, and the pump activates. The pump will continue to run until the system is back up at pressure again (usually 20 or 30mbar). Pumps are rated in terms of the number of litres per minute they can move – if you need a powerful system, this is the figure to take note of when buying, but bear in mind that a more powerful pump will empty your tank quicker.

# Accumulator Tanks

One problem with pressure pumps is that they are sensitive to slight leaks in the system. For instance if a tap is dripping slightly, the pressure will slowly drop to the point where the pump will kick in briefly to top the system back up. This can be annoying at night because from time to time you will hear the pump kick in. In bad cases the pump can get into a frequent on-off cycle. The ideal solution to this is to ensure there are no leaks in the system. The compromise solution is to add in an 'accumulator tank' – this bit of kit evens out the pressure in the system and ensures things such as dripping taps or very minor leaks won't keep you awake at night.

The accumulator tank can be sited anywhere on your plumbing, so it can be added in later if you find you are having problems with the pump cycling on and off. You can install accumulators in-line on a pipe length but you can also just connect them on one side and blank off the other. They are usually installed close to the pump but can in theory be placed anywhere on the system.

An accumulator tank – note it has been installed on its own branch and doesn't need to be 'in-line'.

# Water Purifiers and Filters

If you intend to travel places where you might need to fill up your water from a less-than-ideal supply, you may want to fit a water purifier or filter into your system. Most pressure pumps already have filters attached to them, but these are more to catch grit and other debris that would otherwise damage or clog up the pump. In order to actually treat the water, a more robust filter or water purifier is required. The purifier could just be fitted underneath your primary sink – i.e. in the kitchen – rather than treating all your water even when it is just for showers etc. Note that if you take this approach you will need to install a dedicated 'pure' tap, separate from a hot mixer tap as the water from the boiler won't have been treated.

Try to fill your tank up from a reputable source, ideally marked as 'drinking water'.

There are also a variety of water system cleaners, purification tablets and tank additives available. Campervan water systems have a tendency to develop an unsavoury taste after a while, and if you don't look after the system regularly you may also find them going 'slimy'. Filling up from dubious water supplies tends to exacerbate these problems. As a minimum you should aim to empty and sterilize the system once a year, and you may need to do more depending how you are using it. Consider using tank additives to treat the water as soon as it goes into the tank, and try not to leave water lying in the system for too long.

# Taps

Which taps you choose to install is largely a case of personal taste, and there is certainly a wide variety of models to choose from. If you are installing a basic system, you will probably need a tap with an integrated micro-switch to wire up to your submersible pump. If you are installing a pressure switched pump then actually any taps will work – even domestic ones, though you will have to deploy some pipe adapting skills to plumb these into the system. If you are installing a micro-switch tap into a pressure pump system you can just ignore the wires to the micro-switch or cut them off. Look out for folding taps that tuck away when not in use, high taps that will let you fill up tall juice bottles, and combination sink and shower hose taps for use in bathrooms. You also have the choice between taps that only have one feed – i.e. cold water – and mixer taps that have both hot and cold inputs.

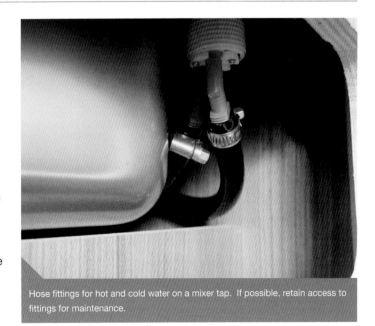

Hose fittings for hot and cold water on a mixer tap. If possible, retain access to fittings for maintenance.

Taps also come with different 'tails' – if you get one with the right tails it will make plumbing into your system that much easier. For example, if your plumbing is 12mm push-fit pipe you should try to get a tap with compatible tails otherwise you will need to use pipe adapters to get it all to fit together. The other thing to be aware of is the different diameters of hole that taps can be installed into – measure the hole in your sink unit (if there is one) and check that it matches the diameter specified for the tap.

# Water Tanks

Tanks come in all shapes and sizes. The smallest tank you should consider is probably around 20litres – enough for a number of days or even a week if you are being careful and only using it for cooking and drinking for one person. A 25 or 30 litre tank in a small campervan will give you a bit more leeway in when you need to fill up. Small tanks have the advantage of being light enough to carry to a tap to fill up, and are also easier to fit into the vehicle. You could consider carrying a spare so you don't get caught short.

Larger conversions where water is being used for things other than cooking and drinking – for example for showers, flushing toilets, bathroom sinks etc. – will need bigger tanks. An 80 litre tank is a reasonable minimum size to serve a conversion with a small bathroom and two people cooking, washing, etc. for several days to (at most) a week. If there are more people, you have demanding water use habits, or you want to go longer in between water fill stops, you might want to consider a tank of 100-150 litres or even much larger (some overland vehicles will carry hundreds of litres), though there are obvious weight and space implications. Some toilets have their own water tanks and this can be useful – it adds extra capacity and you don't want to accidentally use up the last of your precious fresh water by flushing the loo.

Using two jerry water containers is a flexible approach in a small conversion and makes carrying them to a tap to refill easier.

## Conservation

You do need to change your mindset a bit when on the road and start thinking about water conservation. Most people drink 2 litres or so of water a day (or they should) and when at home the average shower lasts around 8 minutes and uses up over 60 litres of water. You don't want to start rationing water for eating and drinking, but when it comes to washing dishes and yourself, you will need to be a little more careful. One solution to this is to swim in rivers or use campsite showers, but with a bit of awareness and frugality you can make an 80 or 100 litre water tank last.

A mid-size 70 litre fresh water tank.

"You need to think about conserving water when on the road... and when you get close to running out, make sure you get the first shower!"

# 38 Fitting Underslung Water Tanks

| | | |
|---|---|---|
| **PREREQUISITES** | - - | |
| **DO BEFORE** | Flooring | |
| **COMBINE WITH** | Plumbing, shower tray, filler inlet installation | |

**MODERATE 3/5**

Large water tanks can be installed underneath the vehicle, and this is a great way to save valuable space inside. There are companies who make tanks to fit the space available under specific vehicles. Under-floor tanks are held in place using long metal straps or brackets which need to be bolted through the floor and fastened in place using good spreader washers. If you are installing very large tanks, be aware of the weight implications and ensure the fixings are adequate.

The only trouble with storing your water under the van is it becomes much more vulnerable to freezing – this can be combated to a certain extent with low-wattage tank defrost elements and insulation blankets, but if you are planning to use the vehicle in cold weather you may find yourself permanently on edge about your water freezing. This is one good reason to consider fitting your fresh water tank inside the vehicle, though often freezing can still be a worry and space considerations may take precedence. If you are worried about your waste tank freezing it is less problematic as you can just leave it open to drain away immediately. If fitting tank defrost elements, ensure they are located near the bottom of the tank so they don't run dry, and ideally place them near the outlet to the pump. Tank defrost elements usually run on a thermostat and will consume 2-3Amps while on – they should be combined with good tank insulation and a reasonable sized leisure battery / battery bank setup.

Large underfloor water and waste tanks shaped to fit around the chassis. Secured in place with robust metal straps and bolts through the floor.

# 39 Fitting a Filler Inlet

| | |
|---|---|
| **PREREQUISITES** | - - |
| **DO BEFORE** | Panelling, flooring |
| **COMBINE WITH** | Installing underfloor tank, cutting holes in vehicle |

The most elegant solution to how to fill your water tank, particularly large water tanks, is to fit a filler inlet point on the side of the vehicle in exactly the same way as your fuel tank (but don't mix them up – diesel has a way of making the water taste funny!). Filler inlets usually feature a lockable cap and use 40mm ribbed hose leading directly from the filler inlet to the tank in order to allow fast filling. An important feature of the filler inlet is a breather vent which lets the air escape as you fill the tank – particularly important if filling it from a powerful source.

It makes sense to carry a good length of hose (in a poly bag or plastic crate to catch any spillage) so that you can park near the tap and fill up with ease. Experienced travellers will carry a small selection of hose fittings so that you can attach to most taps you will come across.

1. Position the inlet – above the top of the tank with a good route for the hose to follow.

2. Measure, mark, and cut out the hole for the inlet (use masking tape as required to protect the paintwork). If the hose is going into the vehicle and then to an underslung tank, you will also need to cut the hole through the floor.

3. File and paint bare metal edges.

4. Fit the filler inlet with plenty of sealant and stainless self tapping screws as required.

5. Fit 40mm filler hose onto the inside of the inlet using large jubilee clips and route the hose into the tank inlet. Test for any leaks.

If you are installing a very large water tank, you may want to consider making the filler hoses a bigger diameter so that you can fill the tank up quicker. If you are going to be travelling in remote places you may also want to carry a portable filter and a couple of 20-30litre jerry cans or even a submersible pump capable of filling your tank from a river or other water source.

A lockable water filler inlet.

Water tank and battery gauge.

# Waste Tanks

The waste tank holds 'grey' water – i.e. water coming from sinks and showers. Note that toilets have their own tanks which are emptied separately. The simplest solution to a waste tank is not to have one – attach a waste hose to the bottom of the sink and stick the hose through a hole in the floor; perhaps not the most environmentally friendly thing to do, and a little awkward if you're in a car park with lots of other people, but a quick and easy solution none-the-less. Another easy solution is to have a small container (e.g. 10-15litres) under the sink with the hose feeding into it. At regular intervals (when you are in an appropriate location) you can remove the container and empty it discreetly outside.

> "The more careful you are with what you put into your waste tank, the less worried you will be about where to empty it."

The more advanced waste tank solution is to fit a proper tank underneath the vehicle. The tank can either be small, e.g. 15 litres or so – little more than a temporary holding tank, or much larger, say 50-70 litres which allows for multiple showers etc. in between empties. Larger waste tanks are best emptied at designated places – campsites usually have a drain that you can drive over for this purpose. The more careful you are with what you put into your waste tank, the less worried you will be about where to empty it.

You will need a good system for emptying the waste tank – ideal is a readily accessible good quality drain tap at the side of the vehicle. The drain hose will need to be a suitable size – for example 3-4" (75-100mm) – with a fall from the base of the tank to allow effective emptying. If you get this wrong it will be both awkward and involve you pouring waste water up your arm every time you empty the tank. Leaving the waste tank drain open when driving will allow it to fully empty. Instead of a drain tap you can use a 'slide drain valve' which allows easy and rapid dumping of the tank contents. It is sometimes useful to be able to attach a hose to the waste tank so that you can lead the waste water away from the vehicle – for instance if you are parked up for a longer period of time.

# Tank Gauges

If you put your tanks somewhere tricky to see into at a glance, it is very useful to install a gauge. You probably actually need two gauges in larger conversions – one to show how full your fresh tank is and the other to warn you when the waste tank is in need of being emptied. Fresh tank gauges usually use three or four probes that are permanently fitted into the tank – you may be able to have these probes ready installed in the tank when you buy it, though retrofitting them is a relatively easy job too. A cable links the probes with the gauge (and the battery). If you situate the gauge somewhere easy to see, you should notice before the water or waste situation becomes critical.

Waste tanks tend to use a couple of stud sensors on the outside of the tank instead of probes – the main purpose here is to warn you when the waste tank is getting full. Again a cable runs from the gauge studs to the gauge and the battery (via the fuse box).

Place tank gauges (fresh and waste water) somewhere easy to see.

# Plumbing

The majority of campervan fresh-water plumbing uses either half inch (13mm) hose or 12mm push-fit pipe. Somewhat confusingly, flexible hose is measured by the inside diameter, whereas push-fit pipe is measured by its outside diameter. For small and basic systems, you will be able to stick to flexible hose throughout. For more complex projects, push-fit plumbing is the way forward (though half inch hose could also be used). The 12mm pipe is semi-rigid – it can bend in gradual curves but anything beyond that you should fit elbows or bends. Push-fit plumbing is very easy – you just need to make sure you push the pipe all the way in, past an initial resistance. Try hard to test the system before any connections get covered up as you can guarantee the leak will be in the one spot you can no longer get at.

If you have used push-fit plumbing in a house, there are a few differences worth noting. Domestic house installations using push-fit pipe usually use 15 and 22mm pipe, but 12mm is most common in campervan and motorhome circles. Another difference from domestic push-fit plumbing is that pipe inserts (that are routinely used with 15 and 22mm) are rarely used with 12mm push-fit. 12mm fittings also rarely have the 'lock-nuts' seen on most domestic plumbing fittings.

# 40 Making a Hose Connection

| | PREREQUISITES | - - |
| --- | --- | --- |
| EASY / MODERATE 2/5 | DO BEFORE | - - |
| | COMBINE WITH | Installing water system |

When making hose connections it is important to check that the nozzle is the same size as the hose being used – if the hose goes on easily it is probably because the nozzle is intended for a smaller size of hose (e.g. 10mm instead of 13mm). Hose reducer fittings are available to handle this issue, or you can change the hose size you are using.

1. Boil a kettle and fill a mug with hot water (make yourself a cuppa while you're at it!)

2. Use your pipe cutters or a sharp knife to ensure there is a good clean cut at the end of the pipe. Dip the pipe in the hot water for 10 seconds or so.

3. Thread a jubilee clip over the hose and then push the hose onto the nozzle, all the way on.

4. Let the hose cool, then do the jubilee clip up tight, but not so tight that it damages the hose.

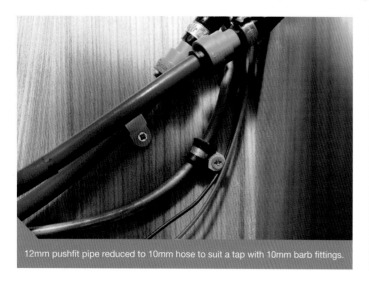

12mm pushfit pipe reduced to 10mm hose to suit a tap with 10mm barb fittings.

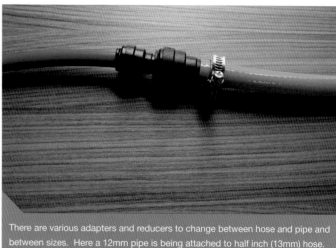

There are various adapters and reducers to change between hose and pipe and between sizes. Here a 12mm pipe is being attached to half inch (13mm) hose.

# 41 Making a Push-fit Connection

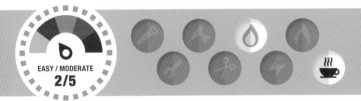

EASY / MODERATE
2/5

PREREQUISITES    - -
DO BEFORE        - -
COMBINE WITH     Installing water system

It is worth buying a pipe-cutter before starting on your plumbing – similar to a pair of scissors but strong enough to cut through most plastic pipes.

1. Use pipe cutters to make a clean cut in the pipe. It is crucial that the end of the pipe is cut square. Scrape off any burrs with your finger nail.

2. Push the pipe into the push-fit connection. It should go in, stop, and then go in again. Give it a tug to confirm the fitting is gripping the pipe.

3. If you need to disassemble a push-fit connection, simply hold the circular collet into the body of the fitting and pull the pipe out.

12mm pushfit pipe held in place with p-clips.

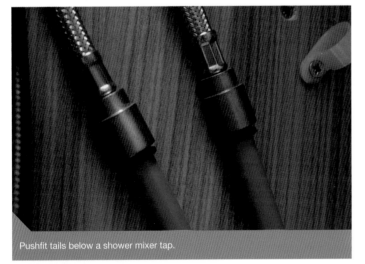

Pushfit tails below a shower mixer tap.

A straight connector with 25mm convoluted waste pipe behind.

Inline taps or valves are useful to close off distinct parts of the water system and to open drain down points.

Non-return valves are useful in a couple of situations but make sure you can still drain down the system when required.

# 12mm Push-fit Pipe Fittings

Numerous different push-fit fittings are available and it's well worth getting a good selection of them at the start of the project so that you don't get caught short for want of an elbow. Some of the pipe fittings available are as follows:

- Equal Ts – lets you split a new section of pipe off at 90°.

- Equal Ys – splits the pipe into two sections but keeps both pipes heading in the same direction.

- Equal Elbows – routes the pipe in a 90° bend, ideal to get your pipe around tight corners.

- Equal Straights – handy connectors that provide a straight connection from one section of pipe to another (does a good job of hiding the fact that your calculations were wrong and you needed to add in more pipe).

- Non-return valve – allows water to only flow one way through your water system. These valves are sometimes used after the pump to stop water travelling backwards through the system when the pump is switched off. A non-return valve can also be useful when fitting a water heater to ensure hot water can't travel back through the system as it expands.

- Inline Tap / Valve – allows you to shut off the flow of water by twisting the tap on the top of this connector. These are ideal if you want to service or change sections of your water system, or isolate your system if you develop a leak. Taps are often placed just after the pump, and can also be used along with a pipe fed through the floor of the van to allow you to drain your water system.

Pushfit Tees, elbows, inline valves (taps), and non-return valves are common fittings. Splitters (Y's) and straight connectors (not pictured) are also useful.

- Hose / pipe adapters and reducers – adapters allow you to switch from pipe to hose and vice-versa when needed, and reducers allow you to change from one size of pipe or hose to another. For example, this would be needed if you are running 12mm semi rigid pipe, but need to change to 10mm or half-inch hose to supply a water outlet such as a tap.

Convoluted waste hose leading to a smell trap beneath the kitchen sink.

A campsite waste water emptying point – you can simply drive over the drain and open your waste tank.

# Waste Plumbing

Campervan waste plumbing is similar to domestic waste plumbing in that there seems to be an unnecessary collection of different pipe sizes, leading to inevitable compatibility problems.

## Waste Water System

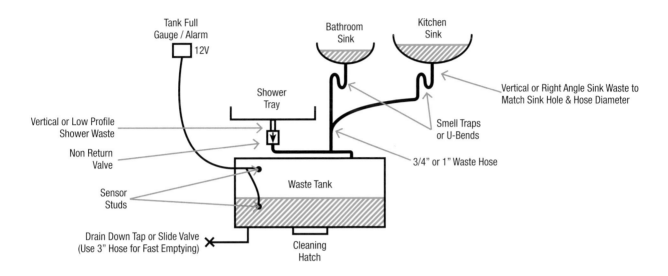

- **Sink wastes** – As with taps, there are two different diameters to consider: the first is the diameter of the hole in the base of the sink; the second is the diameter of the outlet that the hose will be connected to. The hose outlet can either be straight down or right-angled to suit the installation.

- **Waste hose** – Waste hose comes in several diameters. ¾" (19mm) and 1" (25mm) are the most common sizes, though bigger hoses (up to 3") are also sometimes used (for example for waste tank emptying). Just to confuse matters there are other waste hoses and fittings on the market, so you may also encounter fittings for 20mm, 23.5mm, and 28.5mm to name a few. Note that the hose measurements are the inside diameters. If a hose doesn't feel like it goes on the fitting very well, it is probably due to incorrect sizing – you may be able to make this work (either by forcing a tight fit, using adapter sleeves / reducer grommets, or using PTFE tape and tight jubilee clips to take up the slack), but trying to match the right hose to the right fitting is better in the long run.

- **Waste connectors** – straights, Ys, Tees, reducers (and reducing grommets) are all available. You can also get elbows although you often don't need them since the hose is flexible.

- **Smell traps** – below every sink you would be well advised to install a smell trap. The domestic equivalent is the U-bend, however a smell trap takes up significantly less space. They do what they say on the tin and stop bad smells lurking in the waste tank from rising up into the living space.

- **Shower wastes** – the problem with shower wastes in campervans is that usually you are very limited for space. The ideal solution is for the waste to go directly and vertically down through the floor as this will help the water to flow away the quickest. If that isn't possible, you need to fit a right angled low profile shower waste and then ensure the waste hose leads away at a good angle.

- **Shower non-return** – if you're not careful you can get a nasty surprise one day as you're driving along looking for somewhere to empty your almost full waste tank. If you stop too suddenly you may find a significant portion of the waste tank slopping up and into the shower tray. The solution to this is to install a non-return valve on the waste hose below the shower tray.

# WATER HEATING

Hot water in a campervan seems like a bourgeois luxury when you first experience it, especially if you have previously spent a long time travelling without it. Hot water adds a whole extra layer of comfort to a conversion, and as such it may well be on your wish-list. Installing a hot water system is similar to installing a heater, and in reality the steps aren't too complicated.

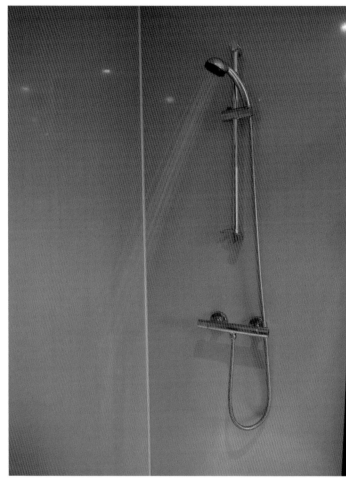

## Types of Boiler

Water heaters (also known as boilers) come in a variety of forms. They are either powered by gas or by mains electricity, sometimes both. Water heaters also use 12Volt electrics but only for the control electronics rather than the actual heating. They come in a range of sizes but around a 10 litre tank is about right in a campervan unless you plan to have several people showering one after the other (in which case you will need a large fresh water tank as well).

The main choices of water heater are:

- Combined heater and water heaters

- Electric water heaters

- Gas

- Gas and Electric

- Diesel

"Hot water in a campervan is like a bourgeois luxury when you first experience it. But once you've had it, it's hard to go back!"

The advantage of combined heater-boilers is that you only have one appliance to install, and in theory it takes up less space. You might hope that a combined heater-boiler will save money as well, but this is often not the case as they are expensive appliances. There are advantages to having these as separate units too – for instance for maintenance purposes. Also, if you keep them separate at least if one stops working you can still use the other.

If you plan to always stay on campsites or somewhere with a mains hook-up, then an electric only boiler may seem like a good solution. At least you don't have to plumb an electric boiler up to the gas. However, if you want to be able to park up in the wilds, away from mains electricity, then going for a gas boiler is really the only way forward. Several of the gas boilers on the market are 'dual fuel' in that you can either run them on gas, or on mains electric, or for fast heat-up times you can even use gas and electric at the same time. Dual fuel boilers have a lot of advantages and are the type most recommended here. Diesel boilers are also available and the gas versus diesel discussion within the Heating and Gas chapters are worth reading if you are leaning in this direction.

A Propex Malaga - one of a number of hot water boilers on the market. Choose one that fits the space available and has a tank of the right size for you.

A Truma Ultrastore. Find a position to install the water heater where you can put the flue through the side wall. Note it mustn't snag the side door or be too close to windows.

When you are buying your water heater, try to get one that comes with the correct connections for the type of plumbing you are using – for instance if you are using 12mm push-fit plumbing, try to get the boiler model with those fittings as this will save a fair bit of hassle adapting pipes etc. At the time of purchase, you should also try to get the right colour of cowl and vent cover to match your vehicle – usually the choice is white or black / grey. Depending on the type of vehicle you are converting, you may need to get an extension for the vent – for instance if the wall it is passing through is thicker than designed for.

# 42 Installing a Water Heater

**ADVANCED 4/5**

| | |
|---|---|
| **PREREQUISITES** | Flooring |
| **DO BEFORE** | Panelling |
| **COMBINE WITH** | Installing water system, fridge vents |

As with campervan heaters, water heaters are 'room sealed' in that the combustion of gas is sealed off from the living space. In order to achieve this, there needs to be both an air intake and an exhaust vent – normally situated through the side of the vehicle. Therefore you will need to find a location for the boiler where it can sit – ideally on the floor or low down, as close as possible to where the other plumbing will be, and note that the exhaust vent mustn't be too close to a window or somewhere it might foul the sliding door. You may find that you need to raise the boiler off the floor in order for the vent to go through above the exterior trim of the vehicle (otherwise the trim will need to be cut around it). You should also try to avoid the vent passing through parts of the vehicle that are excessively curved.

The following installation steps apply to a Truma Ultrastore boiler, but the installation of other models is similar.

1. Locate the best position for boiler – construct a timber pedestal for it to sit on if required.

2. Measure, mark, and cut the hole for the vent. Protect the paint with masking tape and treat the bare metal with primer.

3. If required, build a timber frame around the inside of the vent hole.

4. Secure the boiler to the floor or pedestal.

5. Attach the vent grill or cowl, using sealant and stainless self tapping screws as required.

Cut the hole for the flue and add internal framing as required. File and treat the cut edges before adding the cowl.

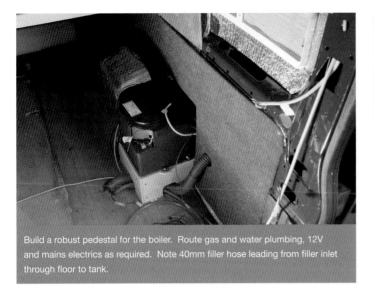

Build a robust pedestal for the boiler. Route gas and water plumbing, 12V and mains electrics as required. Note 40mm filler hose leading from filler inlet through floor to tank.

Install boiler controls somewhere accessible but where they won't get accidentally knocked.

6. Run 12V cables to the controller and thermostat, and link with the fuse box and boiler.

7. Run mains cable from the consumer unit to the boiler and wire up.

8. Plumb in fresh water supply and hot water pipes. Follow the manufacturer's instructions but the fresh supply will usually need a non-return valve as well as a drain / blow-off valve fitted. Installing an isolation tap on the supply is also useful for future maintenance purposes, and for when you don't intend using the boiler for periods of time.

The boiler cowl with cover on (make sure this is removed before starting the boiler).

9. Plumb into gas (enlist a GSR engineer as required).

# Draining, Blow-offs, and Non-return valves

Hot water boilers usually need to have an emergency 'over-heat' blow-off pipe that allows the boiling water to be released out of the system before causing any damage. The blow-off valve will be described in the instructions for your particular boiler, but often it will be positioned in-line on the cold feed immediately prior to the boiler. The pipe should stick down through the floor so that if it ever needs to vent it won't scald anyone. The blow-off valve also doubles as a drain-down point for the boiler.

Depending on the model of boiler, you may need to place a non-return valve immediately prior to the blow-off / drain valve. This prevents expanding hot water from spreading back into the cold water system. It is important that the non-return valve is the right side of the blow-off / drain valve (i.e. the cold side) as otherwise the hot water will be unable to escape and you will be unable to drain the boiler down.

# Hot Water Plumbing

The plumbing for the hot water can essentially mirror the cold pipes. 12mm push-fit pipe is recommended. You may want to use red pipes or you can just use blue with some red tape at intervals to distinguish them. The hot pipes will need to go to each mixer tap, and of course to the shower if there is one. Your hot pipe work will also need to have drain-down points at the lowest parts of the system.

# BATHROOMS

While adding significant levels of convenience and comfort to a conversion, there is no question that adding a bathroom to your project will add a great deal to the effort, and probably budget, required. That isn't intended to put you off, but be aware before you start that your bathroom will add a fair bit of complexity to the task ahead of you. That said, there are major attractions to being able to duck into a cubicle when the call of nature arrives, no matter where you happen to be, and whatever the time of day or night. The cubicle also provides easy access to privacy for instance when changing clothes etc., without needing to start pulling blinds and curtains. Going the extra mile and adding in a shower will, for many converters, be the final step towards creating a true home from home.

Although there are occasional exceptions to the rule, bathrooms are usually only found in high roof campervans. The standard campervan bathroom is basically a small room tucked into as tight a space as possible within the confines of the vehicle. Fitting everything into such a small space, without making it so cramped as to be unusable, is a real challenge and one which even large professional conversion companies have sometimes struggled to get right.

The best advice is to try mocking-up the space before you commit to the final design – get some big bits of cardboard or wood and create the space in the vehicle or just in your living room. You could just mark it out on the floor but having the walls in place gives you a better feel for what is and isn't acceptable space-wise. Try sitting on a box or a chair as if it was the loo and see if you've got enough space for your knees. Try standing up and washing your armpits – will you manage to get clean in this space or just bruise your elbows? After pondering this for a while, you may find that your bathroom requirements feed heavily into what size of vehicle you choose, and also what the ultimate layout will be.

## Bathroom Construction

The campervan bathroom is usually three solid walls with a door in the fourth. At least one of the solid walls will be the side (or back) of the vehicle – construction will be easier if you make this wall vertical, but working with the curve of the vehicle will use up less space.

# Materials

Large motorhome manufacturers making vehicles on an assembly line can afford to construct bathroom cubicles using plastic and fibreglass moulded to their exact design. For most of the rest of us, we are stuck with more conventional materials. If your bathroom will have a shower in it, pretty much everything will get a good soaking from time to time, so you need to be confident that your walls will be up to the job. The big problem is that your walls will also be highly visible from the main living space, so you need them to look good on the outside, while being waterproof on the inside. The main material choices are:

- Lightweight Furniture Ply – this will look great, match the rest of your conversion, comes in loads of different finishes, but isn't designed to get soaked. If you are careful, you might get away with using it if you combine it with a good shower curtain and try to keep it relatively dry. However, over time you may find that the wood starts to suffer as it isn't usually treated to the same spec. as marine ply or shower-wall.

- Marine Ply – marine ply properly sealed and varnished is designed to get wet (you can build a dinghy out of it). It can also look good, though not in the same league and variety of finishes as furniture ply.

- Shower-wall panels – this stuff is used to replace tiles in domestic showers, behind baths etc. It looks great, comes in a variety of finishes, and is designed to get soaked. Various joining strips are available which are fine if you are joining two bits at a right angle. Unfortunately shower-wall is one sided, so you would need to cover the living space side with something else.

- Plastic – PVC boards can be very useful when constructing campervan bathrooms. They are 100% waterproof, and usually the sheets are both thin and flexible which makes them very suitable for curved walls and ceilings. Be aware that plywood butted up against PVC will squeak when driving so careful construction is required.

- PVC cladding panels – these lightweight and fully waterproof panels can be a good option for cladding the inside of a ply constructed bathroom. The cladding panels are slotted together with a tongue and groove system, with the tongue on one panel sliding into the groove of the next panel and so on. They are around 8mm thick, 250mm wide, and come in lengths just under 3metres. These could also be used on the ceiling to good effect if required.

- Vinyl Wall Board – thin furniture ply sheets (i.e. 3mm thick) sometimes come with water-resistant finishes such as vinyl. Be careful not to use paper covered boards as these will suffer badly as soon as they get wet. These thin boards can be stuck onto thicker ply to create the inside of the bathroom.

There isn't really the perfect choice, so you will have to choose an approach that suits you. This may involve laminating (i.e. gluing) a thin waterproof layer onto a thicker living space layer, or it may involve laminating a thin presentable layer on the dry living space side (perhaps even carpet) onto shower-wall or similar. Of course you need to be conscious of weight penalties if using more than one material sandwiched together. Whichever approach you take, it's a question worthy of some careful thought.

A well constructed shower room using PVC bathroom cladding panels on-top of 15mm furniture ply.

# 43 Constructing a Bathroom Cubicle

MODERATE
3/5

| PREREQUISITES | Panelling, flooring |
|---|---|
| DO BEFORE | Installing shower tray |
| COMBINE WITH | Installing cassette toilet, constructing bed & furniture |

Although all conversions will vary, the following steps should give a guide to the basics of constructing the bathroom cubicle.

**1.** Prepare the back wall of the cubicle – usually the side wall of the vehicle. You will need to insulate as usual and then cover with a waterproof and flexible panel – PVC board can be useful here. If a toilet waste door is going through the wall your panel will need to fit around this. You may find it easiest to build a half or full height vertical false wall so that the toilet can sit flush against it.

**2.** Cut your first sheet of plywood roughly to size and carefully scribe it to both the wall and the ceiling of the van. You may find it helpful to do this in two or three stages – scribe a small template piece to the ceiling or wall first, then transfer it to the bigger board once you have the shape right. (See more guidance on scribing techniques in the Joinery chapter.)

**3.** Use the first sheet as a rough guide and modify the next sheet as required to create the other side wall.

**4.** Use right angle brackets or softwood battens attached to the vehicle to securely fasten the side walls in place – take your time doing this as the rest of the cubicle will be built on top of these.

**5.** Create a doorway by attaching a thin rectangle of ply at right angles to both side walls, and at the top and bottom, leaving an opening just big enough for your door. Make sure you have left enough corridor space for the door to swing fully open.

**6.** Cut your door from the ply and hang it using hinges on one side of the cubicle. Add a door handle and catch, and lock if required.

**7.** Construct a false floor within the cubicle, using timber battens to raise the height as required. There should be enough space for all your pipework, shower waste etc., while still leaving enough headroom to stand in the shower. The false floor is also a good way to raise your toilet to a level where the waste door will be above any exterior trim. It is good practice to leave some way of gaining access to the false floor void – even if only enough for inspection purposes.

*"If condensation is the enemy, water vapour is the root cause…"*

The walls of a bathroom cubicle being built out of 15mm furniture ply. This small space (approx 900 x 900mm) is enough (for some) for a comfy bathroom when on the road.

# Ventilation

If condensation is the enemy, water vapour is the root cause… and bathrooms create a lot of moisture. You should aim to have a good source of ventilation specifically for the bathroom. The vent will also help keep your campervan smelling fresh. Your choices are either an opening window, a small rooflight, or a ceiling or wall fan. If you opt for a window, beware that you will need a way to cover it to retain privacy.

In addition to ventilation, you might also want to consider fitting a heater outlet into your bathroom – this will help dry it out and help push the damp air out through the vent. If you do decide to install a heater outlet here, make it low down but out of the direct path of the shower jet. You should use an outlet that can be properly closed for when the shower is in use, and for times when you only want the heat going to the main living space.

# Showers

The simplest shower to install in a motorhome is an external one – you can either use a 'solar shower' (a large black bladder with a hose and nozzle which warms up in the sun on your roof), a portable battery powered shower with a pump dropped into a bucket, or install a proper shower point plumbed into your cold water system on the side or back of the vehicle – great for rinsing off after a surf or for washing dogs. The more sophisticated solution is to have a proper inside hot shower. The reality is that a campervan shower is unlikely to live up to a domestic one – you will need to be fairly sparing on water usage, and with the best will in the world the space is likely to be a bit cramped. That said, being able to have a good wash is a real luxury when on the road, especially if you've just come in from a long walk or run, or to help peel off a wetsuit after a cold surfing session.

A 12V shower featuring a submersible pump – all you need is a bucket of water and a good view!

# Shower Trays

The tray is really the crux of your motorhome shower. The main choices are fibreglass or plastic trays. The key is to find one that fits your chosen design, though another approach is to design the cubicle shape around the size of the tray. It is possible to get replacement fibreglass trays for the majority of popular caravan and coach-built motorhome makes (search online for 'caravan shower trays'). These are usually made to order from moulds and come in a wide variety of different shapes, often to fit round wheel-arches, cassette toilets, etc. Another useful approach is to get a plastic 'universal' shower tray that can be cut to fit most scenarios. There are several plastic universal trays on the market, some of which also have cut outs to take cassette toilets, and these are good options for campervan shower rooms. If you need to you can use bits of PVC panel to supplement the edges of the tray if required. Alternatively you can get fancy and use wet-room flooring or if you have the skills you can even create your own mould for a custom fibreglass shower tray.

# 44 Fitting a Shower Tray

| | |
|---|---|
| **PREREQUISITES** | Construct bathroom cubicle |
| **DO BEFORE** | - - |
| **COMBINE WITH** | Installing cassette toilet |

**MODERATE 3/5**

The shower tray needs to sit on top of a firm platform – in essence this forms a false floor.

1. Use lengths of softwood timber glued and/or screwed to the floor to create a service void. You will need the void to be a minimum of a couple of inches (50mm) and if you have the head space to spare, bigger is better.

2. Then lay a plywood floor (min 18mm) over the battens, ensuring it is well supported – you may want to use marine ply for this for ultimate durability. If at all possible, retain a way to get access to the void though this is often easier said than done. If you are installing a cassette toilet and a tray with a toilet cut-out, the loo will sit on the plywood with the shower tray around it. Leave the board loose until you finish getting the various bits of pipework in place. The platform will need a large hole to accommodate the shower waste, and probably smaller gaps or holes at the back for cold and hot pipes to the shower, plus a cold feed to the loo.

3. If required, cut the shower tray to size and place the tray on top of the plywood platform. Ensure the drain hole is the lowest point of the tray and make adjustments with wedges etc. (under the plywood) if required. Also make sure that any ledges at the edge of the tray will drain back into the tray.

4. The shower will drain best if the waste goes vertically straight down through the floor, ideally with a non-return valve somewhere between it and the waste tank to prevent waste slopping up into the shower tray every time you stop at traffic lights. If you need to, you can use a low profile right angle shower waste instead, but there must be a good run (angle) on the waste hose to ensure good drainage. Consider using wider bore or even domestic drainage pipes to further aid efficient drainage.

5. Once you are ready you can connect the waste up and fix the tray down, often just using sealant (the waste plumbing and toilet will also help hold it in place). Pay careful attention to sealing around the sides.

The battens for the false floor with plumbing beneath.

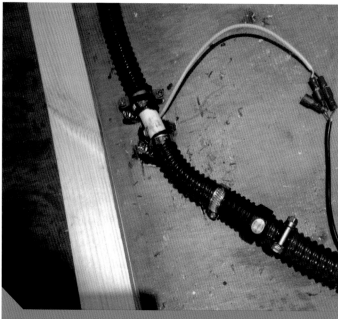

Waste hose for shower and sink going through the floor. Note the non-return valve on the shower waste. A vertical shower waste dropping straight down would be preferable but wasn't possible here.

A false floor made of 18mm sheathing ply ready for the shower tray to be cut to size and fitted. Note plumbing for shower waste, sink / shower tap, and w.c. flush.

Shower tray installed with w.c. sitting on top.

# Shower Taps and Risers

You can choose between a dedicated shower tap or a mixer tap in the sink that pulls out on an extendible hose. In a small space, there is a lot to be said for the latter option – apart from anything else it makes the plumbing easier and means you don't need to hide pipes going up the wall to the shower riser.

Ensure everything is well sealed, including the doorway.

A worktop being prepared for the small bathroom sink.

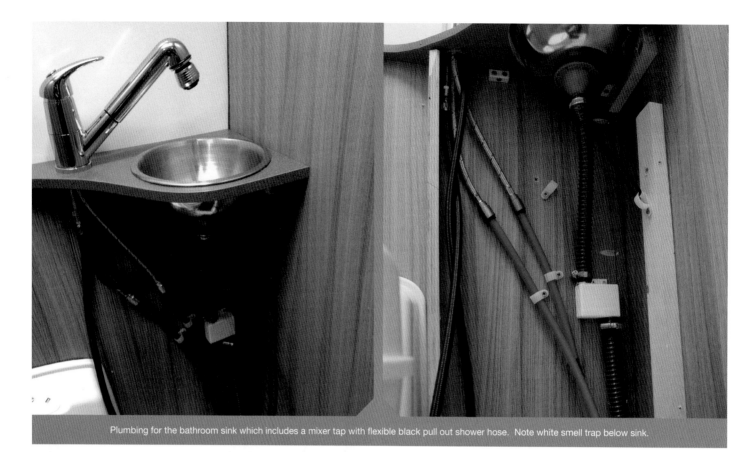

Plumbing for the bathroom sink which includes a mixer tap with flexible black pull out shower hose. Note white smell trap below sink.

## Shower Curtains

If you have managed to use materials that are fully waterproof (e.g. shower wall or PVC panels) you may not need a shower curtain, especially if you have added a rubber seal around the door. However, it is common to add a shower curtain to protect the walls and also stop water spraying through the gaps in the door. Low profile metal and plastic shower rails are available that you can shape to curve right around the bathroom if required. You can also keep things simple by overlapping two curtains. Some shower rails can just be stuck on, but you may want to use a rail that can be screwed to the wall or ceiling for additional longevity (use stainless steel screws so that they don't rust).

The shower riser bar and stick-on mirror installed on the walls.

# Toilets

Most of us have experienced an increasingly frantic search for a lavvy at some point, and for some the thought of going outside has been enough to put them off camping and campervanning for life. Installing a throne in your beautifully constructed bijou bathroom removes these worries for good.

One option is the 'porta-potti' (more on these later), but the all-singing all-dancing solution to campervan loos is the cassette toilet. These consist of the main pan, with a waste tank below that needs to be periodically removed and emptied (more on that later). Some cassettes are fixed in place just like a domestic loo, but a common design in campervans allows the bowl to swivel around – this feature is great for maximising what you can fit in a small bathroom and lets you swivel the bowl out of the way while brushing teeth or showering. These loos are usually designed so that you can give them a good soaking while showering (though you need to remember to put the loo roll somewhere dry).

Cassette loos can be flushed either with a manual pump or often with a small electric pump. The water can either be plumbed from your fresh water supply or some cassettes have their own small flush tanks. There is something to be said for separate flush tanks as they eliminate the potential for wasting your precious last few litres on flushing the loo. If the flush tank is separate you can also pour additives into it which can be desirable. That said, loos with integrated flush tanks take up a bit more space, and require slightly more work to fit the filler inlet.

A swivelling cassette toilet is a great addition to a campervan – make sure you have enough space for your knees!

A neat solution using a small shower tray with a bench cassette toilet.

A cassette toilet mounted side-on with shower tray.

# 45 Installing a Cassette Toilet

PREREQUISITES | Flooring, wiring & plumbing
DO BEFORE | - -
COMBINE WITH | Constructing bathroom cubicle & fitting shower tray

**ADVANCED 4/5**

The cassette needs to be installed against a vertical flat surface. If you think carefully about it you may be able to install it against an internal wall, or perhaps a wall accessible when the back doors are opened – the advantage of this is that you don't need to cut a hole in the side of the van for the waste tank door. If the loo is to sit against an external wall you will need to provide a vertical wall for it to sit against. Before starting, ensure you have any extras that you might need – e.g. cassette shower tray skirt, wiring for an electric flush, and a fresh water feed if needed.

1. The trickiest thing when installing a cassette toilet is establishing the precise location. If you need to install it against the side of the vehicle, you need to find a spot where there is space for the waste tank door. The door needs to sit on a reasonably flat surface and there needs to be a clear route through the wall – i.e. no struts, wheel arches, or other obstructions in the way. Ideally the door should be above any plastic trim passing round the base of the vehicle, but this may raise the floor of the bathroom up too much given limited headroom.

2. Use the template provided with the loo to mark and then cut out the hole for the door. Note that the piece of cut out material will be re-used later so be careful not to drill through except at the edge or scratch it. If there is a separate flush tank you will need to cut the hole for the filler inlet too.

Use the template to mark and cut out the toilet waste tank door. Note that the metal cut out will be reused in the door frame.

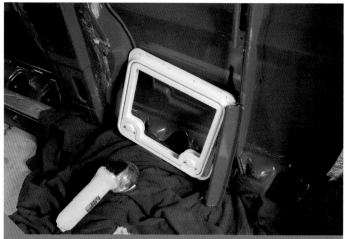

Finding a good position for the toilet can be tricky – here a small section of strut has been removed to make room. Raising the bathroom floor a little provides space for plumbing and brings the wc door above the exterior trim.

3. If required, beef up the inner wall around the new hole with some strips of timber.

4. Get the piece of van wall cut out earlier and use the template to mark and then cut it to size so that it fits in the door frame. You will then need to use the shape created to cut a piece of plywood that will sandwich together with the metal to create the door, surrounded by the frame.

5. Double check that with the toilet sitting in place it is possible to remove the waste tank through the hole. Use sealant and self tapping stainless screws to secure the tank door and frame in place.

An internal softwood frame is clamped to the metal skin.

The waste tank door frame is built using the metal cut out earlier plus a bit of plywood.

The waste tank door is installed and ultimately adds to the appearance of the vehicle.

6. The toilet will be fixed to the floor using screws accessed with the tank removed. Ensure the back of the toilet is adequately pushed against the back wall to create a good seal.

7. If the toilet is sitting on or in a shower tray, use a cassette toilet 'skirt' along with plenty of sealant to create a good seal to stop water getting anywhere it shouldn't.

8. If required, wire up the flush pump and plumb in the cold water feed which should have an isolation valve for future maintenance purposes.

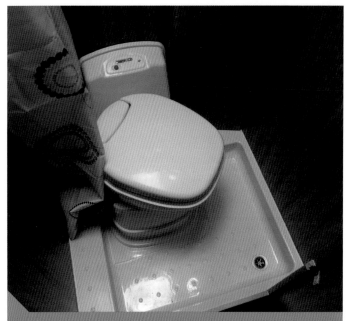

The w.c. is sealed and screwed down from below the waste tank, through the shower tray and false floor. Here a PVC skirt has been added with sealant to create a waterproof seal with the shower tray.

# Porta-pottis

A step down from the cassette toilet, but still a potentially good solution, is the porta-potti (or portable toilet). These come in a range of sizes and the bigger they get the more user-friendly they are. Big guys in particular will struggle with the smaller models. You can use them in conjunction with a bathroom cubicle – for example stored elsewhere but placed loose on the shower tray when required. As a compromise measure you could plan to use a porta-potti in the living space with all the curtains etc. closed, though this is a less than ideal option and requires a rather close relationship with any other van occupants. Another option is to carry a toilet-tent that gets erected beside the vehicle when you park up, with the porta-potti placed inside it. If none of these options seem like a good idea then you probably need to upgrade your plans to include a cassette toilet instead.

Portable loos work similarly to cassettes in that they have a flush tank and a waste tank. The flush on most models is just a manual pump which works quite well. The sizes of the tanks vary and will dictate how frequently you need to fill and empty them.

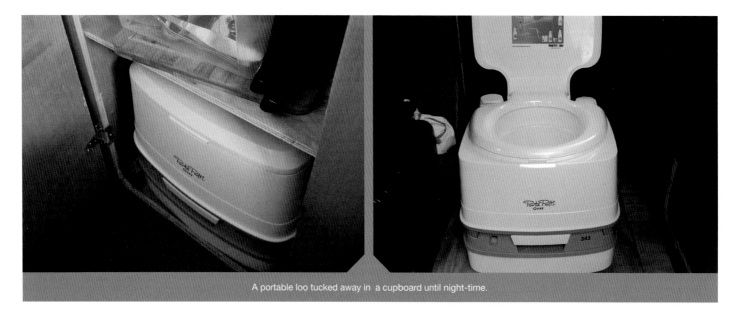

A portable loo tucked away in a cupboard until night-time.

# Emptying

Emptying the loo is a right of passage for many motorhome owners, and it may be fairly off-putting at first glance. Although it isn't the most pleasant task, once you've done it a couple of times it doesn't seem so bad. With both cassette toilets and porta-pottis, you remove the waste tank and then carry it using the handle to an emptying point. Most campsites have a designated facility for emptying chemical toilet waste tanks, often with a hose provided to make rinsing out easier. You can also empty the tank down a conventional toilet, provided you're careful. Be aware that the chemicals are often not suitable for emptying into a septic tank system, but are fine to empty into mains sewerage systems.

The least pleasant job of life on the road, but you get used to it after the first couple of 'empties'.

Before emptying the tank, read the instructions carefully. There is usually a fold out pipe that you take the cap off and this is what gets tipped down the drain. Pay attention to getting ready to press a vent button as you tip the tank over as this will allow air in and stop it from emptying in several lurching gulps. Don't push the vent button in until you tip, otherwise liquid will start coming out there. Get the first couple of empties out of the way and you'll soon learn the ropes – one of the few necessary evils of life on the road.

# REGULATIONS, INSURANCE, & THE DVLA

Having delved through the nuts and bolts of converting vehicles, it is worth running through the various regulations that affect your project. This subject is littered with grey areas and common misconceptions about what you can and can't do as a DIY converter. The following section refers to the situation in the UK at the time of writing – other countries have similar but often slightly different laws.

## MOT

All vehicles more than three years old on the road in the UK need to pass an annual test known as the MOT (which just stands for Ministry of Transport). The MOT test checks the vehicle meets environmental and road safety standards. The MOT doesn't test the habitability of a campervan and nor does it act as a mechanical service, so you should also regularly tick those boxes in addition to the MOT.

## Seating Regulations

Seating regulations are covered in more detail within the seating chapter, however some of the headlines are as follows:

- All seats intended to carry passengers while travelling should have robust 3-point seatbelts (and they should be worn).

- All seats in the vehicle cab should either be original seats or their tested equivalents.

- All seats designated as travelling seats will (in theory) have their seat belt fittings assessed as part of the vehicle's MOT.

- The law does not (yet) insist on rear seats being 'Tested' models. The MOT will not check seats or fixings, just the seatbelts – so the responsibility is yours.

- Tested seats are only as good as their fixing to the vehicle chassis.

## Electrical Regulations

Electrical systems in campervans and motorhomes can be split into 12Volt and mains. There are no legal restrictions on who is allowed to work on 12Volt systems, although if wired badly you risk things not working properly or worse you could start a fire. 12V wiring is a task that many DIY converters will consider taking on themselves, perhaps with some input from an auto-electrician for some of the more complicated aspects.

> "Mains voltage systems are potentially much more dangerous than 12V as an electric shock at this voltage can kill."

Mains voltage systems are potentially much more dangerous than 12V as an electric shock at this voltage can kill. There aren't any legal restrictions on who can wire a mains system in a campervan, although the latest IEE wiring regulations must be adhered to and you should feel confident that you are up to the challenge. If you wouldn't do wiring in a house, you shouldn't do mains wiring in a campervan. The mains system does need to be tested and certified by a qualified electrician. If you intend to carry out the bulk of the mains voltage wiring yourself, you should liaise with an electrician beforehand to check they will be happy to test and sign-off the work that you have done.

# Gas Regulations

There is more about gas in the separate chapter dedicated to the subject. Poorly installed and maintained gas plumbing and appliances can cause explosions, fires, and silent killers such as Carbon Monoxide poisoning. Therefore the simple answer to 'who can legally work on gas installations in campervans' is that **you need to be a Gas Safe Register (GSR) certified engineer** with the correct endorsements. **The "Caravan – LAV" endorsement** (LAV = Leisure Accommodation Vehicle) is a specific category of work that GSR engineers should be qualified for in order to work on campervan and motorhome gas installations.

―――――

"Poorly installed and maintained gas plumbing and appliances can cause explosions, fires, and silent killers such as Carbon Monoxide poisoning."

―――――

In other words, if you stick to the letter of the law, you are going to have to find a certified gas engineer to do your gas plumbing for you. There is a slight loophole to the above rules in that you are also legally allowed to work on gas installations (in a non-paid setting) if you are 'competent'… however, that is not carte blanche for all budding DIY enthusiasts to just get stuck in because 'competent' in this case has been further defined to mean that you should be trained and capable to the same standard as would be required by GSR, so unfortunately this apparent loophole does not apply to the majority of would be converters.

# Speed Limits

The table shown here is a simplified version of the national speed limits published by the UK government at the time of writing. The key take-home message for most of us is:

"The majority of vans have a speed limit that is 10 miles per hour less than that for a car. If the same van is converted into a motorhome, and registered as such with the DVLA, it has effectively the same speed limit as a car."

## UK Speed Limits in mph (Table has been simplified)

| Type of vehicle | Built-up areas | Single carriageways | Dual carriageways | Motorways |
|---|---|---|---|---|
| Car-derived vans * | 30 | 60 | 70 | 70 |
| Motorhomes ** | 30 | 60 (50 if over 3T) | 70 (60 if over 3T) | 70 |
| Vans up to 7.5T | 30 | 50 | 60 | 70 (60 when towing) |

\* (subtract 10mph if towing)

\*\* Note that any motorhome being used as a goods vehicle has the lower speed limit applied to them.

There are a variety of subtleties to the exact classification of some vehicles (for example the definition of 'dual-purpose vehicles' becomes quite complex) and if you are in doubt, either drive at the slower speed limit or seek clarification.

―――――

"If a van is converted into a motorhome, and registered as such with the DVLA, it has effectively the same speed limit as a car."

―――――

# DVLA and Modifying Registration

All vehicles driving on the roads should be registered with the DVLA. On the V5C registration document it lists various attributes of the vehicle such as its body-type, number of seats, colour, engine, etc. If you modify your vehicle in such a way that the V5C no longer accurately describes the vehicle, you should notify the DVLA with the changes. Not only will this help the authorities should your vehicle be stolen or involved in an accident, but it may also be a requirement for your insurance. If those aren't reason enough, then as mentioned above your vehicle is likely to have a higher speed limit applied to it if formally registered as a motorhome. The DVLA usually uses the term 'Motor Caravan' for the new body type and they generally insist on seeing evidence of the conversion (i.e. photos) as well as stipulating some minimum requirements to qualify for the change.

DVLA minimum requirements for body-type of 'Motor Caravan' at the time of writing:

- Sleeping accommodation
- Cooking facilities
- Fixed table
- Storage

While considering these minimum requirements it is also worth checking whether your insurance company will insist on certain criteria which are often more detailed than those of the DVLA. If the vehicle is converted by a professional company, the DVLA will want you to provide a letter from the converters on headed paper. If you convert the vehicle yourself you may be asked to provide proof of the work carried out, including receipts where applicable.

It's a fine line between what will and won't be accepted as a Motor Caravan by the DVLA, but the bar is now set reasonably high.

# Insurance

Historically it has been tricky to find good insurance for DIY campervan conversion projects, with most mainstream insurance companies not recognising the process involved in carrying out a conversion. It often used to be a case of insuring the van as a commercial vehicle initially, and then once the conversion was complete taking out new insurance to cover it as a campervan.

These days there are a number of good insurance brokers around who cater specifically for home conversion projects. Policies vary but some will specify a limited conversion period of between three and nine months, after which you are expected to have completed the project (though extensions to the period may be possible). Some insurers have a set of minimum requirements (similar to the DVLA) which they use to decide whether they are happy to insure your conversion as a campervan or motorhome. Common minimum requirements include:

- Side windows
- Bed of a certain length
- Table and dining area
- Cooking facilities
- Storage

As with the DVLA, insurers will often want to see photographic evidence.

After your conversion is complete your vehicle is likely to be worth substantially more, so you should make an effort to re-value it and make sure your insurance policy is updated to reflect the new value.

Remember to ensure your insurance reflects the value you have (hopefully) added.

# Example letter to DVLA

DVLA                                                      Your Address

Swansea                                                   Postcode

SA99 1BA                                                  Date


Dear Sir / Madam,

I am writing to update the details on the enclosed V5 logbook for the vehicle with registration **XXXX XXX**. This vehicle has been fully converted from a panel van into a motorhome. I have **attached some photographic evidence of these changes** and note some of the main features of the conversion below:

**Motorhome – Main Features**

Fixed double bed (1.9m length)

Dinette rear passenger seat (folds out to form extra bed)

Two rooflights

Two side windows

Two rear windows

Four seats with 3 point seatbelts

Dining area for 4 people with fixed table

Kitchen including stove, sink, storage, fridge

Lighting throughout

WC and Shower room

Fresh and waste water tanks

Gas and electric supply system

Please can you update the V5 to reflect these changes, particularly with regards to **the new body type of 'Motor Caravan' as well as the number of seats including the driver which is now 4**. I confirm that all work has been carried out by competent and experienced people, and that the conversion has been completed to a high, safe, and robust standard.

Please don't hesitate to contact me should you require further information.

Yours faithfully,



Your Name

Phone: 0777 XXX XXXX

Email: youremail@address.com

# CONVERSION DIARY

It is useful to have a look at the progression through a real conversion project, both to get an idea of the timescales involved, but also to get a good feel for the order things should be done in. Although each project will vary, the order things are carried out is often similar. Things like fitting the windows or a heater which require cutting holes in the van and are messy are best done first – they also dictate the position and height of things like the stove and units. Insulation and wiring need to be done before the panels and furniture go in. Soft furnishings can generally be left till last.

A professional converter can rattle through a fairly basic but high standard conversion in a couple of weeks or less, perhaps running to a couple of months or more for a complex and big custom project. However, for the average DIY converter a project like this can take a considerable amount of time and effort, and in some cases the conversion becomes an ongoing process throughout the life of the vehicle. An experienced DIY converter can push through a conversion to a reasonably good level in a few weeks of solid work, however if you only have weekends and the odd evening (and are perhaps new to the process) the project may well take you six months or more.

It is important to recognise your goals with a project such as this. For some, a major part of the reason for taking the conversion on is to enjoy the process of carrying out the work. For others, doing the conversion yourself is a means to an end and your goal is to go away and use the van, not spend too much time stuck at home doing the conversion. Either way, keep your eye on the prize – by all means put lots of effort into a high standard conversion, but make sure you don't obsess over it so much that you never get away in it.

The ideal rough order to carry out a conversion is as follows, although there is always loads of crossover, parallel tasks, and no single absolute correct order.

1. Cut holes – fit windows, heaters, etc.

2. Insulate

3. First fix wiring

4. Seating & Flooring

5. Lining and Panels, First fix plumbing

6. Furniture

7. Second fix wiring & plumbing

The following page shows a rough diary of a recent conversion project, but as you can see the 'ideal' order suggested above wasn't strictly followed here, and there was much overlapping of tasks going on. In particular the wiring was done later than usual in this project, perhaps because the design was still evolving until quite late in the construction.

———

"Keep your eye on the prize - put lots of effort into a high standard conversion, but don't obsess so much that you never get away in it."

———

| July | |
|---|---|
| | Started looking for vehicle – attended several auctions, looked at private and trade sales. |

| August | |
|---|---|
| 3rd Aug | **Bought vehicle at auction** |

| Week 1 | |
|---|---|
| 5th Aug | Preparation, removed bulkhead, removed front passenger bench seat |
| | Sourced replacement single seat and two swivel plates |
| | Removed existing panels, planned layout |
| | Cut bars to form main bed frame |
| 9th Aug | Insulation & vapour barrier |
| 10th Aug | Bed boards cut |

| Week 2 | |
|---|---|
| 13-14th Aug | Constructed kitchen unit |
| 15th Aug | First side window in |
| 16th Aug | Panels cut |
| 18th Aug | Picked up van seat, mattress, etc. |

| Week 3 | |
|---|---|
| 20th Aug | Fitted front single passenger seat, fitted front seat swivels |
| | Mocked up rear bench arrangement |
| 21st Aug | Waste water and gas prep |
| 22nd Aug | Water prep, fitted bed boards |
| | Constructed porta-potty cubbyhole |
| 23rd Aug | Wiring, carpet panels |
| 24th Aug | Fitted second side window, heater installed, carpet struts |
| 25th Aug | Bed board refinement |
| | Investigated solution to swivel / handbrake issue |
| | Constructed rear seat platform, cut ceiling panels |

| Week 4 | |
|---|---|
| 26th Aug | Discussed swivel / handbrake issue with local engineering company |
| 27th Aug | Platform & rear seat fitted, cut mattress |
| 28-29th Aug | Wiring |
| 31st Aug | Water plumbing, rear platform apron, table |
| 1st Sept | **First overnight test trip** |

| Week 5 | |
|---|---|
| 6-7th Sept | Constructed rear storage unit |
| 8th Sept | Exterior decals |

| Week 6 | |
|---|---|
| 9-10th Sept | Unit doors and hinges |
| 20th Sept | Van kit out |
| 22nd Sept | Cruise control retrofitted |
| 23rd Sept | **Ferry to Spain for 6 week maiden voyage!** |

It's worth noting that the swivel / handbrake issue mentioned wasn't resolved until into November, and the vehicle was used for some time before various small finishing touches were all finalised and the 'snagging' list was completed.

# CONVERSION BUDGET

At first glance, the cost of professionally built campervan and motorhome conversions can seem eye-wateringly high. The price tags can seem pretty hard to justify until you start to add up the cost of the vehicle plus all the expensive parts and the amount of labour required. Before getting carried away with your own project, make sure you try to be realistic about what things cost. At the same time, you need to be careful not to put yourself off the idea completely before you even get started.

> "…if you don't want to spend too much, then make sure you match your conversion plans to your wallet, otherwise you'll spend your diesel money on parts."

To help you get a better feel for how much your own project might cost, the rough budget breakdowns of a couple of real projects are shown here. It is important to recognise that conversions are possible at all budget levels – from very low cost shoestring vans, right through to exorbitant, no expense spared, all singing all dancing projects. These figures were roughly correct at the time of writing, but will of course need to be factored up with inflation as time goes by.

The major savings you can make when converting yourself are on labour costs. You can also scrimp and save on trying to buy parts as cheaply as possible. The key message however, is that certain types of conversion are only possible for certain budgets – if you don't want to spend too much, then make sure you match your conversion plans to your wallet, otherwise costs can quickly spiral and before you know it you'll have spent all your diesel and travelling money on parts.

## Example Budget 1

### A mid spec. 2 berth campervan conversion

Vehicle – VW T5, 6 years old, 85k miles, bought privately for roughly £9,500

Conversion Budget - £5,000

All prices approximate at time of writing (2017) – adjust for inflation as required.

| Item * | Amount |
|---|---|
| Single passenger seat | £300 |
| 2 swivel plates | £250 |
| Sink / Stove combi | £220 |
| Heater | £550 |
| Small Fridge | £550 |
| Battery | £90 |
| Charging (using VSR) + Wiring | £300 |
| Lights | £85 |
| Folding rear seat / bed | £1200 |
| 2 bonded side windows | £250 |
| Timber – 3mm ply panels, 18mm marine ply bed board, softwood battens, 15mm hardwood ply for furniture | £400 |
| Water – tank (large jerry canister), small waste tank, submersible pump + plumbing | £100 |
| Gas | £80 |
| **Total Conversion Cost** | **£4,375** |
| **Total with Vehicle** | **£13,875** |

* Some of the items above were new, some ebay, gumtree, etc. Wherever possible good prices were sought out.

# Example Budget 2

## A high spec. 4 berth motorhome conversion

Vehicle – Fiat Ducato LWB, 4 years old, 40k miles

Bought at auction for roughly £9,000

Conversion Budget - £10,000

All prices approximate at time of writing (2017) – adjust for inflation as required.

| Category | Description | Amount |
|---|---|---|
| Bathroom | Toilet + surround, PVC boards, Taps etc., Shower Tray | £750 |
| Bed | Mattress, bedding, etc. | £300 |
| Chassis | Bolts, paint, metal struts | £170 |
| Electrics | Leisure Battery | £150 |
| Electrics | Mains System - Inlet, hookup leads, consumer unit, cables, mains charger, inverter | £500 |
| Electrics | Charging – B2B charger, charging cables, maxi / midi fuses + holders, isolation switch, etc. | £420 |
| Electrics | 12V Wiring - Cables, Bus bar, Fuse box, Fuses, Fuse holders, terminals, etc. | £350 |
| Electrics | Sockets, switches, etc. | £120 |
| Electrics | Lighting – mini spots, strips, reading lights, spotlights | £180 |
| Furniture | Table leg, edge trim, hinges + handles etc. | £150 |
| Furniture | Misc Timber (plywood, softwood, etc.) | £200 |
| Furniture | 15mm furniture board etc. | £1,100 |
| Furniture | Worktop + table | £150 |
| Gas | Underslung gas tank, tank pipes, internal gas plumbing | £450 |
| Heating | Heater + fittings | £550 |
| Insulation | Insulation | £180 |
| Insulation | Cab Window Mats | £70 |
| Kitchen | 80L Fridge + vents | £600 |
| Kitchen | Sink / stove combo | £220 |
| Misc | Bolts, screws, sealant + adhesives | £250 |
| Seating | Dinette Seat | £1,100 |
| Seating | 2 x Captain Seats | £800 |
| Seating | Seat Runners, swivels, belts, boxes | £600 |
| Trim | Carpet Lining | £180 |
| Water | Underfloor Fresh + Waste Tank Kits | £220 |
| Water | Pump, fresh plumbing, waste plumbing | £250 |
| Water | Water Heater | £500 |
| Windows | 2 x Double glazed Side Windows | £550 |
| Windows | Mid-size Rooflight | £400 |
| Windows | Small Rooflight | £80 |
| Windows | Rear Windows, blinds + parts | £320 |
| | **Total Conversion Cost** | **£11,860** |
| | **Total with Vehicle** | **£20,860** |

As you can see from the examples above, even when you are doing the work yourself it is easy for the costs to quickly escalate. Bear in mind that professional conversion companies will usually be able to source parts cheaper than you (unless you buy second hand etc.) so in some cases the difference between what they will charge you and the DIY cost won't be as wide as you might first expect; having said that, all but the smallest converters will also usually need to charge VAT on-top of their fee, which will largely eradicate any savings they made on parts.

# Cost Control Suggestions

It has been said of boats and yachts that they are just holes in the water, surrounded by wood, into which you pour money… and unfortunately some conversion projects can end up being similar money-pit follies. Carrying out your conversion yourself is the first big way to save money, and there are some other areas listed below where you can make decisions that will help keep your budget under control.

- Don't install a bathroom, or keep it very simple – adding a shower and hot water adds both significant cost and complexity to a project.

- Don't do a fancy and costly conversion on an old vehicle – match the conversion to the vehicle and vice-versa.

- Minimise number of windows and rooflights installed.

- Keep electrics and lighting simple. Try to install a basic system initially that will allow for later date additions.

- Find cheaper seating solutions.

- Use standard hardwood plywood instead of lightweight furniture ply – it won't look quite the same, but can save a significant bit of cash. Clever use of paint, varnish, stains, and carpet lining can all help create a classy finish in a budget conversion.

- Keep gas and water installations simple – use in-board removable tanks / cylinders.

Many cost-cutting measures will go against your concept of your ideal campervan, but if your budget is limited you may need to find aspects that you can compromise on. Sometimes items on your wish-list are perceived essentials that when it comes down to it are secondary to your main aim of owning a campervan that you can actually afford to go away in.

---

"There are some obvious areas where key decisions will help keep your budget under control."

---

However much you spend on your conversion, you'll all end up at the same beach!

# TOOLS

In an ideal world, you would have access to a large, well lit, indoor garage space where you can drive your van in and carry out the conversion in the spacious dry and warmth, with easy access to both the roof and the chassis, surrounded by a well equipped workshop with access to every tool you've heard of and more. The reality for most is that you'll end up with the vehicle parked out on the street or on your drive, constantly trying to fit jobs into tight time and weather windows, sometimes in the dark and cold evenings of winter, using a ramshackle collection of tools that seem to continually lack the exact implement you could do with. Such is life!

"…it is perfectly possible to carry out a high standard conversion with a fairly limited set of resources…"

Thankfully it is perfectly possible, if not quite as luxurious, to carry out a high standard conversion with a fairly limited set of resources. This section tries to highlight a small list of the most important tools, without which you may struggle to complete the project. Of course if you don't personally own all (or any) of these tools, you can usually find a friend, relative, or neighbour that can come to your rescue… and often through borrowing tools, you may also gain valuable help and advice from those more experienced, so never be afraid to ask.

# Key Power Tools

A small selection of good power tools will make your conversion journey a far smoother ride. The following few tools are the key ones used, are relatively affordable, and these will prove valuable and well used additions to any DIY tool collection.

- Cordless Drill
- Jigsaw
- Circular Saw

Alongside these essential tools, you should also gather together:

- Gloves & Goggles
- Ear Defenders
- 1st Aid Kit
- Fire Extinguisher
- Extension Cable
- Work Light

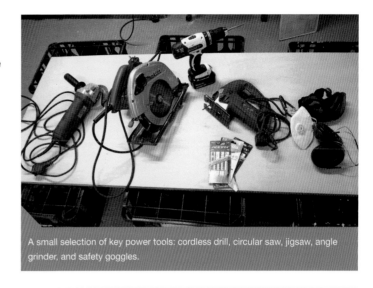

A small selection of key power tools: cordless drill, circular saw, jigsaw, angle grinder, and safety goggles.

## Cordless Drill

Probably the one power tool no-one should be without, the cordless drill / driver is all but indispensable to the point where most of us wonder how on earth we managed prior to their appearance in our toolboxes. It makes the author's elbow ache at the thought of using a screwdriver for everything now screwed in using a cordless drill / driver. Mains powered drills tend to be more powerful than their cordless cousins but these days a good quality battery drill is more than capable of the vast majority of conversion tasks. Make sure you get two batteries with the drill so that you can always have the spare on charge.

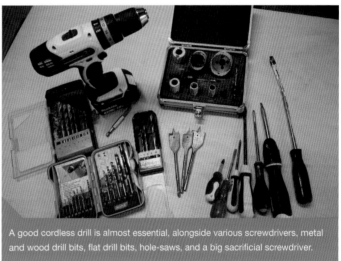

A good cordless drill is almost essential, alongside various screwdrivers, metal and wood drill bits, flat drill bits, hole-saws, and a big sacrificial screwdriver.

Get a set of HSS (High Speed Steel) drill bits in sizes from 2 or 3mm up to 10mm, plus a set of brad-point wood bits in similar sizes. Be aware that bits wear out fairly rapidly (especially when drilling metal) and should be replaced as soon as you sense you are struggling to drill the hole. Small drill bits frequently break so having spares is a good policy to adopt. A small selection of flat wood bits for cutting bigger holes – e.g. a set of five or six bits in a range of sizes from 13 to 25mm will come in useful. Note that flat bits are particularly bad for splintering when they exit so always drill through into a scrap offcut. If you will cut a particular sized hole a lot it may be worth getting a hole saw (or a set of them) to use with the drill – great for cutting holes for spotlights, heater vents, etc. – though most big holes can also be cut with a jigsaw or fashioned with a round file after starting with a flat bit.

> "…the cordless drill / driver is all but indispensable to the point where most of us wonder how on earth we managed before…"

You will also need a set of driver bits to cope with various different screw heads encountered – as a minimum make sure you have Phillips (PH), and Pozi (PZ) bits in sizes 1, 2, and 3. You can also get driver bits to fit all the weird and wonderful heads encountered in vehicles including flatheads, allen key heads, torx, hex, square, and others. Another useful addition to your accessories collection is a socket set adapter that will let you tighten and undo bolts using your drill.

# Jigsaw

The trusty jigsaw is one of the key tools in a converter's armoury. You can use a jigsaw for many conversion tasks from cutting holes in the van for windows or hookup sockets to cutting cupboard doors and curves out of plywood. The exact model of jigsaw doesn't really matter although in general you get more powerful ones with more control as they get more expensive. You will probably use it a lot while doing a conversion, so try to get one you like.

In many ways more important than the tool itself are the jigsaw blades – you will need some fine toothed metal blades for cutting holes in the van, some mid-sized timber blades for clean straight cuts in plywood, plus some fine and thin 'scroll' blades for cutting tight curves in plywood. You can start your collection by getting a selection pack containing a range of blade types.

> "The trusty jigsaw is one of the key tools in a converters armoury."

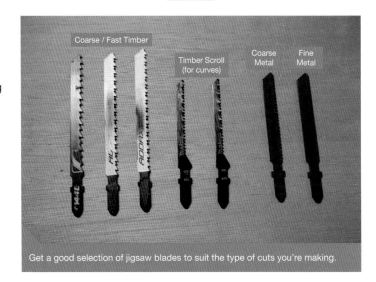

Get a good selection of jigsaw blades to suit the type of cuts you're making.

# Circular Saw

Circular saws are the tool for the job when long straight cuts in timber are required. A mains powered corded one coupled with an extension cable is fine. It is possible to cope without a circular saw, and use a handsaw instead, but they aren't hugely expensive and they make cutting up sheets of plywood far quicker and easier. Try to get one with a reasonably fine toothed blade as you will get a cleaner cut – if you find that the saw is making a mess of your wood it's probably time to get a new blade.

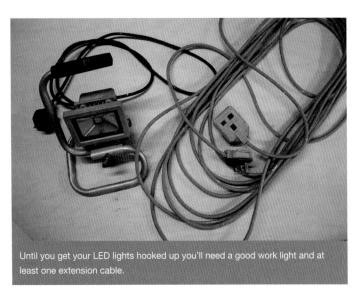

Until you get your LED lights hooked up you'll need a good work light and at least one extension cable.

If you get stuck and you're not sure what to do next... tidy up!

# Additional Power Tools

A well equipped workshop will have a variety of other tools which undoubtedly make the job easier but are probably luxuries for most DIY-ers unless they can justify them for other projects as well.

## Angle Grinder

You won't use an angle grinder all that often so this may be something you can borrow the occasional time you need one. When you do need one – for instance for cutting struts out when fitting windows, or cutting a seat girder to suit your project – there is no better tool for the job. You should pair the grinder with some metal grinding and cutting discs and pay careful attention to protecting the van from all the filings produced. There is also a fire risk when using angle grinders so take care and have a fire extinguisher to hand just in case.

When you do need an angle grinder, there is no better tool for the job

## Mitre Saw (Chop Saw)

For making quick and accurate cuts to lengths of timber, mitre saws are great. However, you can easily make all of these cuts with a handsaw so unless you will use one a lot they shouldn't be seen as essential.

## Table Saw

A table saw is even more of a luxury item than a mitre saw and you need a space where you can use one. If you have access to one already, then great – they do make tasks like panel cutting, unit construction, and ripping softwood down easy – but the number of DIY converters owning a table saw will be a minority.

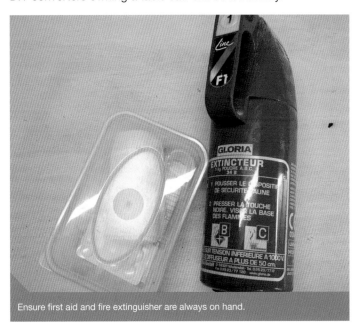
Ensure first aid and fire extinguisher are always on hand.

A vice on a good workbench and a mitre or chop saw are great additions to a workshop.

# Other Power Tools

There are loads of other power tools out there that you may or may not feel you need. It all depends what you're doing and how advanced your skill levels are. Tools such as pin guns, routers, power planes, compressors, reciprocating saws, power shears, welding kit, power washers and even shot blasters may come in useful but are beyond the scope of this book.

# Hand Tools

There are too many useful hand-tools to list them all here, and a good way to approach your collection is to build it up over time, buying good quality individual tools as and when you find a need for them. Some of the most useful are listed below to help get you started.

———

"…build your collection up over time, buying good quality individual tools as and when you find a need for them."

———

| Tool | Description |
| --- | --- |
| Crates or trestles | Some old milk or beer crates are great for laying sheets of plywood etc. on, and can also be useful for standing on. Some people prefer trestles, but in many ways crates are more useful and versatile. |
| Workbench and vice | The pillars of many good workshops – a portable bench can be just as useful if not as sturdy. |
| Molegrips | Brilliant for getting a firm grip on something. |
| Pliers | Not quite as good at gripping as molegrips but more versatile. As well as a standard pair of pliers, having a pair of long-nose pliers can be a great get-out-of-jail-free card for when you need to get hold of something small and just out of reach. |
| Screwdrivers | The cordless drill / driver has made screwdrivers far less important than in the past, but they will always be useful as there are many situations where you won't be able to use the cordless. Having a couple of stubby short ones is also often handy. A cheap old large flathead screwdriver specifically set aside for use as anything other than a screwdriver can end up being one of the most useful tools in your collection – the perfect tool for levering, hitting, scraping, and generally abusing. |
| Hammer | If you don't already have a hammer, you should get one… simple as that! A basic claw hammer that feels good in your hand will do the trick. Other hammers such as pin hammers and rubber mallets are also useful on occasion. |
| Files | Flat and round files are useful tools to have for tidying up both metal and wood edges, or for widening out holes etc. |
| Hand saw | Another cornerstone of any tool kit, a good general purpose hand saw can do pretty much everything you can do on a mitre saw, circular saw, or table saw for a fraction of the cost… it just takes a bit more effort. For finer joinery work you may also want a tenon saw, and coping, fret, and pad saws can also be useful on odd occasions. |
| Hacksaw | For cutting anything metal or plastic, a hacksaw is indispensable. You may want to pair a standard hacksaw with a smaller 'junior' hacksaw which can be useful for cutting smaller objects or in tight spaces. |
| Plane | You can get away without a plane, but if you have one and know how to use it there are many circumstances where it comes in handy – such as shaving the edge of a bit of ply down to better fit against a wall, or fine tuning the size of a shelf being fitted to a cupboard. |
| Chisel | Having at least one sharp chisel lying around can come in handy for cutting notches out of bits of timber as well as a myriad of other tasks that crop up from time to time. |
| Set square | A precision machined set square for making sure your cuts are at right angles. For bigger pieces you can use a bit of plywood offcut so long as you only rely on original factory cut edges. |
| Compass | Used to draw circles, but also very useful for scribing shapes. Purpose made scribing tools are also available. |
| Pencils | Everyone has their own preferences but every converter should always have a good selection of pencils to hand, not to mention a good sharpener and eraser. |
| Sandpaper | For getting rid of splinters and tidying up the edges of ply, keep a stock of bits of sandpaper to hand. Get a couple of different 'grades' for fine and coarse sanding. |

Sometimes the simplest tools are also the most useful – old crates are great for supporting boards, standing and sitting on, and generally making your life better.

A good socket set and a selection of adjustable spanners and mole-grips will come in handy.  As will a set of 'special' bits to undo bolts such as hexes, torx, etc.

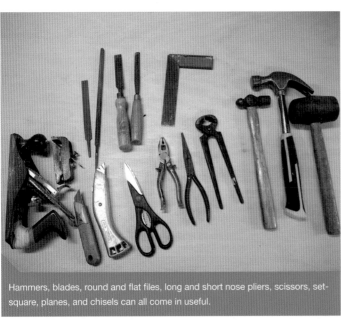

Hammers, blades, round and flat files, long and short nose pliers, scissors, set-square, planes, and chisels can all come in useful.

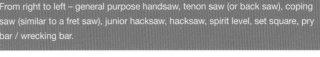

From right to left – general purpose handsaw, tenon saw (or back saw), coping saw (similar to a fret saw), junior hacksaw, hacksaw, spirit level, set square, pry bar / wrecking bar.

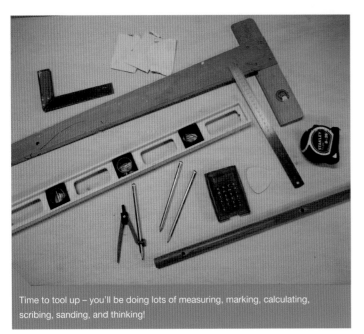

Time to tool up – you'll be doing lots of measuring, marking, calculating, scribing, sanding, and thinking!

A good selection of clamps is essential for certain tasks – get a couple of mid-sized quick release type clamps for starters.

# Electrical & Plumbing Tools

In addition to the conventional tools listed previously, you are likely to need a small collection of electrical and plumbing tools as well. The items below are all you need to do the vast majority of electrical tasks, both in a vehicle and at home. Note that all electrical tools should have good insulated handles.

| Tool | Description |
| --- | --- |
| Crimps | For attaching terminals onto cables. |
| Large crimps | Needed for putting terminals onto thicker cables such as those for charging – if you are only doing a few you can get away with using a combination of pliers, flat screwdriver and a hammer. |
| Pliers | A small pair of pliers always comes in handy when wiring. |
| Snips | A small pair of snips for cutting the cable – they can be combined with the pliers but having a dedicated tool can be useful. |
| Strippers | To remove the insulated sheath from the end of the cable. Standard wire strippers are tried and tested and perfectly adequate, though the recent innovation of combined strippers (mainly designed for domestic mains cable use) are worth a look. Flex strippers are also useful tools when stripping the sheath from thicker flex and cable. |
| Screwdrivers | It's useful to have a few dedicated electrical screwdrivers with insulated handles. |
| Multimeter | For testing battery condition, voltage, and fault finding. These are only any use if you also read-up on how to use one. |
| Soldering Iron | Not used in day to day wiring, but can be useful, for instance to fix a connection on a faulty appliance. |
| Pipe cutters | Water pipe cutters are particularly important if using push-fit plumbing – they are relatively cheap and well worth it to get a good straight cut every time – these can also be used to cut water hose and rubber gas hose. If you are taking on any preparatory gas plumbing (see safety notes elsewhere!) you will need a copper pipe cutting tool as well as a pipe bender. |

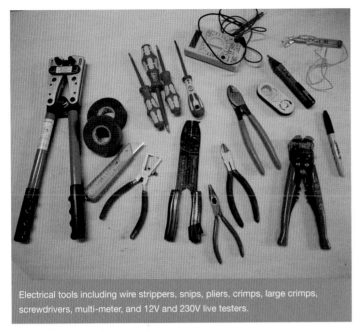

Electrical tools including wire strippers, snips, pliers, crimps, large crimps, screwdrivers, multi-meter, and 12V and 230V live testers.

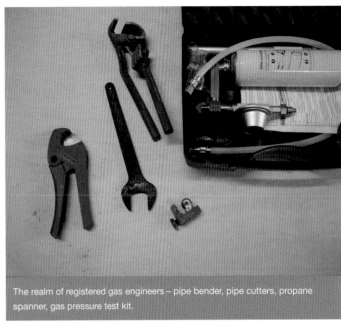

The realm of registered gas engineers – pipe bender, pipe cutters, propane spanner, gas pressure test kit.

A selection of ring and spade terminals with large and standard crimp tools.

The essentials for any conversion project – adhesive sealant, masking tape, and high temperature spray adhesive.

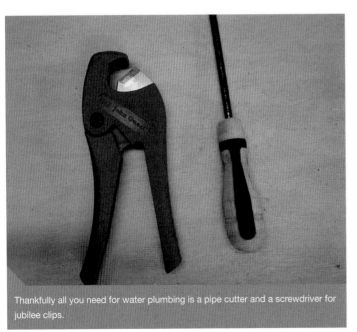

Thankfully all you need for water plumbing is a pipe cutter and a screwdriver for jubilee clips.

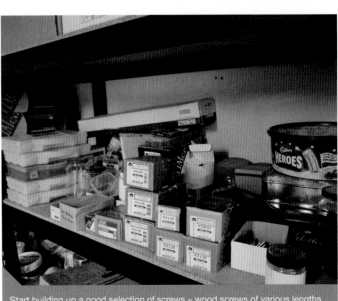

Start building up a good selection of screws – wood screws of various lengths, self-tappers, stainless steel countersunk screws, to name a few.

"Throw your belongings in the back, get on the open road, drive to a beach, a mountain, or a sunset.  Go for a night or go for a year... wait and see what the weather does, follow the surf, see where the road leads.  Spend the night and watch the sunrise in the morning. Meet new people, explore new places, have new adventures... with your own campervan at your disposal, who knows where you might end up?"

# EPILOGUE

I am only around five miles from home, and yet as I drive northwards in my newly converted van, with the sun shining through the window, I recognise a familiar sensation beginning to wash over me. The tension seems to drop from my shoulders and a sense of calm optimism begins to seep into my pores to replace the previously ever-present (if poorly acknowledged) stress and grumpiness. I have felt this happen many times before, but today the sensation is all the more welcome having been absent for a prolonged period – like a long-missed good friend appearing unexpectedly at the door, just when they were needed the most. It is hard to find a single word to explain and encapsulate the good vibes that are beginning to flow freely around the vehicle, but I know from previous experience that the closest I can get to a one-word definition is 'freedom'.

Of course there are other ways to achieve similar sensations – for instance when your flights have been delayed and you finally arrive at the beach in the sunshine on a long-awaited vacation; or when you walk out through the school or college gates at the start of summer holidays; or when you walk away from your last day of a job that you couldn't wait to escape from. But the thing I love about experiencing it this way, in my newly built campervan, is the sheer reproducibility of it – not only am I feeling it now, but in theory I can throw my belongings in the back and re-create it time and again: every good forecast; every weekend; every holiday; indefinitely!

For anyone who has a sense of needing adventure, escape, or just a way to access the places and activities they love, owning a campervan is a fantastic way to help make your dreams and ideal lifestyle become that bit closer to reality. Not only does converting your van yourself make it far more affordable, it can also be hugely satisfying and ensure that you end up with a vehicle that truly suits your needs.

This book is unashamedly aimed at the DIY or self-build converter – it doesn't necessarily show how to achieve pristine professional finishes, or extol the virtues of expensive components and complicated techniques, but in keeping things relatively simple the hope is that the book remains accessible to the largest number of budding converters (while still providing a good grounding for more advanced conversion projects).

A project like this book has a habit of rapidly growing arms and legs and (perhaps inevitably) there were a number of chapters that I wanted to include that have fallen by the wayside – for instance dealing with prolonged off-grid living and renewable energy (solar panels and wind turbines); generators; overlanding; fitting awnings, roofracks, and towbars; air-con, satellite TV, and mobile wifi; not to mention all the fantastic and varied conversion examples that could easily have made the book twice the size. However, these chapters will have to wait – leaving them out in this edition has allowed the core pages to get onto your bookshelf in time to inform this year's crop of conversion projects.

As I am writing this and preparing the book for the printers, there are numerous news items that may well affect the future of campervan converting: the UK is poised to leave the EU with as-yet unknown implications to laws affecting converters; following on from France's lead, the UK has stated a target of phasing out new petrol and diesel cars and vans by 2040; the Scottish government has an even more ambitious target of achieving this by 2032; at the same time, companies have begun serious testing programs of autonomous (driverless) vehicle technology; not to mention the glut of dot-com billionaires that are driving a new space race with the very real possibility of there being a colony on another planet before we stop using diesel.

Despite all the intriguing futuristic possibilities, something tells me that people will still be converting campervans for a long time to come, and with luck tasks such as cutting bits of plywood, using pushfit plumbing, and installing cassette loos, will stay reasonably relevant for a while yet.

Who knows where we'll be and what we'll be travelling in during this book's lifetime – I, for one, am looking forwards to unplugging my newly charged campervan pod, throwing my surf board in the back, and asking my Chauffeur-come-Satnav to plot a course to the new space port on the Outer Hebrides, before tucking myself into the comfy bed in the back. "Let's go... wake me up when we get to Mars!"

Happy converting & bon voyage!

"Electric campervans and renewable energy…
a glimpse of the future?"

## Feedback

We have put a lot of effort into producing this book, and we hope that it is a high quality and (most importantly) useful addition to your book shelf. If you find any corrections, have some feedback for us, or want to share your project with us, please email us at publish@renwicksguides.co.uk